WHITE DOVE CROW
4623 STREETER RD
MANTUA OH 44255

# PRAYER TO THE GREAT MYSTERY

*Edward S. Curtis titled one of his finest photographs, that of a Sioux medicine man beseeching his maker,* Prayer to the Great Mystery. *It is an appropriate image for the title of this book, since the underlying belief of all indigenous people is that the gift of life is sacrosanct. To the Sioux and the other Plains people, the buffalo was a symbol of all good given by the Creator. Thus, the skull, raised to the sun in such a way, was neither question nor answer, but rather a simple act of faith. It did not matter that the great herds were, as Curtis put it, "swept from the earth as in a twinkling." For the elders to whom he spoke were convinced of but one thing: the Great Mystery. And what the Great Mystery took away, He would, one day, return.*

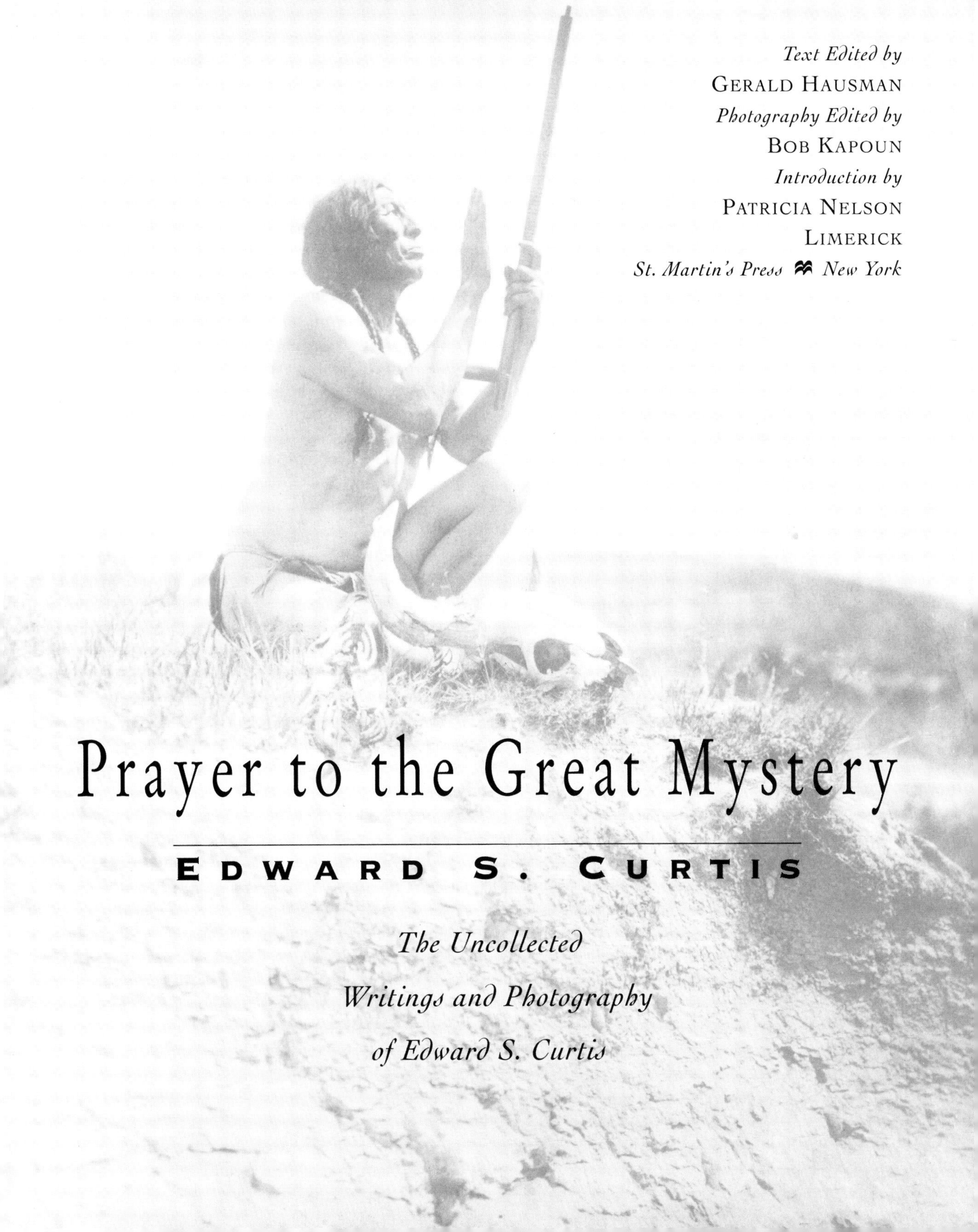

Text Edited by
GERALD HAUSMAN
*Photography Edited by*
BOB KAPOUN
*Introduction by*
PATRICIA NELSON
LIMERICK
*St. Martin's Press* ❧ *New York*

# Prayer to the Great Mystery

## EDWARD S. CURTIS

*The Uncollected*

*Writings and Photography*

*of Edward S. Curtis*

*Design by* JAYE ZIMET

*Endpapers:* On the Custer Outlook

Library of Congress Cataloging-in-Publi-
cation Data

Curtis, Edward S., 1868–1952.
    Prayer to the great mystery: the un-
collected writings and photography of
Edward S. Curtis / Gerald Hausman,
text editor; Bob Kapoun, photography
editor; introduction by Patricia Nelson
Limerick.
        p.   cm.
    Includes   bibliographical   references
and index.
    ISBN 0-312-13591-2
    l. Indians of North America — Pictor-
ial works.   2. Indians of North America — Folklore.   3. Indian   mythology.
4. Legends — North America.   I. Hausman, Gerald.   II. Kapoun, Robert W.
III. Title.
E77.5.C83   1995
970.004'97 — dc20                95-32877
                                 CIP

First Edition: November 1995

10   9   8   7   6   5   4   3   2   1

*For Marianne and Lorry*

# CONTENTS

## V—THE NORTHERNMOST COAST  195

## INTRODUCTION

Since the Edward S. Curtis revival began in the early 1970s, a movement that rescued this great American photographer from virtual obscurity, he has been the focus of numerous recent studies and exhibitions. The value of his original books and prints has soared into the realm of fine art, and his name has become synonymous with the renaissance of interest in native peoples worldwide.

With all that has proliferated recently, it seems almost strange that it would be possible to bring into print yet another Curtis volume. Nonetheless, over three years ago, Ted Spiegel, a leading consultant with the Library of Congress, mentioned to Bob Kapoun, a vintage-photo archivist and major collector of Edward S. Curtis, that the Library of Congress had an impressive collection of unpublished Curtis photographs. Seeing this collection of hundreds of prints that had never been taken out of the Library of Congress and had never appeared in any book form, including Cur-

*Povi-Yemo ("Flower-Falling"). San Ilde-fonso. 1905.*

tis's major opus, the twenty-volume *The North American Indian,* Kapoun realized the need to focus on "the unpublished Curtis." Thus, a book has been created that contains ninety-three photos from the unpublished archive, never reproduced in any form, and a hundred and fifty "unknown" prints, which have appeared only in the limited edition of *The North American Indian* but have never been published in any other popular venue before. The philosophy underscoring this new volume is to present the work of Curtis that shows his humanity as a photographer rather than his well-known brilliance as a stylist and as a superb technician.

What is additionally revelatory about *Prayer to the Great Mystery* is the interpretive use of Curtis's text for the first time, showing his breadth as an historian of native peoples. Recent Curtis works have focused only on his photography, ignoring the fact that he was also a writer of considerable distinction, whose special interest lay in storytelling and mythology. No other work since the beginning of the Curtis revival of the 1970s has attempted to draw together the finest text of all the volumes and to merge Curtis's words with his unknown images. All of the ethnographic text within this new book comes from the twenty volumes of *The North American Indian* and has been edited and abridged to reflect contemporary usage. The language has been simplified for clarity, but the descriptions of the tribes are Curtis's own and the words of the elders he recorded are put down as they told them. The original encyclopedias, in fact, contain literally millions of words, often recording minutiae that readers even during Curtis's own time found unreadable (and there were only 272 numbered sets of these encyclopedias made in the first place). Given this abundance of descriptions, geographies, tribal renderings, and detailed linguistic instructions, Curtis's thoughts have never been presented before in one unified body. Excerpts describing the various tribes and histories of North America have been assembled from nearly all but a few of the original encyclopedias, and they show remarkable insight into tribal living. Here is Curtis at his humanitarian best, recording not only how the people looked but also how they talked, how they dreamed, and how they really lived from day to day, for so many of his classic photographs suggest a "noble savage" motif that Curtis himself would have railed against had he known how his photographs would be misinterpreted later. Thus, the larger goal of this work is to challenge many of the prevailing theories that Curtis was merely a romanticist. And the combination of these new, or virtually unknown, photographs with an edited and modernized text that has the same intent should help bring about a new impression of the great American writer and photographer.

Curtis's obsession *to be a witness* compelled him to do the work he did—to see, through the lens of his eye, that which was passing out of sight; to witness the presence of the American Indian in the tribal dress of a century that had come to a close. This ephemeral vision was still available, albeit barely, at the turn of the century, and he sought to preserve the beauty of a past that had been all but deracinated by the white man.

Between 1889 and 1930, Curtis visited Indians from such disparate tribes and such diverse landscapes as Kwakiutl, Comanche, Apache, and Cree. There was no end to his passion in recovering what was lost; there was no limit to his apprehension that tribal life in America would soon be gone from this earth. Hence, in each weighted volume of *The North American Indian,* which commenced publication in 1907, he painfully recorded the tribal census, lamenting the loss of people stricken by famine, disease, warfare, genocide, and, worst of all, the debilitating passage of time. A once-great people—in fact, America's indigenous population—he believed, were about to leave behind little more than a moccasin print, unless something could be done to preserve their memory. He knew that he would have to record the whole history of the North American Indian, for he believed—and he was probably right—there was no one else at that time capable of undertaking such a monumental task.

The value of Curtis's efforts remains pristine through many of the narratives of tribal elders that are reprinted here for the first time. Their stories beg to be told, and in most cases, Curtis's subjects sought him out, rather than the reverse. These are the great moral tales of tribal migration; some of the experiences, in fact, recounted by elders and storytellers may contradict much of what is currently thought to be true in contemporary anthropology. For example, we are told the story of the Mandan, a tribe of the plains, whose origin is cast in obscurity. Curtis's sources, however, reveal a surprising mythological starting point, which is perhaps the Gulf Coast of the United States. Here, then, in this book is the Mandan admission of their migration up the Missouri "from the place where the river flows into the great water." The Mandan elders further told Curtis of a "land to the south where the green of the trees never faded and the birds were always singing."

A Cheyenne narrative, which appears in the book, reveals an equally startling truth about the Cheyenne origin myth involving Niagara Falls:

The history of the people and their life cycle, from eastern mountain to southern and northern plain . . . it is highly probable that the tribe once inhabited the Algonquian territory of eastern Canada; there may be a hint of Niagara here, as well. In various versions of the same tale, we are told that the seeds were brought out of a lofty waterfall, or in the depths of a spring flowing from a hillside; or that the heroes went into a butte and got them; and, finally, that the butte was on the eastern margin of the Black Hills. Here we have, in effect, a panorama of the changing environment of the people as they moved from lake, river, and cataract to the semiarid plains west of the Missouri. Thus the great waterfall loses its immensity; it becomes a spring within a hill. Then it changes again and becomes the hill itself. After this, it is localized to the earliest-known home of the narrator. A man who has lived all his days on the prairies of Dakota finds a bold butte an easier feat of the imagination than a roaring mountain of water.

The miracle of such a record is that Curtis was able to hear, firsthand, several accounts of the Cheyenne migration. In the hearing, he recognized the shifting cultural parallels of myth in the making. His record is all the more valuable for his own interpretation, for he himself was there. In Montana, he recorded Tearing Lodge, a Piegan elder, who said: "Our three tribes came southward out of the wooded country to the north of Bow River. We began to make short trips to the south, finding it a better game country with much less snow. Finally, we gave up our old home. This happened in my grandfather's time."

Once more, time, in the telling, is foreshortened; history is carried on the stream of the human voice. There is, moreover, the narrative of Running Fisher, the Atsina elder, who speaks of his tribe crossing the Saskatchewan:

Among those in the act of crossing the ice was an old woman leading her grandson, who, seeing a horn protruding through the ice, asked his grandmother to cut it off for him. The woman at first paid no attention, but the boy's plea was so insistent that she turned back and began to chop off the horn. As she cut, blood commenced to flow, and suddenly a great monster heaved itself out of the water and glittering ice and drowned all of the people.

The outcome of this story is that only a part of the tribe journeyed farther to the South, thus completing their migration. The rest stayed on the other side, in Canada, which explains, in part, the tribal divisions that are so often accounted for inaccurately by white historians, although not by Curtis's informants.

There is material in this book, which I, as an archivist and historian of Native America for over thirty years, have not seen anywhere in print, nor heard on any reservations. The reason goes back to the lifelong obsession of Edward S. Curtis: to capture the light before it faded, to the extent of often talking to people over the age of one hundred. As these pages demonstrate, Curtis sometimes returned to a site as many as ten times in the same number of years, in order to gather the best possible example of tribal life. He was a man of his time, in addition to being an escapee from the moral reasoning that reduced his subjects to poverty and humiliation. And he was, after all, one man, trying to do the work of an institution. In appraising his worth, we ought to remember that, like the faces he captured on film, he is no longer with us, and, therefore, he is unable to speak beyond these pages, which finally, one feels, reflect Curtis not as a romantic but as a witness. His work, however, is a testament to an ideal, one that, though imperfect, sheds light and shadow on an unrecoverable past.

—GERALD HAUSMAN
Tesuque, New Mexico

It has been over one hundred years since Edward S. Curtis took his first photograph of an Indian subject. Between 1895 and 1928, Curtis took very likely over forty thousand negatives. At first glance, this number seems an unbelievably high figure. When divided, however, over thirty-three years, or just over twelve hundred images per year, this total number is not unimaginable.

Yet what remains perplexing is the way Curtis continues to be perceived by the American public: as a photographer known only for his highly romanticized images of Indians—perhaps of which no more than two hundred are considered part of the "classic Curtis oeuvre." Therefore, one of the foremost goals of this new book is to dispel the image of Curtis as the stereotyped, highly stylized photographer he is still thought to be. The previously unpublished photographs that are included here—and that were first shown to me by Ted Spiegel at the Library of Congress from the collec-

*Navajo Woman. 1904.*

tion of original Edward S. Curtis photographs—were the primary inspiration for this book. Edited out for some reason—and therefore relegated to total obscurity—these ninety-three photographs reveal dimensions to Curtis's life that are not traditionally associated with him—particularly his less-posed, more candid and realistic images. In addition to the previously unpublished photographs, an additional one hundred and fifty images have been culled from twenty text volumes of *The North American Indian*. These one hundred and fifty images, selected from approximately fifteen hundred small photogravures from the books, have never been published in any previous form. They suggest a greater dimensionality to Curtis's work than might be gained from the classic "hit parade" images that have been constantly republished over the last thirty years.

Take, for example, a group of five photographs taken by Curtis for his documentation of the Hopi

*A Navajo Smile. 1904.*

people. Sequentially listed by negative number, these photographs of two Hopi children eating watermelon offer us a rare opportunity to see Curtis, the photographer, at work. Note that the five images are like a time line, showing the children in different poses and actions. It is interesting to note that only the last image was selected to be included in *The North American Indian;* it was titled "The Delights of Childhood," printed in volume twelve, page 36. I find these other images more revealing, because they show the subjects in more natural poses.

Another striking example of naturalism in Curtis's work can be seen in the contrast between two photographs taken of the same Navajo female subject. In the previously unpublished Curtis photograph, the viewer sees a subject who appears not to be intimidated by the camera and is in a relaxed posture. The second portrait is more formal, and even stultifying. The smiling portrait ultimately shows a woman who trusts the photographer, but

this photograph may be truly atypical of his style.

The reader of this book must remember that it was not Curtis's intent to photograph an Indian subject exactly as he or she looked or dressed on a particular day; but rather, it was to reveal how he or she would have looked *before* any "white contact." This required, by necessity, a willing subject. In fact, American Indians, certainly by the end of his career, were very much aware of Curtis's goals. "Tribes that I won't reach for four or five years," he once mentioned at a lecture, "have sent me word to come and see them." He well understood why they would petition him, for they, better than anyone, fully understood that their history was an oral and not a written one.

The first event in Curtis's life that illustrates his career as an Indian photographer occurred in 1898. While hiking on Mount Rainier, Curtis, then a young man, came upon a group of scientists lost in an early snow squall. Guiding these men to safety, Curtis realized that one of the men was Dr. C. Hart Merriam, physician and naturalist, who was the head of the United States Biological Survey. Merriam, a man of considerable cultural influence in late-nineteenth-century America, directed E. H. Harriman, the famous railroad tycoon, to ask Curtis to be the official photographer of the Harriman expedition to Alaska in 1899, which launched Curtis's career.

Merriam was not the only man to help shape Curtis's future. George Bird Grinnell, editor of *Forest and Stream*, and also a conservationist and naturalist, was also on Mount Rainier that day. Grinnell in time became Curtis's mentor and, more than anyone, influenced his photographic destiny. In 1898, Grinnell had already spent over twenty years visiting and living among the Blackfeet, and he and Curtis became good friends as a result of the expedition. Later, Grinnell invited Curtis to witness the sacred Sun Dance ceremonies of the Blackfeet, and this event marked a turning point in Curtis's career as a photographer. Curtis was so taken by the experience that he formulated an idea that he expressed to Grinnell:

> I don't know how many tribes there are west of the Missouri, Bird—maybe a hundred. But I

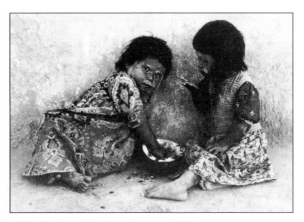

want to make them live forever—in a sort of history by photographs. No, I mean in both photography and words, if I can write them. And if I live long enough. You and I know, and of course everyone does who thinks of it, the Indians of North America are vanishing. They've crumbled from their pride and power into pitifully small numbers, painful poverty and sorry weakness. There won't be anything left of them in a few generations and it's a tragedy—a national tragedy. Thinking people must realize this. So, I want to produce an irrefutable record of a race doomed to extinction—to show this Indian as he was in the normal, noble life, so people will know he was no debauched vagabond but a man of proud stature and noble heritage. Bird—I believe I can do something about it. I have some ability. I can live with these people, get their confidence, understand them and

*Moki Melon Eaters (A). Hopi Pueblo. 1900.*

*Moki Melon Eaters (B). 1900.*

*Moki Melon Eaters (C). 1900.*

*Moki Melon Eaters (D). 1900.*

*The Delights of Childhood. 1900.*

photograph them in all their natural attitudes. It's such a big dream I can't see it all, so many tribes to visit, so many strange people. But I can start—and sell prints of my pictures as I go along. I'm a poor man but I've got my health, plenty of steam and something to work for.

Subsequent to Curtis's experience on the Blackfeet reservation, Theodore Roosevelt's wife noticed a photograph taken by Curtis in *Ladies' Home Journal*. His photograph had just won a prize, and Mrs. Roosevelt asked Curtis to come and photograph her children. During the photo shoot, Curtis and President Roosevelt became friends, and thereafter, Roosevelt became an avid supporter of Curtis's projects. Ultimately, Roosevelt wrote a letter of introduction that allowed Curtis to meet the financial mogul J. P. Morgan, who would become the primary backer for *The North American Indian*.

Between the years 1898 and 1906, Curtis had used his own limited funds to launch his ambitious project. After his meeting with Morgan, Curtis be-

lieved that his financial difficulties were over, for the industrial financier promised to underwrite all of the photographer's working expenses with a stipend of fifteen thousand dollars per year. Curtis did not anticipate the difficulty that would result from being his own publisher. From the outset, costs for field supplies, field assistants, editors, travel expenses, and, finally, production costs would more than absorb monies pledged by Morgan. So stressful was the project, financially and psychologically, that it eventually left Curtis a shattered man.

Throughout the pages of this new book, the reader will discover many fine Curtis photographs—ones that heretofore only a few people knew existed. I find these images utterly beautiful. They should provide the viewer with a totally different perspective of an enduring American artist .

—BOB KAPOUN
Sante Fe, New Mexico

# The Great Mystery: Edward Curtis and the Curious Customs of the White Photographer

When it comes to mysteries, great or small, no nationality or ethnicity holds a monopoly. If Indians have mystified and puzzled Anglo-Americans for several centuries, then Anglo-Americans have surely invested a proportionate amount of time in mystifying and puzzling Indians. As any neutral observer would have to conclude, white people practice very curious ways and habits. They have, for instance, placed tremendous faith in the power of the written word, sometimes behaving as if they believed that an event had not really happened unless it had registered in a written record. For a century or so, white people have also been very fond of an interesting mechanical invention called the "camera," a device that seems to allow human beings to break a number of the usual laws of the universe, freezing time and bequeathing to posterity visual images that long outlast the image-makers themselves. At the foundation of this fondness for the camera has been a willingness to believe that a photograph, even more than a written document, captures reality and holds it in place, whether or not that is reality's preference.

In future studies of the mental world of white Americans, the ethnographers of the twenty-first century will have to ask how photographers—and Edward Curtis would be a prime example—came to hold such power in the shaping of public thinking. Vast numbers of people, who may not recognize the name Curtis, still have minds well-stocked with images drawn from Curtis photographs, images that rush to consciousness when the word *Indian* is invoked. The occasion for the publication of this collection, then, is not merely to make the most of the unearthing of many previously unpublished Curtis photographs, nor is it simply to reunite Curtis's written work with his visual work, though either of those goals would make the project well worth doing. But this book also provides a prime occasion to contemplate Curtis himself, and to consider him as an instructive case study in the power and influence wielded by photographers in white American culture.

The present opportunity thus requires us to reverse the usual direction of vision. Curtis spent much of his time looking through a camera lens at Indian people. Now comes our opportunity to take up the questions: What did the people who appear in his photographs see when they looked back at Curtis? How did the objects of his interest assess him and his curiosity? Just as important, what did Curtis's various sponsors and patrons see in him and his projects? What about his determination to preserve memories and images of a defeated people that so engaged the support of that archetypal winner J. P. Morgan? When the editors of this volume tell us that Curtis had an "obsession to be a witness," they raise a question that goes to the heart of the project of understanding the United States. What kind of nation, after the violent conquest of indigenous people, would send out "witnesses," and obsessed witnesses at that, to record what the nation as a whole had just tried to destroy? In the same spirit, when Curtis divided his written presentations between narratives of the "history" of a tribe and retellings of the tribe's creation myths and origin stories, what clues does this division give us to Curtis's belief in a fundamental difference between white people's ways and Indian people's ways of remembering the past?

A great deal of what we know about Indian people in the past comes from the work of people like Curtis, white people who seemed to feel most fully alive when they were in the company of Indian people. While we would like to hear, directly, the voices of nineteenth-century and early-twentieth-century Indians themselves, we still must listen to them through the interpretations and translations of these white mediators. Even the photographs—perhaps especially the photographs—cannot bring us into direct, intense contact with the people photographed, since Curtis—like any photogra-

pher—arranged and selected, omitted and emphasized various aspects and qualities of the scenes he recorded. There is, in other words, no way of separating our understanding of the people photographed from our understanding of the photographer. There is no way of separating the study of Indian people from the study of the white people who shaped our images of North America's natives.

In the complicated workings of the conquest of the American West, Indian people's history got thoroughly tangled up with white people's history. Thus, in thinking about American Indian history, it has become essential to follow the policy of cautious street crossers: Remember to look both ways. When we look at and think about these photographs now, we are also obliged to look at and think about the photographer. In Curtis's case, that curiosity is particularly well-rewarded. On every page in this book, Edward Curtis proves to be just as interested as the native people whose lives he felt compelled to witness and whose stories he felt driven to record. Elements of the "great mystery" lie in Curtis himself.

—PATRICIA NELSON LIMERICK
Boulder, Colorado

# PRAYER TO THE GREAT MYSTERY

# I—The Southwest

Of all the material that Edward S. Curtis gathered on North American Indian culture, perhaps the hardest won, in terms of mythology, came from the people of the southwestern desert region. Geographically, these are the tribes stretching from the high desert canyons of New Mexico to the sandy bottomlands of Arizona.

As Curtis himself readily confessed, "The Pueblo Indians of the Rio Grande Valley, so far as their religious beliefs are concerned, remain the most conservative of all tribes of North America." And he goes on to say in the pages of this book that at Santo Domingo a proclamation was set forth that banned the release of any information to white people, with the punishment, in at least one instance, of execution for the Indian with a loose tongue.

However, if the work itself was difficult, the path invariably thorny, the result, under Curtis's watchful eye, bore beautiful fruit. For example, he celebrates and magnifies the midwife ceremony of birth, the bringing of a sacred name; he dutifully records the solstice ceremonies of Winter People and Summer People; and he delves deeply into the rites of the Pufonu secret society of shamans. By the time the interviews were conducted, these latter were reduced in number to nine members, with no future initiations in sight. This points, once again, to the prescience of Curtis's work; he knew that time was running out to record the moment of magical power, the merging of man and animal, the fusion of myth and traditional practice.

The coverage of a Tiwa peyote society is no less dramatic and ethnologically fascinating; in fact, its magnificence stems from the fact that it is a direct transcription from the visionary experience of a young Taoseno participant. These, like the Rio Grande snake myths told by tribal elders from Tesuque and Nambé, belong to an ephemeral and fractional time, now long past.

The Keresan history of Cochiti/Santo Domingo seems to read like a Native American version of *Crime and Punishment,* and his Zuni histories correct many of the errors implanted by white historians, giving us an intimate portrait of life during the first Christian contact with the Spanish. Gathering Hopi myths was something that Curtis did over a number of years, perhaps twenty in all, during which time he saw the erosion of the old ways, the constant entrenchment of the new, yet his reportage bears the stamp of authority and an intimate identification with his subject.

Pima, Yuma, Apache, and Navajo are also recorded faithfully, and as Curtis says, he often corroborated his material by repeated sessions where his stories were told and retold for veracity and tribal consensus. The result, overall, gives us the origin tales of a people who have told their story with a sense of pride as well as an intimation of finality, knowing that the myths are being spoken so that they may then be written for the generations to come.

**Tewa**
**History**

Of the Indian tribes whose ancestors came in contact with Europeans during the sixteenth century, only the Pueblo people have preserved their aboriginal customs with any degree of purity. Indeed, a great many tribes that suffered such contact are no longer known by name, yet the Pueblos have changed relatively little during the intervening centuries.

During this time, however, the Spaniards tried to lead the Indians toward Christianity by abolishing their native ceremonies. By the time the English colony had been founded at Plymouth, a number of Pueblos along the Rio Grande supported resident Franciscan friars, who not only brought their own religion to the villagers but the arts and trades of "civilization" as well.

Resentful that their faith should be assailed, the Pueblos accepted the Christian teachings in outward form only. Within, they jealously guarded

*Tablita Dancers. San Ildefonso. 1905.*

their own beliefs and native ways, continuing secretly to practice them. There seems little doubt that the hatred toward the priests was a major factor in the Pueblo revolt of 1680. The Indians avenged the overbearing attitude toward their religion by visiting death upon every Spanish missionary whom they could seize.

With some exceptions, the attitude of the Spanish toward the Pueblos was not a beneficent one. Witness, for example, the atrocities by the army of Coronado in 1540, and by Vargas and others during the reconquest of 1692. Yet in spite of all this—the shifting village sites and the consolidation of pueblos so they might be more readily missionized—the Pueblo people have clung tenaciously to the religion of their forefathers.

The Pueblos of the Rio Grande and the Rio Jemez, together with Acoma, have become most protective of their rites and ceremonies. Zuni, so long on the frontier of New Mexico province, does not seem to

*In the Village of Santa Clara. 1905.*

in Arizona, was founded by refugees from the Rio Grande after the Pueblo revolt of 1680. Pojoaque, another Tewa pueblo east of the Rio Grande and north of Santa Fe, has, within the present generation, become almost entirely Spanish. Onate in 1598 mentioned eleven Tewa villages; Benavides, a generation later, credited eight.

The farther north one goes among the Tewa, the more evident becomes the strong infusion of Plains Indian blood. The resemblance of most San Juan men to the Plains people is striking. They wear wrapped, or tied, braids, which are bound with strips of fur or cloth. They dress in hip-length leggings and shirts of deerskin; presently, however, these are now worn only on gala occasions.

The following material on the customs of San Juan, San Ildefonso, and Nambé make no pretense at completeness. Among the New Mexico pueblos, the investigator learns what he can, and is grateful when the door is left ajar for a few moments.

The civil officers at San Juan Pueblo are the governor and two lieutenant governors, who are regarded as his right and left arm. There are also a peace officer, or *alguacil*, and two church officiates, or *fiscales*.

The native officers are the summer and winter cacique; one is called "summer strong" and the other is "ice strong"; the war chief, "country leader head," and two assistant war chiefs, "country leader arm"; there are also four deputy war chiefs, "country little(s)."

The governor and his staff, subject to advice of the two caciques, control the civil affairs of the community. The caciques are spiritual leaders, who divide the year between them, by equinox. The summer cacique, usually addressed as "my old woman," is the religious head of the pueblo from February until the middle of October. The winter

possess such guardedness. However, it is true today that the Zuni will not permit a Spanish Catholic person to witness the religious performances that are open to other "foreigners." And while they will explain sacred beliefs and customs, they will not exhibit the objects associated with them.

The information recorded here covers the Tewa group of Pueblos: San Juan, San Ildefonso, and Nambé; and also Zuni, which, however, are from a different linguistic stock.

It is evident that the Tewa practiced an elaborate snake cult, perhaps with associated human sacrifice, which still survives in certain esoteric rites, the end of which seems not far off. Of all the secret rites of the Rio Grande Pueblos, none has been more difficult to track down than this one. The native laymen have small knowledge of the subject, and even among these individuals, there are few who would risk forfeiture of their lives by revealing the little they know.

The Tewa Indians, a branch of Tanoan linguistic stock, occupy five villages in the Rio Grande Valley north of Santa Fe, and a single pueblo adjacent to the Hopi villages on East Mesa in Arizona. The Tewa pueblos in New Mexico, from north to south, are San Juan, Santa Clara, San Ildefonso, Nambé, and Tesuque. Hano, the Tewa settlement

cacique, addressed as "my old man," is even more deeply venerated than his fellow high priest; and he rules for the remaining four months of the year.

It is the duty of the caciques to see that the numerous ceremonials are maintained in unbroken sequence. Specifically, the summer cacique prays for rain and growing crops. In his rituals, he uses meal made of blue corn, which represents the blue summer sky. The winter cacique prays for snow and fertile seeds, using meal of white corn, symbolic of snowy fields.

There are two main ceremonial societies that constitute the general population of the pueblo. They are the Squash, or Summer People; and the Turquoise, or Winter People. Normally, a child be-

*Whyay-Ring. Santa Clara Pueblo. 1905.*

*Santa Clara and the Rio Grande. 1905.*

longs not only to his father's clan but to his ceremonial society as well. However, an adult may
change his "party affiliation," if he finds his father's
society uncongenial.

The main clans of the Summer People are: Sun,
Moon, Star, Cloud, Earth, Corn, Blue Corn, Yel-
low Corn, Red Corn, White Corn, Black Corn,
Squash, Grass, Cottonwood, Aspen, Badger,
Weasel, Eagle. The clans belonging to the Winter
People are: Spruce, Oak, Bear, Wolf, Coyote,
Cougar, Elk, Mule Deer, Eagle, Chicken Hawk,
Eagle Mountain, House, Wood, Red Stone,
Turquoise.

Like all Indians, the Pueblo people take special
pride in their children. On the fourth morning after
a child is born, the two midwives who attended the
birth return for the name-giving ceremony. During
the night, some holy herbs are placed in a bowl of
water, and now the sacred cornmeal is laid out in
readiness. At the first streak of dawn, the two
women step outside the house, one with the child
in arms, the other carrying a torch taken from the
fire.

The torch brightens the predawn sky, and calls
the attention of the sacred powers to the newborn
child. The woman holding the baby tosses a bit of
meal to the cardinal directions. Then both women
turn slowly toward the left, the heart side. Doing
so, they catch sense impressions—a sun-streaked
bough, a smoke mist by the river, a windblown cottonwood leaf. These things, their colors, their presence may suggest a fitting name for the child. Or
they may bestow a name esteemed by the parents,
or some occurrence surrounding the birth itself.
Having thus announced the name to the listening
spirit powers, the women return to the house in the
dawn light. Once inside, the torch is put back into
the fireplace. The women offer the infant and the
mother a sip of the medicine water that was prepared the night before; the bowl is then passed
among those who are present in the house.

Tewa children are kept in laced cradle boards,
which are often hung from the vigas, or roof beams
of the house. Corn is placed at the head of the cra-
dled female child; a bow with arrows at the head of
the male child. These, they say, guide the thoughts
of the children in the proper way, so that they may

*Oyegi-aye ("Frost Moving"). Santa Clara Governor. 1905.*

think in the right direction when they grow older.
The shed milk teeth of boys, when cast away, are
done so with a prayer to the sun, to ensure the
strength of incoming teeth. A similar supplication
to the moon is made for girl children.

At the appropriate time, all boys and girls are
initiated into the Ohuwa, the Tewa equivalent of
the Hopi kachinas. The Ohuwa—Tewa for
"cloud"—are masked personators of the cloud
gods, who perform in the kivas; the Summer People in April or May, the Winter People in December. Before this, they do not know the deep
religious secrets, though they have witnessed, to
some degree, many of their manifestations in the
dances.

The rite occurs every seventh year, each society—Summer and Winter—initiating its own chil-

dren. The ceremony begins with the boys (but not girls) stripped to the waist. Two masked figures of the Winter People, who represent White Fir Cloud and Douglas Spruce Cloud, appear. Using bundles of yucca leaves for their whips, they deliver four vigorous strokes, as an awakening to the youths. Afterward, they remove their masks to show that they are human beings, rather than the gods they represent.

Once the initiates have been instructed in the lore of the kiva, they practice dancing. The elders, watching them, select the best ones to be the dancers in the coming ceremony. The initiates, thus selected, spend that night (as well as four following days and three nights) in the kiva, practicing songs and dances.

The Payooke, or Summer Society, is held in very high esteem, for its function is to pray for rain, and for the growth of the cultivated and the wild. They also pray for the good of the world, regardless of tribe or race. At the summer solstice, the summer cacique and his delegates make a pilgrimage to a lofty peak about twenty miles west of the pueblo. On this mountain, known as Tsi-kumu-pi, Obsidian-Covered Mountain, the sacred shrine of Yellow Cloud Man is located.

The cacique prepares the medicine in a bowl while the others watch him. He fills a blue stone pipe with native tobacco and blows smoke on the shrine and the medicine bowl. Then he sprinkles medicine in the six directions. Throughout the day, intervals of song are interspersed with prayer. Cornmeal is offered and prayer feathers are given to the cardinal directions.

Finally, the cacique sings this song:

*Morning big youths, get ready;*
*Your deerskin moccasins,*
*Your sparkling porcupine quills,*
*Your gleaming quilled leggings,*
*Your dark eyelashes —*
*Bring all people to life!*

Another ceremony connected with the summer solstice takes the form of a relay race in the plaza. This is for the purpose of giving strength to the sun from his return across the north. Formerly, the contestants were opposed — Winter People against Summer People — but this opposition is said to have been abandoned. The reason, they say, is that the Winter People's practice of tying yucca leaves to their ankles had more power than the Summer People's withered grass anklets. The race now occurs on the twenty-fourth of June, the feast day of the village patron, Saint John.

When the irrigation ditch is opened in the spring, the summer cacique, along with his winter brother, attends the ceremony of opening the water flow. The summer cacique goes around his colleague to the head of the line, and they proceed, walking in the middle of the ditch, to the other end. While walking, the summer cacique scatters cornmeal and fish scales along the way. In the fall they "close" the ditch by starting at the lower end, and walking to the source under the leadership of the winter cacique.

*Tse-ka ("Douglas Spruce Leaf"). Cacique of San Juan. 1905.*

In the spring the summer cacique fills a large deerskin ball with seeds of various kinds. Starting from the plaza, two groups of young men from the two societies drive it with clubs into all the houses. A woman of each household wraps a piece of thin bread about the ball and throws it out, and the young men scramble for the prize. Then they drive the ball over the fields until finally it bursts, and the seeds are scattered far and wide. Everyone is eager for the ball to be dispersed. How, otherwise, could they hope for good crops? Since it is sometimes two days before the ball is broken, the two societies must alternate in their work, taking time to rest and eat.

The Pufonu are a society of shamen, who are greatly valued at the pueblo, for it is through them that many healings take place. The Pufonu-sendo, the leader of the society, is nearly as important as the caciques. In 1909 there were about fifteen shamans; in 1924 the number was reduced to nine. There has been no initiation since about 1918.

A candidate for initiation spends eight days under the instruction of the Pufonu-sendo, during

*Chit Songwi. Nambe Pueblo. 1905.*

*Tablita Dancers Returning to the Kiva. San Ildefonso. 1905.*

which time his only food is boiled corn. Early in the morning of the last day, he goes to the river with the other members. Once there, he wades out until the water touches his mouth. He drinks and spews the water to cleanse himself; then all return to the leader's house for a feast provided by the initiate's family.

Each shaman possesses a *yiya*, or "mother," his personal fetish in the form of an ear of corn. The white downy underfeathers of the eagle are held to the corn by strings of beads—turquoise, garnet, and quartz—and the whole thing is encased in parrot tail feathers, rising from the base to beyond the tip of the ear. Highly prized, along with the mother fetish, is a small white soft-stone bear, the animal spirit that gives great power to the shamen.

When a sick person requires the help of the Pufonu, a messenger—the father or friend of the sick person's family—brings a gift of cornmeal and tobacco to the shaman. That night, unless the patient is too ill to be moved, the Pufonu shamen meet at the house of the Pufonu-sendo. There they arrange an altar, upon which they set their stone bears and around which they put flints and skins from the forepaws of an actual bear. The shamen sit in a row behind the altar, and their corn mothers are placed upright in a row between them. In the center of the altar is a bowl, in which, while singing, each shaman places a bit of ground root and herb. Each man carries a gourd rattle in his right hand and a pair of eagle tail feathers in his left. While everyone sings, the leader dips his feathers into the medicine, and with an upward motion against his rattle, he scatters the sacred water in the six directions.

Two men, one from each end of the row, the youngest, rise and dance about the room, striking one feather against the other, as if to rid the room of evil influence. They turn, dancing at the outer corners of the square altar, and then sit down. During the third song, the leader again disperses the medicine water in the six directions, and a man from the right side of the row takes up two lightning stones, made of flint and pyrite. These he strikes, sending a spark in each of the directions; then toward each shaman. After this, he dips a feather in the medicine and draws it across the lips of each man.

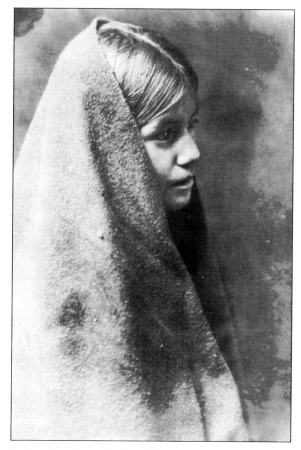

*Nahkat Sheh. Nambe Pueblo. 1905.*

The leader next gives each of his helpers a sip of the root medicine and a bit of bear medicine from his pouch, which they retain inside the lower lip. This gives them the power to detect and drive out sickness. Now all but the leader move about the room, stroking the patient with their feathers. Some have drawn the bear forepaws over one arm; these they use to cuff the patient, in the manner of a bear. Then, from the sick person's body, they begin to extract stones, bones, rags, and thorns. These, the story goes, have been injected into the patient's body by sorcerers; they are now broken up and deposited on a cloth spread on the floor.

Next the Pufonu-sendo announces that witches and wizards are trying to prevent a cure. The shamen, crying fiercely, rush about the house and go outside, searching for the evil ones. They re-

*Fo-e ("Snow Child"). Santa Clara. 1905.*

trees begin to leaf. First, the war chief summons a number of unmarried girls, each of whom names a male companion for the dance. On the fourth morning, the girls dance alone on the plaza while their leader sings; at night, they dance in the kiva with the men they have chosen. After this, they carry baskets of cornmeal to the homes of their partners; and the men return the baskets, filled with meat, to the homes of the girls.

On the last initiating days of the ceremony, the girls grind corn for the men, while a fire of juniper boughs gives forth a black smoke. It is from this that the Tesuque name of smoke-grind dance is derived. The girls who dance in the plaza wear men's clothing: deerskin shirts and leggings, buffalo-fur headbands, an upright turkey feather in the hair, and faces painted white.

The following is one of the songs used in the smoke-grind dance:

> *At big morning lake, Lake Peak,*
> *High up in the clouds*
> *The cloud boys come.*
> *Here they are!*
> *We sing, we dance;*
> *Cloud boys and girls.*
> *Here we are at Lake Peak,*
> *The home of White Cloud Man,*
> *The beautiful cloud-filled lake.*

In the dance in the kiva at night, a woman beats a drum and sings, and occasionally whips the girls. This is the song sung at that time:

> *Far to the east, Old Sun, we are friends.*
> *We are your children, Old Sun, dancing.*
> *Our enemies came to whip us,*
> *We went to drive them*
> *Down at the plum trees.*

Then the masked men come and dance while the girls rest. Afterward, the girls are sent to the cacique's house to remain with the maskers. In 1909 six mothers were pointed out as former participants in the smoke-grind dance; there were several infants said to have been begotten in the

turn, exhausted, holding up a figure made of rags, which they tear to pieces, depositing the fragments on the cloth. After this, they sit down again and begin another song, during which they rise and dance about the room, stroking with feathers the bodies of those who are watching them. Two young men rise and gather up the cloth, which contains the evil objects extracted from the sick person. They take these into the night and cast them away somewhere outside the pueblo.

The shaman (who was originally sought by the family of the patient) now gives the patient his stone bear, which is to be kept on his body for four days. Afterward, it is returned to its owner with whatever payment the family wishes to make for his shamanic services. At the end of the healing ceremony, all the shamen take home large baskets of cornmeal as their fee.

*Three Tewa Myths* | *The Smoke-Grind Dance of Tesuque* — This fertility dance occurs in the spring when

ceremony of 1908. However, membership in this society is limited to only seven women, corresponding, perhaps, to the myth of the seven daughters of the sun.

*The Snake Dance of Nambé*—This information was given in 1905 by a Nambé woman:

"There was once a male snake in one of the houses of this pueblo. If there had been a woman snake, there would be many people here today. The snake was fed ceremonially with cornmeal and pollen.

"When they practice for the dance, they feed meal to the feathers they wear on their heads, also to their drums. The dancers are kept shut in a house for four days, during which time they are not permitted to see or touch a woman. When the dance is ended, they must bathe in the river.

*Winnowing Wheat. San Juan Pueblo. 1905.*

*The Fruit Gatherers. San Ildefonso Pueblo. 1905.*

"Santa Clara has two snakes, and two women who are called Snake Mother. One of these walks as if she had no bones. When we make bread cakes with snake symbols, we bring them to the kiva and feed them to the snake, which has been taken there. The women are not permitted to see it. It is black and white, thick and long. It has a rattle. When the snake becomes old and will not eat, they take it away and get another. This is done in October, very early in the morning, and the men are absent for three days.

"If the cacique did not take care of the snake, finally releasing it and getting another, the people at the pueblo would die. This is why we believe in the snakes. When the men go to work in the fields, they first chew a weed and spit it out in the thick grass, so that the snakes will not bite them. If a man kills a snake, he kills it completely, and puts its head where the ants will not eat it. Otherwise, it would follow and spit its poison on him, and he would swell and die."

There used to be snakes kept in Nambé, and the snake dance, a relic of this custom, is still given once a year. The summer cacique had charge of the male snake; the winter cacique of the female snake. The present summer cacique did not believe in the custom and let his male snake go. The other had died, or gone away, and for a long time there had been but one in Nambé, which, they say, was the cause of the steady decrease in population.

The same Nambé woman had this to say about the snake dance:

"The snake dance occurs about New Year's, and at present only three men take part. They do not handle snakes, but imitate the former ceremony in which the snakes were used. In preparation for this dance, the men are confined four days and nights in the house of the war chief, and during this time they must not touch a woman. If one is bitten by a snake, or has any kind of wound, it will become very bad. The dance begins about the middle of the morning, when the singers stand on the south side of the plaza and the dancers come out of the house into the center of the plaza and dance. They come out four times, returning to the house to rest. They imitate snakes in the movement of their bodies. After the fourth time, they go to the houses of the village and receive food, which they carry to the war chief's house. Then they go to the

*Mowa ("Shining Light"). Nambe. 1905.*

river, where they throw cornmeal into the water. After doing this, they bathe, first asking the river to take away all sickness and to give them good health.

"The men wear white moccasins and a white loincloth, which ends in a long tail; their faces are painted half white and half red or blue. The hair is left with the side locks hanging, and eagle feathers are made into a peak on top of the head. Colored yarns hang from the arms at the elbows, and bells and shells are attached to their ankles. Their legs and arms are white; feathers hang from yarn bands below the knees. In the right hand, they have a gourd rattle, and in the left, a painted stick with eagle feathers at the ends and middle. Singing, they raise their voices: 'Like snakes, you are sent as snakes; come, do what you were sent to do. We are real snakes, born of a snake mother; you are a grandchild of a snake mother.'"

*A Kiva at Nambe. 1905.*

*Pose-aye ("Dew Moving") Profile. Nambe. 1905.*

*Snake Tales of the Tewa* — A Tesuque man once told me the following story:

"Once upon a time, a handsome youth came into a house and asked a girl to be his lover. She consented, and he told her to keep him secreted in a large jar. She locked him in an unused room, but when she returned to visit him, he was not found. Remembering his words, she peeped into a vessel and saw a large snake coiled there. In due time, she gave birth to two snakes. Her father angrily reproved her. He took the snakes into the hills, released them. Then he gave them cornmeal and begged them not to harm the people.

"It is in memory of this incident that the village of Tesuque keeps two snakes. The cacique feeds them and prays for their goodwill. The snakes are brought together for breeding, and the young are released in the mountains with prayers, meal, pollen, and feathers. They are asked to send rain, to remain in the mountains, away from the village. We do not kill snakes. We give them meal and ask them to go into the mountains and not harm us. A man who is bitten by a snake goes at once to the summer cacique, who knows how to cure him with herbs. He is kept in seclusion until he recovers, and

he must not be seen by a woman, nor come in sight of fire, lest he die."

A San Juan man added the following narrative:

"When I was a youth of about fourteen, I herded my father's cattle. It was in the month of August and just about midday. Going down an arroyo, I saw a track, as if someone was dragging a heavy log. It was strange that the track was not in a straight line. I went up on a small hillock to see where the cattle were, and I was just about to jump down the slope when I saw in front of me, under an overhanging rock, a very large snake. I could not run. It was coiled. It had an arrowhead mark on the back of its head and smaller ones on its body. Its head was raised. It did not rattle. It seemed a long time before I could jump back and run home."

The San Juan snake was killed in 1884 by a Frenchman quarrying rock. He was cooking his supper, and the snake came to the door of his cabin. Almost paralyzed with fright, he seized a sharp pinch bar and struck. The bar passed through its neck, but the snake was so large that the implement simply punctured instead of severing it. The snake was seven feet six inches long and "as thick as a stovepipe." The place from which the

snake had come, he discovered, was a small cave in the rocks, walled in with stones and pots.

The Santa Clara Indians say that by inserting into a snake's mouth the tip of a twig moistened with saliva, they can render the reptile unconscious. In order to convince a skeptical American neighbor, a young man caught a nonvenomous snake. He took a toothpick, placed the tip in his mouth, then in the snake's. The reptile almost at once grew motionless, and then it became as limp as a piece of rope. It lay on the patio some hours before it disappeared unnoticed.

*A San Juan Home. 1905.*

**Tiwa History**

If one reads the accounts of the first Spanish explorers, it is no surprise why the Pueblo Indians of the Rio Grande Valley, so far as their religious beliefs are concerned, remain the most conservative of all tribes of North America. Most Indians are loath to reveal their religious beliefs. However, with tact, patience, and tenacity, one can often obtain valuable information. On the Rio Grande, though, one meets organized opposition to the divulging of anything pertaining to ceremonial life. At Santo Domingo, proclamations have been issued against affording material to white people, and at one pueblo, tribal members who violated the code were executed.

The Tiwa were unfortunate in their first contacts with "higher civilization." Coronado's force passed the winter of 1540–1541 in a "Tigueux" village, the houses of which had been vacated for the Spaniards by the Indians. The ensuing events were the direct cause of nearly four centuries of resistance, usually passive, but nonetheless, resolute and bitter. The vast silent opposition of the Pueblo Indians stems from their regard of what they view as a grasping, faithless race, whose first chronicler, Casteneda, tells the tale all too well:

> The horsemen on the plain with many of the Indian allies from New Spain smoked them [the Tiwa Indians] out of their cellars [kivas], so that they begged for peace. They then put down their arms and received pardon. They were taken to the tent of Don Garcia . . . he had been ordered not to take them alive, but to make an example of them so that the other natives would fear the Spaniards; he ordered 200 stakes to be prepared at once to burn them alive. Nobody told him about the peace that had been granted them, for the soldiers knew as little as he, and those who should have told him about it remained silent, not thinking that it was any of their business. Then when the enemies [Indians] saw that the Spaniards were binding them and beginning to roast them, about a hundred men who were in the tent began to struggle and defend themselves with what was there and

*A Tesuque Ancient. 1925.*

with the stakes they could seize. Our men who were on foot attacked the tent on all sides, so that there was great confusion around it, and then the horsemen chased those who escaped. As the country was level, not a man of them remained alive, unless it was some who remained hidden in the village and escaped that night to spread throughout the country the news that the strangers did not respect the peace they had made, which afterward proved a great misfortune.

The people of Taos, the northernmost of the pueblos, and those of Picuris, a mountain village about twenty miles to the southeast, speak the same tongue, a dialect of Tiwa. Taos lies about seventy miles north of Santa Fe. Mountains are visible in every direction, and the peaks and crags of the Sangre de Cristo are forbidding and sublime. Climbing the canyon road, the traveler soon sees the twin pueblos of Taos, one on each side of a musical brook. A few thin columns of smoke rise high in the quiet air. A horseman approaches, swathed in a white cotton sheet; only his face is visible. The facial features are those of a Ute, while the garb is Cheyenne. Walking beside him is a woman wearing flapping white deerskin boots, such as no woman of the plains ever wore.

Soon the road is dotted with figures clothed in the same way. Nearly all, especially the men, have Plains Indian features. One realizes that this nevertheless is the Taos type, but harbors a feeling that there must be a group of tepees behind the clump of willows down by the stream. The plaza is nearly deserted, but on a fourth-story roof there is a young man, whom you are told is keeping a watchful eye on his girlfriend. But if you know anything of Taos, you suspect that his eye is missing nothing of your own movements. Taos shares with Santo Domingo and Jemez the distinction of being the most recalcitrant of the pueblos—which, if you knew the others, is quite a distinction.

The name Taos is a Spanish plural, first recorded by Juan de Onate in 1598. The Tewa name, Ta-wii, means "dwell gap," for the situation of the village at the mouth of the canyon. Their own name for themselves is simply Taina, "people," or "red-willow people." Taos was "discovered" in 1540 by Hernando de Alvarado, a subordinate of Coronado. He described it as he first saw it: "... the houses are very close together, and have five or six stories, three of them with mud walls and two or three with thin wooden walls, which become smaller as they go up, and each one has its little balcony outside the mud walls, one above the other, all around, of wood. In this vil-

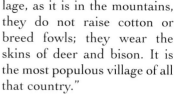

*Wyemah. Taos Pueblo. 1905.*

lage, as it is in the mountains, they do not raise cotton or breed fowls; they wear the skins of deer and bison. It is the most populous village of all that country."

Prior to the year 1680, Taos became a city of refuge to Pope, a San Juan shaman, who was charged with some crime by the Spanish authorities. From this time, he devised the plan for the general revolt of all the Pueblos, and the killing of all missionaries and colonists. When the plot ripened, Taos played a major role, its warriors joining in the siege of Santa Fe. The reconquest by Vargas in 1692 was accomplished without conflict in Taos; however, on his second visit there, he found it necessary to despoil it and carry away its stores of corn. This happened because the people refused to come out of their temporary refuge in the canyon.

In 1847 a number of influential Spanish conspired to overthrow American authority in the territory. They had the cooperation of Taos, and the resulting armed conflict has become known as

*A Corner of Taos and a Kiva Entrance. 1925.*

the Taos Rebellion. Early one January morning in the Spanish village of Fernando de Taos, Indians and Spanish killed six persons, including Charles Bent, governor of the territory. The insurrection had a final engagement on February third at the pueblo of Taos. There, Colonel Sterling Price with 353 men, a six-pounder cannon, and several howitzers began to bombard the church at 250 yards and throw grape at the village itself. In the end, 150 Indians were killed, while only twelve of the attacking force died.

From the earliest times Taos and Picuris were exposed to the attacks and cultural influence of various Plains Indians. Possibly this was merely the continuation of an even earlier contact when they themselves were plainsmen, who, constantly harassed by their enemies, ultimately crossed the mountains to the headwaters of the Rio Grande. There is no historical evidence supporting this conjecture, which is based primarily on the universal Pueblo tradition of a northern origin.

*Old House and Kiva at Picuris. 1925*

There is a record of the temporary migration, about the middle of the seventeenth century, of a considerable body from Taos to El Quartelejo, a district in what is now Scott County in western Kansas, where the Jicarilla Apache then ranged. In 1704 the village of Picuris, for some reason, fled to the same place, but they were soon persuaded by the governor of the province of New Mexico to return. In 1695 Vargas wrote: "While I was absent from this city (Santa Fe) there arrived a band of Apaches from the east, who are called Chiyenes, and they told . . . how some men, white and light-haired, had destroyed a very large tribe of the Apaches Conejeros, living much further inland than their own."

The translation of the above is that some Apache at Picuris Pueblo informed the people there that some white men had come to the banks of the Arkansas River and made war on the Wichita Indians of Kansas. The account given by the

Apache was fully accredited by the Spanish officials, who regarded the white men as French. The name Apache is misleading here because the Spanish referred to any warlike Indians as being "Apaches."

At the beginning of the eighteenth century, the Ute were causing considerable trouble by running off the horses at Taos, and the Comanche were so persistently attacking Pecos that by 1790 its population had decreased from 2,000 in 1680 to 152. Much of this diminution was due to the Apache tribe, who prior to the year 1700 had periodically raided Pecos and the other Pueblos east of the Rio Grande Valley.

The Cheyenne ranged on both sides of the Arkansas and in the Panhandle of Texas. The route from Taos to Texas and Oklahoma was through Taos Pass to Cimarron, thence to Springer, and then heading eastward through open country to the northwest corner of Texas. This trail was used by white traders and buffalo hunters, as well as Indians. Taos, situated between mountain and plain, became a meeting point, the rendezvous of white trapper and Indian trader alike. Thus Taos was influenced by blood and custom from all the cardinal directions.

One of the more controversial ceremonies at Taos is the ritual of peyote, which has become a kind of latter-day religion among many Indian people. Peyote is a small cactus, native of Texas along the Rio Grande, and also Mexico. Among the Southern Plains tribes, the upper part, the button formed after flowering, is sliced and dried, and ceremonially eaten for the purpose of curing disease. It possesses an intoxication that induces hallucinations. To a devotee, the word *peyote* means not only medicine but a person, the deity who works wonders through the substance of the cactus.

The cult, which has become popular at Taos, was introduced there about 1910 by young men, who had been initiated in Oklahoma by the Cheyenne. At Taos the peyote group builds a circular, roofed lodge of green boughs, large enough to accommodate, with a little crowding, a circle of thirty or forty men. In front of the small central fire, they make a half-moon by heaping dry earth and wetting it so that it will retain its form, and on this symbol the leader places a peyote button. This is, in effect, the altar of their church. The opening of the shelter and that of the half-moon are toward the east.

The leader, who sits at the back of the lodge, is provided with a bag filled with dry circular slices of peyote. He passes four to the man at his left, who lays them on the ground before him. He passes four more, and the man at his

*Tull Chee-Hah. Taos Pueblo. 1905.*

left gives them to his left-hand neighbor; and so it goes until each person has his four. The leader then rolls a cigarette and lays it beside his peyote buttons, and hands the tobacco and a package of corn-husk wrappers to the man at his left, who rolls his cigarette and passes the materials on. When all are ready, the leader issues the word to raise the cigarettes. He then directs the fire-keeper, who sits at

the north side of the entrance, to bring him a light. The fire-keeper carries an ember from one to another, beginning with the leader and passing in a clockwise direction. They smoke, and all pray in subdued voices while smoking.

Following this, the peyote is cleaned, the "cotton" removed from the center. The outer skin is taken off. The remainder is rolled into a pellet, which is held in the right palm. The individual gazes at the pellet while praying to the deity Peyote. He hopes that the pellet will go down easily and not become lodged in the throat, and that he may sit without growing weary. All together four buttons are ingested and each of the men then sing four songs while a drum is beaten. As one Taoseno initiate has explained:

"While the drum was going round the first time, I asked for two peyote buttons. On the next round, I asked for three; the next time, four. It seemed that I wanted to sing all the time. I was happy. When the drum came to me, I sang either five or six songs, which was passing beyond the rule. The others were laughing at me. The next time I asked for five. The leader looked at me and laughed, and after considering a moment, he took five from the bag and passed them to me. He thought he had played a trick on me by passing three green and two dry ones, for the green are stronger and will not roll into a ball.

"I chewed up a green one and swallowed it, then the other two, and made the dry ones into balls and swallowed them. Then I asked for tobacco, and smoked and prayed. Everybody was listening to me. I was happy. Words came to me. While I prayed, I heard someone behind me singing. It sounded like an old man. But it is against the rules to turn about. We must sit upright without touching the wall or turning the head.

"Then I happened to look at the peyote on the

*Iahla ("Willow"). Taos. 1905.*

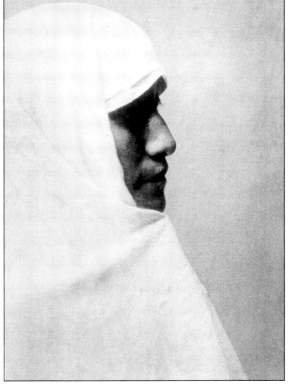

*Pavia. Taos. 1905.*

half-moon. I had a vision. The world stretched before me, a broad, flat expanse, white and covered with flowers. Here and there were deer, elk, buffalo. Several men on horses appeared. They rode toward me, then turned and disappeared. A single man then appeared, walking toward me and looking at me as if he intended to speak. I glanced away for an instant at the people around me, and when I looked back, he was gone. I had lost it. That singing behind me was something sent by Peyote. If I had kept my eyes on the man who was coming to me, I think he would have given me new songs or a message of some sort.

"It was nearly midnight, the time for bringing water from the creek. All this time, from the beginning, I had not stood up. Suddenly, I felt that my knees were stiff, that I must stand up. I asked the leader for permission. He said, 'Wait a little. The water will soon be here.'

"'I must go out. Please let me.'

"'Well, go, but come back quickly.'

"So I went out. The fire-keeper went along and asked, 'What is it, brother?'

"'Somebody is calling me,' I said.

"I felt that someone or something in the air was calling me. So we went out, and I walked about for a few minutes, but saw nobody. We came back, and I sat down again. The fire-keeper then brought a pail of cold water, drank, and gave it to the leader, who drank and passed it around. I took a large quantity, and immediately felt as if we were just starting. There was no stiffness or weariness in my body."

The leader now gives permission to stretch the limbs, and the people extend the legs straight before them without getting up. After a few minutes, he bids them resume the original posture, legs doubled up beneath them. It is now about one in the morning. The leader sings his Morning Star songs, holding a bunch of eagle feathers, as well as some green leaves and a cane. These and the drum and the rattle are passed around. The ceremony continues until gray dawn, the devotees asking for peyote and tobacco at will.

At the first sign of dawn, the fire-keeper fetches another pail of water; everyone drinks deeply. They sing again until full dawn, when food is brought by a woman—bowls of boiled meat, of chopped meat sweetened with sugar, of parched corn in sweetened water. The woman receives a cigarette, smokes a puff or two, then prays for health and strength for each of these people. Then the bowls are passed around, and each person takes one small handful, and no more. The leader now sings his finishing song, and when the people step out into the light of the sun, they form two lines facing eastward. The leader sets down the drum at the end of the path. They then stretch their limbs and, for the first time, speak to one another. It is the time for congratulations, good wishes, warm greetings. They walk in small groups or sit quietly in the shade of the lodge. Now and then, a few of them sing softly into the rising wind, waiting for the feast that comes with the noonday sun.

*A Taos Girl. 1905.*

to dig with his digging stick. He kept singing and digging and making circular motions all around the place where the root was supposed to be. At last, digging vigorously, he found the root that he was looking for. When he found it, he chewed it and spat on his hands and rubbed the root juice all over his body. He could feel the people watching him, which was good.

Finally, his work done, Bear Old Man put his pack on his back and went homeward, singing contentedly. From the village, the people watched him, and they said, "Bear Old Man came for his medicine root; now he goes back to his timber den."

Bear Old Man did that thing, just as they said he would. But just before he entered his den, he sang one last song, which goes like this:

## Three Animal Myths of Taos

*The Bear*—Bear Old Man lived in the mountains at Burnt Timber Hill. One day, he decided to come down near the village where the people lived to find some medicine roots. Early in the morning, he showed up, and he began to sing, shaking his digging stick. He put medicine in his mouth and spat in the four directions. Then he sang again.

"Surely," he said, "the people must be looking at me." And he danced and he sang, and he started

*In the Forest. 1925.*

*I am Bear Old Man, Old Man Bear*
*Since the beginning, this has been my home*
*It is still my home.*
*I am Old Man Bear, Bear Old Man*
*I live here, I will always live here.*

And then Bear Old Man went into his den, and the people said, "We know his medicine ways now, for he has shown them to us. May we live long, as he does. May we always live here with him."

*The Rabbit*—Many animal people were being killed. They did not know how this happened; they just knew that it did, because members of their group were missing from time to time. So one day, they tracked Mountain Lion and discovered that he was doing the killing. "What shall we do?" the animal people asked each other. And they decided that it was best to kill one of their children, so that they could feed their enemy. One child daily was what they thought best, and they did this. But before each animal family had taken a turn and given up a child, their number dropped very low.

"What shall we do?" they asked again. This time they decided to hunt for game, birds, and such, but they came upon Rabbit. As they were about to kill him, he said, "Brothers, do not kill me. I will help you if you let me go." So the animal people released Rabbit, and he set about to work his plan to help them.

The next morning, he was leaping around, playing, when Mountain Lion pounced on him.

Rabbit said, "Father, do not kill me. I will help you fight the great giant, who is known as Wood Person."

"Where does Wood Person live?" Mountain Lion asked with gold-eyed interest. His long tail was twitching, side to side.

"Come," Rabbit announced, "I will show you."

Then Rabbit took Mountain Lion to a blue pond in the forest. The water was very still and so deep that it appeared bottomless. Mountain Lion

*Taos Children. 1905.*

scowled at the quiet pond. He spoke up, "Wood Person does not live here."

"Oh, but he does," Rabbit protested. "My father, look in the still water, and you will see him."

Mountain Lion edged himself to the end of the ledge where he was seated and peered over. Immediately, he caught his reflection quivering on the calm blue surface. What he saw had black-tipped ears and a snarling face, full of anger. Yes, he thought, Rabbit is right. Wood Person lives in this very pond. And then he sprang from the ledge with

*A Taos Maid. 1925.*

his claws extended and his teeth all ready to tear Wood Person apart.

Rabbit watched with satisfaction as Mountain Lion tumbled, clawing, into the water, where he sank and was not seen again. "Well," he said, "now that I have killed that unfriendly fellow, the animal people will be most pleased."

And they were, for they could at last move about without danger of being killed. "Rabbit is smarter than he is small," they agreed; and that is why the animal people do not judge a person by the length of his shadow.

*The Deer*—The people were worried. There were sorcerers among them who killed whenever they desired, and so the people were few and the sorcerers many. To make matters worse, these sorcerers were invisible and they could change into anything they wanted to. So the people consulted Deer Woman, who was very wise. "What shall we do?" they asked.

Deer Woman replied, "You shall have a great race, and the winner will banish the loser. I will offer my own two sons, so that there will be no chance of the sorcerers taking the lead." She spoke the truth: No living thing was faster than a deer. And so the race was arranged one early morning.

The sorcerers came as two skeletons with the flesh hanging off their bony limbs. They were frightful to look at, all rotten and oozing blood, but the people figured the two Deer Boys could outrun them. At the start, the deer took the lead and held it well for a while. But soon the evil sorcerers, tired of being skeletons, turned themselves into falcons that soared swiftly past the deer.

However, the deer had been well taught by their wise mother in their own arts; and now they opened up a bag of medicine with five kinds of magic. These they put into their mouths, spat them in the four directions, and prayed for heavy rain. Soon black clouds covered the sun; lightning ripped the sky; rain fell. The falcons' feathers were soaked, and they took refuge in a tree.

The rain continued, and while the sorcerers considered what next to change into, the deer bounded halfway around the world, and won the race. But the sorcerers were very bad losers. After their feathers dried, they changed back into bloody skeletons, and they cried out: "For beating us in this race, we will kill all of you!" They had huge clubs made of cactus spines, and they got ready to use them. But now the people surrounded them and with clubs of their own, they took them by surprise. The sorcerers had no chance to change into anything more threatening than bones; presently, they were beaten down to little chips of white, which were perfectly harmless.

There was, however, one sorcerer left. He begged piteously that his life be spared. Some cried out to kill him, too. But there were those who thought that he ought to be spared when he said, "My brothers, let me live and I will promise to do my part to be at peace with you." And so the people gave in and let him go. "What is one little sorcerer?" they said with a shrug. But from that one come all those that are with us today.

# KERES

**Keres
History**

The Keres Indians are found in seven distinct pueblos. The eastern group are Cochiti, Santo Domingo, San Felipe, Santa Ana, and Zia. The western pueblos are Acoma and Laguna. The original home of the Keres was in the canyon of Rito de los Frijoles, about fifteen miles north of the present Cochiti. According to Bandelier:

"The whole length of the village is about two miles, more or less. . . . Here was a little world of its own. The bottom afforded a sufficient extent of very fertile soil; there was enough permanent water to permit irrigation, and there are even traces of acequias on both sides of the brook. Trees stood in front of their homes, and the mesas above are well wooded. Game of all kinds, deer, elk, mountain sheep, bears, turkeys roamed about the region in numbers, and the brook afforded fish. The Rito is cool in summer and not very cold in winter, compared with the surrounding table-lands and the Rio Grande Valley."

*Kayati-Sia. 1925.*

No one knows exactly why, but there was dissension among the people, and what was perhaps some fifteen hundred individuals divided into various groups. The malcontents included ancestors of San Felipe, who later rejoined the main village in a place known as "mountain lion village," a tonguelike mesa called in Spanish Potrero de las Vacas. The native name of this ruin refers to a remarkable shrine, a circle of stones enclosing two crouching mountain lions sculptured out of bedrock that forms the surface of the mesa.

But, here again, as one Indian put it, "trouble came; their hearts were not one." Those who later were to found Santo Domingo went a short distance eastward to Ipani; the others, ancestors of Cochiti, moved about three miles southwest and founded the Red Village, or Potrero San Miguel, Pueblo. At the same time, the San Felipe people went about three miles west of the present village of Cochiti.

Old Cochiti, Potrero Viejo, where the ancestors of Cochiti settled finally, was well situated for defense. The Keres name, Hanat-kotyiti, translates to "high above Cochiti." Here the Indians resided, moving but once, down to the Rio Grande around the time of the revolt. Near the close of 1681, after the general uprising of the Pueblos, Governor Otermin, in his abortive attempt to reconquer the country, found San Felipe, Santo Domingo, and Cochiti abandoned. He sacked them and consumed their grain and burned their *estufas*, or kivas, which he referred to as "houses of idolatry."

In 1689 Governor Cruzate destroyed Zia and slaughtered a large number of its inhabitants. Diego de Vargas, the new governor, found all of the Keres pueblos deserted once again in 1692. When he returned the following year, Cochiti and San Marcos had banded together and were ensconced at Potrero Viejo. Again according to Bandelier:

"The resistance offered by the pueblo proved fruitless, and three hundred and forty two women and children fell into the hands of the Spanish, together with seventy horses and nine hundred sheep. A considerable portion of Indian corn was found in the pueblo. . . . Vargas ordered the prisoners to shell it on the spot. . . . When Vargas at last evacuated Potrero, with his booty in corn and the

*Santa Ana and Jemez Rivers. 1925*

*A Santo Domingo Man. 1925.*

murder he put the dress on the priest, conducted him to the river and urged him to keep traveling southward. A short distance below San Felipe the priest hid at daylight among the cottonwoods on a small island. Some San Felipe rabbit hunters found him, took him to their pueblo, and promised to protect him.

Later in the day the Cochiti Indians followed the priest's trail, and when San Felipe refused to deliver him up to them they laid siege, camping at the river so that the women were prevented from getting water. On the fourth day the water stored in cisterns on the mesa was nearly exhausted. The priest was told that he would have to be given up unless he could bring rain by prayer. He asked for a tanned rabbit skin, and on it he wrote with blood from his own veins. He told his San Felipe friends to hang it on the church tower, which they did. A heavy rain soon filled the cisterns, and the Cochiti guards withdrew. Most of the inhabitants of Cochiti then fled to the mountains, after breaking up the furnishings of the Cochiti church. Some of the statues were made, as they said, of "sweet stuff," which they ate. They made moccasins of the parchment paintings, and that same year they returned to their pueblo on the river.

remnant in captives, he set fire to the pueblo. He burned the grain that could not be taken 'in order that the rebellious enemy might not find any sustenance in it, nor be able to take up his abode without being compelled to rebuild.' Old Cochiti was never occupied again."

There was a minor revolt at Cochiti (the present village along the Rio Grande) in 1694, which Bandelier has described in the following manner:

A priest sent from Mexico, who lived at the pueblo, had a different woman servant each week. . . . A man thought that his wife was intimate with the priest, and he asked that the council either order him killed or send him away. . . . When it was decided to kill the priest, the Indian sacristan provided a woman's dress, and in the middle of the night appointed for the

*A Sia Man. 1925.*

*Timu. Cochiti. 1925.*

Thus the meandering days of the Keres people seemed to be at an end, but the tone of their wandering, put into effect by Spanish depredations, would not be forgotten, and today it is still a palpable memory.

| *Two Keres Tales of Justice and Deliverance* | *The Boy Who Ran Away*—The past is never forgotten in the desert; it is etched in rock, and though attacked by wind and weather, it remains, a tes- |

tament, like the great carved lions of the Keres. The following story was told by a man from Cochiti, who was a participant. It seems that some years ago, around 1914, a young Santo Domingo man named Diego, who was working for a Spanish employer a few miles away from his village, was summoned by the governor of the pueblo. He ignored the summons, and the next morning, the governor and four others showed up at his place of work.

"Diego," the governor said, "why didn't you come when I asked for you?"

Diego made no reply. The governor then told

*Tsipiai. Sia. 1925. (left)*

*A Santa Ana Man. 1925. (right)*

the other men to bind his hands behind him. Afterward, they fastened a rope around his neck and tied it to a wagon. Then they drove off so rapidly that Diego had to run to keep up with them. In the village, Diego was tried by a pueblo council, whose verdict declared that he was guilty of working for a Spanish employer. He was asked to remove his shirt and pants, whereupon his forearms were bound together, each hand on the opposite elbow, and thus they suspended him from a roof beam. They then flogged him and left him hanging there, unconscious.

Eight days later, after Diego had recovered from his punishment, his nephew came to him and said, "Uncle, I am sent here by my father, the war chief, to tell you that they are going to try you again. I am going to tell you what they talked about in the council this morning. The council decided that they will try you tonight. They said that if the governor did not kill you last time, this time he surely will do so. Now, my uncle, if I were you, I would try and run away. As soon as it is dark, try to do that. If you don't, they surely will kill you."

Now Diego was still badly bruised from the beating he had endured. Gathering his thoughts, he spoke to his wife: "My dear wife," he explained, "my nephew has told me that the war chief is going to try me and punish me tonight. He fears that they will kill me. So I must try and run away. As soon as it is dark, I must go."

Shortly after, he ate and departed, picking his way carefully into the hills toward Penablanca, the Spanish village where he had lately worked. There, he went to the house of his former employer's father. The old man was sitting in the kitchen before a lighted lamp.

Diego knocked on the door, and the old one said, "Who is it?"

"I, compadre."

"Who goes there?"

"I, Diego."

The old man opened the door and Diego entered and sat down.

"What is the matter, compadre?" the old one asked.

Diego then told his tale and showed his badly swollen arms and legs, and asked what he should

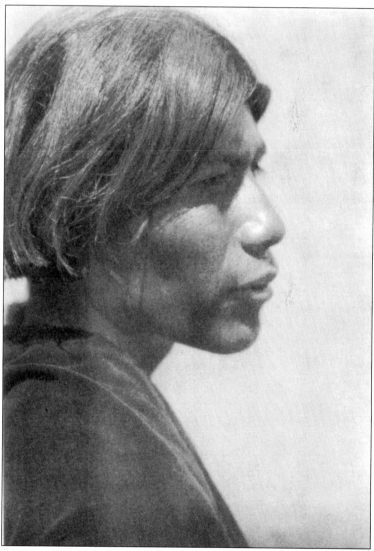

*Sotsona (Fox). Santo Domingo. 1925.*

do, for in the morning, he said, they would be coming for him. "Well, then," the old one said, "I will tell you what you shall do. Before daylight, you must rise. I will make you some coffee and some bread. Then go into the hills back from the river and, on the plain at the top, turn northward to the bridge and go to Cochiti. Once there, tell them you wish to become a Cochiti man. They will put you under their protection. As you know, they are not so bad as your people; they will protect you."

Diego did what the old one told him to do, but before crossing the bridge, he saw some smoke rising from the top of a hill. He approached it and found an old woman building a fire.

He gave her a traditional greeting: "Koatsina."

"Rawa-aa," she responded, which means "good."

"Who is the man that lives in this house?"

"My husband," she told him.

He nodded.

"Then who is the war chief in this village?" For only he could give Diego the necessary blessing of amnesty.

She answered, "My husband is war chief, but he is away for a little while."

"Ahh," Diego whispered with satisfaction. "Then I will await his return."

After a time, the war chief appeared, and Diego introduced himself and explained his predicament. It was still early morning. Immediately, a council was summoned at the governor's house, and after everyone heard Diego's story, it was agreed that he should become a member of Cochiti Pueblo.

Now it happened that Diego confided his situation to the superintendent of schools in Santa Fe. A meeting was arranged, whereby Diego could hide himself behind a door while the superintendent interviewed the governor of his pueblo. The conversation began with the superintendent asking the governor where Diego had gone. He did not know, he said.

"Did you punish him?"

"No."

"Somebody told me you nearly killed him."

"That is a lie," said the governor.

"Well, where is Diego now?" the superintendent said.

*Santana Quintana. Cochiti. 1925.*

"We do not know. He ran away."

"Would you like to have him come back?"

The governor replied, "Of course we would."

"What has Diego done to injure your people?" the superintendent asked.

A man stepped forward and said, "Well, Diego was working for some Spanish, and we do not like our people working for them, nor for white people. The governor and the other officers have prohibited it."

"I see. . . . And you say you cannot find Diego?"

The Santo Domingo people nodded their heads in agreement.

"Well, let me see if I can help you," the superintendent remarked, and he opened wide the door behind which Diego was hiding and listening. There was a commotion then, a stirring of voices, with many faces showing surprise.

"So," the superintendent said, "is it true, Governor, that you would like Diego to go back home with you?"

The governor did not answer.

The superintendent pressed on. "Diego, do you want to go home with them?"

"No," he answered, "I would not like to go home and be killed someday."

The superintendent then asked, "Where are you going to live?"

"I am going back to Cochiti. I am under their governor, their war chief now. I am one of their men. I cannot go back to Santo Domingo; I will never go back."

The superintendent nodded and said, "Governor, do you understand?"

The governor said nothing.

"Governor," the superintendent told him, "I believe you cannot take Diego back with you. You must go to Cochiti and see the governor, the war chief, and the *principales.*"

So Diego returned to Cochiti.

Two days later, however, the Santo Domingo governor and his officers came to Cochiti and met with their leaders. There was a council and Diego was asked to tell his story all over again, which he did. The governor of Santo Domingo listened, and did not deny anything. Then he and his men went away. The next day, however, they returned and begged Diego to go back with them. They begged for his forgiveness. He asked what he should do, and those who had taken him in at Cochiti told him that he should return only if they would not punish him. And that day Diego went back to Santo Domingo.

*Near the Ruin of Old Cochiti*—A Cochiti man went out one night after a late-fallen snow and came upon the tracks of four Navajos driving off pueblo cattle. He knew they were Navajos by the imprint of their moccasins. After following them until he was sure who they were, he ran four miles back to the village. As he neared the pueblo, he cried out a warning: "Aaa . . . ai!"

Arriving at the village, they found the men assembled in the plaza. He told them what he had discovered. Immediately, a party of young men set out to find the thieves. The trail of the Navajos led up into a gorge. Here, the men had let go of all but one animal, a calf, which they had killed.

The Cochiti pursuers looked among the steep cliffs and saw a Navajo high above them. The hunters were hidden in the shelter of some piñons, so they were not detected. The eldest warrior now

*Tyooni-Shiwanna Mask. Cochiti. 1925.*

*Old Cochiti. 1925.*

thus encircle the thieves. Although there was only one rifle in the party, the man who owned it was a marksman. Taking aim, he fired; a Navajo fell into the fire. The others leapt up. One of them seized a bow and arrow, and, jumping over the cliff, escaped. Another ran straight ahead into the Cochiti circle, broke through, and ran off. The fourth leapt over the other edge of the mesa and landed on a ledge. He crept into a small cave but could go no farther. Unarmed and trapped, he finally surrendered.

A Cochiti man extended his bow over the rock edge; the Navajo caught hold of it and was pulled to the top. Suddenly, the outraged Cochiti warriors set upon him. He fought back bravely, but it was no use—they shot him full of arrows. And so the theft of a calf, a meal on the windblown mesa, found feathered retribution. This true story of Pueblo justice happened near the ruin of old Cochiti, Potrero Viejo, where the ghosts of slain warriors still linger in the stillness of a moonlit night.

assumed command. He sent half of his men to the right, where a small canyon mounted nearly to the level where the Navajo had been sighted. Then the leader and some others went to the left to climb the mesa.

The leader's party arrived first and crept up quite close to the four Navajos, who were roasting meat over a small fire. The Cochiti men waited for the other party to get up out of the canyon, and

*Zuni History*

Zuni, lineal descendant of the glamorous Seven Cities of Cibola, is in the extreme western part of New Mexico, not far from the Arizona boundary. The name Zuni was first recorded by Antonio de Espejo, who visited the village on his way from Acoma in 1583. He noted that it was known to the Spaniards as Cibola. *Zuni*, the word, is derived from Keres and Tewa origins, meaning "a rock slide" or "coasting place for children." Cibola is believed to come from the word *shiwinna*, referring to the individual of a tribe. Transmitted to the Spaniards from the lips of Piman Indians of southern Arizona and Sonora, this became Cibola.

Castaneda, in his account of the events leading to the expedition of Coronado, had this to say of the myth of Cibola:

"An Indian by the name of Tejo, a native of the valleys of Oxitipar, was the son of a trader.

*Zuni Girl with Jar. 1903.*

When he was a little boy, his father had gone into the back country with fine feathers to trade for ornaments, and when he came back, he brought a large amount of gold and silver. The boy, Tejo, went with his father once or twice, and saw some very large villages, which he compared to Mexico and its environs. He had seen seven very large towns which had streets of silver-workers. It took forty days to go there from his country, through a wilderness in which nothing grew, except some very small plants about a span high."

Nuño de Guzmán, President of New Spain, hearing of this tale of tantalizing silver, headed an imposing but abortive expedition in search of these fabulous riches. However, the Seven Cities remained undiscovered. In 1536 a hearsay report of the populous villages was brought to New Spain by Alvar Nuñez Cabeza de Vaca and his three companions. Near the end of

*Zuni Pottery. 1903.*

their stupendous eight-year wanderings from the Texas Gulf Coast, they came across a tale told by natives of Corazones Valley in Sonora.

Interest was thus revived in Cabeza de Vaca's story—to such a pitch that the new viceroy, Antonio de Mendoza, purchased the black Barbary slave Estevan, who was one of the four wanderers. In 1539 he was sent as a guide to accompany the Franciscan friar Marcos de Niza. Together, they set out with about three hundred Mexican Indians, who attached themselves to the exploration party as they continued on their march to Cibola.

As they neared the jail, the priest sent Estevan ahead with his Indian entourage. A few days later, messengers returned with the news that Estevan was dead at the hands of the Cibola Indians. The tale of his demise is shrouded in mystery, but the strands of it that exist are here revealed. From the "relación" of Friar Marcos:

> One day previous to reaching Cibola, Estevan sent, as he was wont to do always, his gourd, in order to show them in what quality he was coming. The gourd had a few strings of rattles and two plumes, one of which was white and the other red. When they reached Cibola and pre-

sented the gourd to the person whom the lord has placed there in charge, he took it into his hand, and, seeing the rattles, with great wrath threw the gourd on the floor, and said to the messengers that they should forthwith leave the town, that he knew what kind of people these were, and that they should tell them not to enter the place, lest they should all be killed.

The messengers returned and reported to Estevan what had happened, who said that this was nothing—that those who at first displayed anger always received him in the kindest manner. So he continued his road until he reached the city of Cibola, where he met people who refused to allow him to enter, and placed him in a large house outside, taking from him all he carried of objects for exchange, turquoises and other things received from the Indians on the journey. There he was all night, neither food nor drink being given to him nor to his escort. The following morning Estevan endeavored to escape and was pursued by the people of the city, who were killing some of the people of his company.

In spite of these ill tidings, the friar pressed on. "With my Indians and interpreters I followed my road till we came in sight of Cibola." At last he beheld one of the Seven Cities, gleaming in the sun, and making such a brave showing in the distance that his subsequent report was entirely misleading. Partly, though, this was due to those that interpreted it—minds predisposed to the superlative by what had been found in Mexico and Peru.

In their precarious wandering life among various tribes, Cabeza de Vaca and his companions had more than once saved their lives by posing as medicine men. It was natural that Estevan, on entering the Zuni village, should make much of his shaman's rattle. But the symbol, formerly so potent, proved his undoing; for the Zuni priests, enraged by the presumption of the alien, possibly suspecting him of being a sorcerer, decreed his death.

The existence of a strange race in Mexico was already known to the inhabitants of Cibola through the Sonoran Indians, who regularly visited the pueblos, buying turquoise and buffalo skins. Coronado reported to the viceroy: "They declare that it was foretold among them more than fifty years ago that a people such as we are should come, and the direction they should come from and that the whole country would be conquered." And so, perhaps because of this, the Zuni shamans took prompt steps to discourage the threatened invasion.

Friar Marcos returned to New Spain, and his report aroused such expectations that there was a bitter contest before the Crown for the right of conquest, Mendoza, Cortés, and Hernando de Soto urging their claims. Eventually, Francisco Vásquez de Coronado led an expedition in 1540. Pedro de Castaneda, a member and annalist, wrote the following:

". . . when they saw the first village, which was Cibola, such were the curses that some hurled at Friar Marcos that I pray God may protect him from them. It is a little, unattractive village looking as if it had been crumpled up together. It is a village of about 200 warriors, is three and four stories high, with the houses small and having only a few rooms."

The Zuni discovered, however, that "turquoises and poor mantles" held no bargaining power for Governor Coronado in his gilded and glittering armor. In less than an hour—but not without considerable bloodshed—the inhabitants evacuated the main portion of the village and the Spaniards took possession. The name of the mesa to which the Zuni people retreated is called Corn Mountain. Nine hundred feet in height, a mile long from north to south and a half mile in width, Corn Mountain represented more than a geographical refuge. According to a sacred legend, the ancient ones fled to the mesa to escape a deluge, carrying with them large stores of corn.

The water rose higher and higher, threatening to overwhelm the mountain, and at last the principal priest, the rain chief of the north, decided to make the necessary sacrifice. He dressed his youthful son and daughter in the finest garments and ornaments, and they stepped over the cliff edge into the water, where they became the two striking columns now seen at the west side of the mountain. The water was checked, but in the long years before it receded from the plain, the people had to remain on the mesa, where the power of their chief priest made it possible to raise small crops. It is in memory of this legend that the priest of the north now has the title Corn Chief and the mesa is called Corn Mountain.

In the end, Coronado's advance to glory culminated in the siege of a Tiwa village and the slaughter of its surrendered defenders, the futile search for gold on the plains of Kansas, the disillusioned retreat to New Spain in 1542. His departure had left the Pueblo Indians with an ineradicable hatred of the race that respected not its word and burned at the stake those who foolishly put their faith in it. Yet, when Diego de Vargas, the reconqueror, returned to Zuni in 1692, he found them on Corn Mountain, and was well received.

He climbed the trail, which he found difficult, and he and a cooperative cacique sponsored the baptism of 294 persons. In his own words:

*Zuni. 1905.*

"My fellow godfather and the captains asked me to mount further and in a room on the second floor and a balcony I entered and found an altar with two large curtains burned by wax candles and retaining some bits of ornament."

Along with the altar of the church, which had been established earlier at Zuni, the Indians had carried away to their stronghold on Corn Mountain three effigies of Christ, a painting of John the Baptist, a reliquary, three silver chalices, an enameled chalice, a missal, seventeen other books, two brass candlesticks, two bells without clappers, and a tiny little bell.

This record, which the Spanish chroniclers noted so meticulously, is not without the semblance of importance. The Zuni relate a story of one of the missionary priests whose life was spared during the revolt of 1680 on the promise that he would accept a Zuni wife. He, therefore, according to the tale, accompanied the tribe on its flight to Corn Mountain, where he remained until Vargas appeared on the scene in 1692. However, no mention of this man is made by any of the Spanish chroniclers.

Theodore Kroeber, the anthropologist, stated in 1917:

> The Zuni are professedly anti-Catholic and anti-Christian. During the summer of 1916, the proposed establishment of a Catholic mission incurred the displeasure of the whole tribe except a small minority. . . . Yet every Zuni that has died within the past two centuries lies buried in the unkempt little graveyard that was first consecrated by Catholic fathers, and in the center of which a constantly renewed cross rears its beam. The mission church in the heart of the town is to us the ever impressive reminder of the Christian influence imposed on the nation for many long generations; to the Zuni it is anything but a symbol of the alien religion which they struggle toward from themselves.

> They make attempts, mostly ineffectual, it is true, to roof and preserve the crumbling structure of adobe. Some years ago, a wider passage was wanted between its altar end and the nearby houses. The western wall was therefore torn down. But it was re-erected in its entirety, a few feet farther in! The northern face gives evidence of being similarly shifted. This by a people that resent the coming of the priests, that will not tolerate a Catholic Mexican within view of their religious observances, whom only playing boys, hens, and hogs trouble to enter the edifice which they toil to preserve. We face here a strange conservatism indeed; but it is a conservatism of the present, with no feeling for the past. The church, the graveyard, the cross are not Catholic; they are Zuni; therefore they are clung to and treated as things integrally and inherently Zuni.

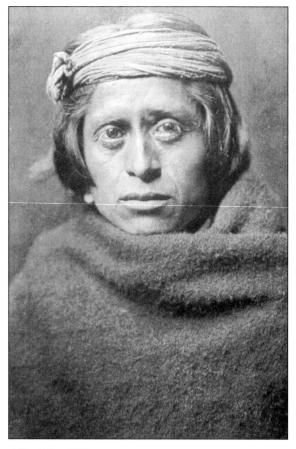

A Zuni Man. 1903.

Subsequent to the reconquest, modern Zuni was erected on a part of the ruins of Halona, a fragment of the original pueblo. Here the entire population of the tribe was concentrated. In a century and a half, then, the Seven Cities of Cibola had disappeared. Along with them, the legend of Estevan vanished; well-informed men profess never to have heard of him. Coronado's invasion appears to be an unknown episode. The last time the stone houses on Corn Mountain were inhabited was 1703. However, the myth of the deluge and the corn shaman who saved the people is fresh as the summer rain of a day ago.

### The Zuni Creation Myth

*Four Worlds* — There were four worlds beneath the earth. The people were living in darkness. They could not see one another; it was as if they were blind. They would step on one another, spit on one another, urinate on one another, all because they could not see. The warriors known as the Great Fathers decided to take the people out where there was light.

They pondered and sent Kwalashi, Raven, around the north side of the world to see if there was a hole through which they might escape. Raven went around from the north to the west and on to the starting point. Four times he went around the world in narrowing circles, until he returned to the people, who were assembled at the center. However, Raven was unable to find an exit.

The Great Fathers then sent Pipi, Chicken Hawk, who started in the west and passed to the south, and so on around the world four times to the center, but he also failed. Next they sent Anehlawa, Sparrow Hawk, who started in the south and passed around the world four times, but he also returned unsuccessful. Muhuqi, Owl, was the next. He started in the east, but went four times around the world without finding a passage into the world above.

Then the Great Fathers went to the west and they asked Pearl Shell Chief to come to the center of the world with his fetish. They gave Coral Chief, to the south, the same invitation; and Light Salt White Chief, who lived in the east. Finally, they

*Zuni Girls. 1903.*

asked Above Chief and Underworld Chief to come. And all came, each with his fetish, and met with the Great Fathers in the center of the world.

"Is it better to go up to the light or to remain here?" they asked.

The North Chief answered, "I should like to go to the light."

The Great Fathers said, "How shall we do so?"

The chiefs replied, "Get our great old grandfather."

So the Great Fathers brought Chumali, Small Locust, and he asked, "What do you wish to do?"

The chiefs answered, "We wish to get out of this world and go where it is light."

"If that is what you wish, I will try to do it," Chumali replied.

And he began to bore through the roof of the lower world, but when he came out of the top of it, all was still dark. He went back and told the chiefs, who said, "You must go still farther, and you will see the sun." So Chumali bored through the second earth, and saw a faintly gleaming light. He went back and reported this, but the chiefs told him, "Go farther, and you will see the sun."

Chumali then bored through the third earth. He went back to the chiefs and said that he had seen light but not the sun, and that the air was not warm, but cold. "You must find the sun," the chiefs told him. Now, when he went back and bored into the fourth earth, he became exhausted from his work and could not continue. The chiefs were sad to hear this. "What shall we do?" they asked one another.

But soon after, they found a cane and pushed it through the hole made by Chumali. The sharpened point broke the ground like sprouting corn. They returned, then, to the people and told them, "We have seen the sun, let us go out." They planted a Douglas spruce, which served as a ladder from the first to the second world; and they called the first world Darkness. All the people climbed up the tree and passed to the second world, where they remained four years.

After this time had passed, the Great Fathers asked what they should do next, stay or continue upward? It was decided to go up, closer to the sun. They called the second world Soot World, because it was soft and dark as soot. Then they planted a jack pine, and all ascended to the third world, where they could see very faint light, a glowing up above. Four years they stayed there and then the Great Fathers asked the familiar question: "Shall we remain or go up?"

"We wish to see the sun," the people said. So the Great Fathers planted an aspen tree, and they called that third world, which had been their home, Dark Light, because seeing was still hard to do in that place. Now they climbed up into the fourth world, and there they found light.

In the fourth world, the Great Fathers sat in four concentric circles, and they began to sing. Those in the first circle heard well, but those in the third could barely hear because the wind rose in the grass and made a singing sound of its own. Those on the outside heard nothing at all. And that is why some people cannot sing and do not try to learn the sacred songs.

After four years, the Great Fathers asked the people whether they wished to remain or to go closer to the sun. "We wish to see the sun," they responded. So the Great Fathers planted a yellow pine. The people then named the fourth world, which had been their home, Light-Before-Dawn, because they had seen the light of the sun but not the sun itself. Now, as they passed upward, climbing into this world, the sound of their coming forth was the low rumbling of distant thunder, the buzz of swarming bees. The earth vibrated with their footsteps.

They found the earth already inhabited by the Old Ones. But these soon fled eastward. The people who came up from below were green and their hair came out from their forehead in a shape like a grinding stone cov-

*Corn Mountain. 1925.*

*Zuni Bread Maker. 1903.*

ered with rock slime; behind them, they had tails like horses. At the place where they emerged, they stayed four years, but after that time, they wished to find the center of the earth. There, it was decided, they should place each of their sacred fetishes.

The people were about to start eastward, in search of the center of the earth, when they heard a rumbling, like thunder. They waited, watching, and out of the emergence place, they saw a man whose hair stood out from his head and in whose hand was an ear of corn. Next to him was a woman of the same appearance. "This one is a sorcerer," the people protested. "We do not want him to travel with us." But the sorcerer said, "This which I have is corn. It is good to eat. If you do not let me go with you, you shall never have this to eat. Instead, you will live on weeds."

The people considered what the sorcerer said, for there was a certain wisdom in his words. He went on: "Besides, if there were none among you such as I, you would increase like ants. There would be no room for you to live." It was agreed then, among the Great Fathers and the people, that the sorcerer and his woman should continue along with them in their search for the center place.

Now the people started eastward. In time, they came to a spring. Here the Great Fathers washed their bodies and then bathed the people's as well. The spring water ran down their sides and they came clean, removing all the green slime that was on them. This spring they named Green Slime Spring, and after remaining there four years, they resumed their journey.

At another spring, which they called Big Wood Spring because a great, long prayer stick was placed there, they also remained another four years. There the Great Fathers washed themselves, and all the people; and they cut off the shocks of hair that jutted from their foreheads and their long tails that hung from behind. This spring they named Leaving Hair Spring because they dropped their hair into the water after it was cut.

The next spring they reached was where they invented the game of Kick Stick, in which runners use their foot, while running, to hurl sticks before them. The game was played to bring rain; and at the end of four years, they put their sticks into the spring, naming it Game Stick Spring.

At another spring, they stopped for another four years. Here they played the game of Hoop Stick, a woman's game—each one throwing a small hoop with a stick—and thus, the spring was known as Hoop Stick Spring.

And so the journeying continued, stopping at many springs, until, at a certain place called Fog Spring, a group of young women stayed behind while the rest of the people moved on. The two sorcerers were following behind as usual, and they came upon the women, sitting by the water's edge. "Who are you?" they asked.

"We are Corn Girls," they replied.

"But you have no corn," the man sorcerer said.

And he gave to one an ear of yellow corn; to another, a blue ear; and to the rest, one to each, an ear of red, white, many-colored, black, and sweet. In addition, he also gave beans and squash seeds. The Yellow Corn Girl then arranged her sisters in two lines facing the east, and all night they danced. In the morning, the sorcerers went on, leaving the girls by the spring.

As the people journeyed, the Great Fathers said, "We are growing very tired," so they ap-

*Zuni Girl. 1903.*

pointed a youth and his sister to go on ahead and take the lead. One day the youth said, "I will go to the top of the hill and see how far we must travel." While he was gone, she fell asleep; he returned, saw her sleeping on her side, and wished to make love to her.

Now the moment he touched her, she cried out, and their faces became like masks. At once, ten children were born. One of them was normal; the other nine were grotesque, like their father. And thus it was the handsome youth and his sister, in their changed form, became God Husband and Dance Old Woman. These two, dancing today, are clowns, like the Tewa Koshare, and they are meant to excite sexual desire and bring the blessing of birth to the pueblo.

God Husband then drew two furrows in the sand with his foot and scraped out a small hollow, which formed two rivers (Zuni River and the Little Colorado) and a lake (near St. Johns, Arizona). When the people saw what had happened, they said, "Too bad that our leaders have turned into these creatures." But God Husband and Dance Old Woman just urged the people to go on across the water, which they did, but whenever a mother carrying an infant on her back got to the middle of the river, the baby—touching the water—would change into a water snake, a fish, turtle, or some other water creature that would bite the mother's back until she dropped her burden.

The Great Fathers observed this with much concern; now half the people were on one side and the other half on the other; and those who had crossed were crying bitterly for their lost children. So the Great Fathers said, "Let all the people cross, and if the children turn into snakes and turtles, do not let them go, but hold them fast. Perhaps, once over, they may then turn two-legged again." The people agreed that this was the thing to do. They began to cross, but again, the children became water creatures, which bit the women. But the mothers, crying out, held on, and soon, when they had crossed over, the creatures turned again into children.

And so it was that God Husband and Dance Old Woman went down under the waters, where they were joined by their misbegotten children—Bat, Bow Chief, Shrew, and others—as well as the changed-shape children, who had become water creatures. All of these, today, are gods and live at the bottom of the sacred lake, which the people call Listening Spring.

## Afterword: The Myth Revealed

Frank Hamilton Cushing, an expert on Zuni culture, who was adopted by a Zuni family, wrote about their devotion to the myth of the lost brothers and sisters in the sacred lake of Listening Spring:

A procession of fifty men went hastily down the hill, and off westward over the plain. They were solemnly led by a painted and shell-bedecked priest, and followed by the torch-bearing God of Fire. Four days after, toward sunset, they returned in file up the same pathway, each bearing in his arms a basket filled with living, squirming turtles, which he regarded and carried as tenderly as a mother would her infant.

Some of them were wrapped in soft blankets, their heads and forefeet protruding. Others were mounted on the backs of the plumed figures, humorously solemn caricatures of little children being carried across the river of ancient myth.

The governor's brother-in-law came in. He was welcomed as if a messenger from heaven. He bore in his tremulous fingers a turtle. Paint still adhered to the man's hands and bare feet, which led me to infer that he had been part of the sacred embassy. He sank on a roll of skins that had been placed for him, and tenderly laid the turtle on the floor. No sooner did the creature find itself at liberty than it made off as fast as its lame legs would take it. Of one accord, the family forsook dish, spoon and drinking cup, and grabbing from a sacred meal-bowl whole handfuls of the contents, hurriedly followed the turtle about the room, praying and scattering meal as they went. At last, strange to say, it approached the foot-sore man who had brought it.

"Ha!" he exclaimed, with emotion. "See, it comes to me again. Ah, what kind favors the Great Fathers grant me this day," and passing his hand gently over the sprawling animal, he inhaled from his palm, deeply and long, at the same time invoking the favor of the gods. Then he leaned his chin upon his hand and with large, wistful eyes regarded his captive as it lay blinking its meal-bedimmed eyes, and clawing the smooth floor.

At this juncture, I ventured a question: "Why don't you let him go, or give him some water?" Slowly the man turned his eyes toward me, a mixture of pain, indignation, and pity on his face. The whole family stared at me in surprise. "Poor younger brother!" he said to me at last, then: "It cannot die."

"It will die if you don't feed it and give it water."

"I tell you, it cannot die. It will only change houses tomorrow, and go back to the home of its brothers. But how would you know?" he mused. Turning then to the blinded turtle, he spoke softly: "My poor dear lost child or parent; my sister or brother you could have been! Who knows which? Maybe my own great-grandfather or -mother!" With this, he fell to weeping, and as he buried his face in his hands, his cries were echoed by those of his family. Filled with sympathy for his grief, I raised the turtle to my lips

and kissed its cold shell; then depositing it on the floor, I hastily left the grief-stricken family to its sorrows.

## Hopi History

The Hopi are one of the very few Indian groups who live the way they did a hundred years ago. They call themselves Hopitu, "the peaceable people," and peace-loving they have always been. True, their history contains pages darkened with warfare, but their military activities were invariably either for defense of their fields

*Walpi Maidens. Hopi Pueblo. 1906.*

*Burros and Moki Men on the Road. Hopi Pueblo. 1900.*

and flocks from the forays of Ute and Navajo or for what they conceived to be just punishment upon some component members of their own tribe.

Affability and sunny disposition are apt to be one's first impression of the Hopi character, at least at Walpi, the destination of most observers from the culture at large. However, this affability can turn to cold reserve or outspoken resentment when ill-treatment, or breach of manners occurs. Numerically few, poor in worldly goods, the Hopi are nonetheless the possessors of true moral courage.

From the time of the Conquistadores, they have been commonly known as Moqui, originating, perhaps, from the Zuni word *Amu-kwe*. The Hopi themselves heartily dislike the designation, which, they believe, originated in the error of the first Spanish visitors. The Spanish mistook the

Hopi word *moki*, "dead," for their tribal name. The Hopi language is composed of diverse tongues, the main branch of which is Shoshonean. This was spoken in a large part of the Great Basin between the Rockies and the Sierra Nevada; also southwestern Oregon and southern California, even to the coast, and on Santa Catalina Island. Hopi speech has roots, as well, in the great Aztecan language. A linguistic map would represent the Hopi as an isolated people surrounded by alien tongues.

Since they were "discovered" in the sixteenth century, the Hopi have occupied their present habitat in northeastern Arizona. Their neighbors on the north, west, and east were the predatory Navajo, alternately hostile and friendly, now raiding the Hopi fields and sheep ranges, now visiting the pueblo festivals, sometimes receiving Hopi migrants and marrying them. From the north and east came also the warlike Ute. Southward, the country was overrun by nomadic bands of Apache, who frequently swooped down from the mountains south and west of the present Winslow.

About a hundred miles to the southeast were the Zuni villages; beyond them along the Rio Grande, the Pueblos with whom the Hopi shared a kind of common bond. Far to the west, in and about the Grand Canyon, were the Havasupai and Walapai, whom the Hopi traders regularly visited to exchange yarn and blankets for deerskins, and who, in turn, annually brought roasted mescal and piñon nuts to the Hopi.

The reservation lies in the eastern watershed of the Little Colorado, but at no point does it extend to the river. There are few perennial streams within its borders. The country, then, is typical of the semiarid Southwest. Broad sandy wastes are broken by rocky buttes and fantastically shaped mesas, rising abruptly from the desert floor. Some seventy-five miles to the southwest, the white, winter-capped San Francisco mountains are visible. The summer days are hot and the nights are crisp and cool. As the country lies at an elevation of 6,500 feet, winter nights can be chilling, yet sunny days follow one another in an almost endless procession.

There are eight Hopi pueblos, all of them on the tops of mesas. On East Mesa are Walpi and Sichomovi (also Hano, a Tewa pueblo founded early in the eighteenth century by emigrants from the Rio Grande); on Middle Mesa are Mishongnovi, Shipaulovi, and Shongopavi; on West Mesa are Oraibi, Hotavila, and Pakavi.

The first white men in the Province of Tusayan, as the Spaniards called Hopi country, came in 1540 under directives from Coronado. The first horses were unknown to the Indians, and legend holds that the Spaniards took advantage of the Indians' awe by telling them that the horses could become angry and devour them. Naturally, the usual depredations took place; Indian tradition says that many tortures were perpetrated in order to learn

the secret of the gold mines that were supposed to exist there.

For roughly a century and a half, contact with the white race had been at long intervals and of an incidental nature. With the attempt to Christianize, however, a new era dawned. The old gods were threatened. From 1629 to 1919, missionary work among the Hopi has never been a sinecure. In "The Memorial of Fray Alonso de Benavides," the following commentary states the situation very well:

"Porras is declared to have immediately cured a case of blindness in a Hopi boy by spitting on his hand, rolling a little mud, and placing it on the eyes of the lad while uttering the word Epheta—resulting in the conversion of a thousand of the Indians. But the old men, evidently enraged at the loss of power through the adherence of so many of their tribe to the missionaries, poisoned some food, which the Father ate. Realizing his fate, he immediately went to Fray Francisco de San Buenaventura, who administered the last sacraments. The date of his death is June 28, 1633."

*The Stairway Trail at Walpi. 1921.*

*Hopi Children. 1905.*

less complete because of the large numbers of occupying forces. However, the contest there ended with the Indians in control and the Spanish giving up the province until the year 1692, when General de Vargas returned and reconquered the territory once again. It was during the interim that throughout the Pueblo region numerous bands fled from the Rio Grande to the less accessible Hopi land. Many of these subsequently returned, but others became permanent residents of the west.

For nearly two centuries longer, the Hopi remained practically out of contact with the white race. The Hopi reservation was established in 1882, but until the beginning of the twentieth century, the people were practically independent of governmental authority. Since that time, however, the old order has had, and will continue to have, many challenges to face, not the least of which is the presence of the alien culture that surrounds them. Safe on their rock, the Hopi wait. And while they wait, the tides of change, like the great sea of sand that embraces them, comes ever closer.

The missionaries had less success here than they wished. The Hopi resented being forced to carry vigas—building timber—from the mountains and drinking water from distant springs. Yet another source of irritation, according to the Hopis themselves, was the priests' summoning of their women for sexual relations. Like other tribes, they were tolerant, at first, of the new religion—perhaps mildly interested and amused by the drama of its ritual. However, when the priests tried to suppress their own ancient rites—the forbidding of planting *pahos*, the plumed prayer sticks, for example, then the seeds of revolt were sown. It wasn't long before an unusually dry season and the consequent failure of crops pointed to what the Hopis had known all along: The attempted overthrow of the old ways was leading to a new evil.

In 1680 messages were exchanged among chiefs, and at the appointed time, there was a concerted attack on the would-be conquerors. In Hopi country, every mission was burned and every Spaniard who could be found was killed. On the Rio Grande, the success of the Pueblo revolt was

## Three Migration Myths of the Hopi

*The Rattlesnake Clan*—When the human beings emerged from the lower world at Sipa-nuni (in the Grand Canyon), the tribes scattered, each going in the direction it chose. The Cougars and Doves went northward along the east side of the canyon. On a high mesa at Tokonabi, they built a village of stone houses, and called it Tokona.

One day the son of the Cougar chief stood looking down at the rushing river, and he began to wonder where all the water went. He told his father, "I would like to find where all this water goes."

The chief said, "My son, you cannot go."

"But I must," the son answered.

The chief knew that it was useless to argue with the passions of youth. "When, then, will you start?" he asked.

"I shall start in four days," said the son. And

then he instructed his sisters to prepare food for the journey and he asked his father to make *pahos*. Afterward, the youth went down to the stream and found a large cottonwood log, which he fire-hollowed and fashioned into a boat with a round door at each end. At the end of four days, the *pahos* and food were ready; the chief's son climbed into the log with a gourd full of water and a pointed stick. Then he sealed both entrances with piñon gum from within. His sisters and the people wept to see him leave. But the men rolled the log into the river, and it drifted away with the current and soon disappeared.

*Nova-Walpi. 1906.*

For many days, the log drifted on the surface of the water. Then, at last, it stopped. Little by little, the youth opened one of the sealed doorways, and no water entered. He removed the door altogether and found himself on the edge of a great waterway, an ocean. I wonder where I should go now? the youth asked himself. Then he beheld a ladder in the middle of the ocean. Opening his bundle of *pahos*, he selected the one that had been made for the ocean person and fastened it to his belt. Next, he made an offering ball of cornmeal and cast it to the ladder.

The ball rolled away toward the lad-

*lpi Snake Chief. 1921.*

der and, upon reaching it, descended down the rungs. As it did so, the waters divided and the youth approached the ladder and discovered that all around it the earth was dry. Now he saw that the ladder went down into a kiva, out of which came a woman's voice: "So, you have come."

"Yes," he answered.

"You arrived a long time ago," she explained as he entered the kiva, "but you did not know it. I am called Shell Woman."

The chief's son gave her the special *paho* fixed to his belt. "This is for you," he said. "My father made it for you."

"Thank you," she replied. "Nobody has made anything for me in a long time, and I am glad to have it."

Then the ladder began to shake. The youth watched as a handsome man came down with many *pahos* and much cornmeal, which he gave to the woman, who, at once, began to sort them out. "Ah," she exclaimed, "one for rain, another for crops. Here is one for children, and one for game." Then she made a disgruntled face and said, "These are bad—ahg!" And she threw away the *pahos* that had been planted by a sorcerer.

Now the handsome man turned and faced the youth, who understood that he was the Sun. "For a long time," the Sun said, "it has been your desire to come, and now you are here. You must listen carefully and heed what I say. Your father has made these *pahos* for the chiefs of the underground. I will give them to whom they are sent. Tell your father that all will be well with your people."

The Sun sighed then, and paused. Continuing on, he explained: "You have seen that there are *pahos* for good, and those also for evil. People who ask for long life, for good crops, and for all that is good, these people shall ask only in the morning. But, remember this: Those people who ask for bad shall ask at noon, evening, or anytime they choose.

These bad things, I have sometimes granted. Now, you must return home; much time has passed since you departed, and the people are worried."

And with that, the Sun approached an entrance that led farther down, below the level of the kiva; and he disappeared. The following morning, Shell Woman told the youth that he would find his home by seeking a mountain to the north. This he did, by casting a fresh ball of cornmeal in the direction he wished to travel.

Finally, he arrived at the foot of the mountain to the north. He looked around and saw many rattlesnakes lying everywhere. Then he asked if they meant to do him harm, and one of them said that he could pass and go on his way, which he did, threading his way carefully among them. The higher he went up the mountain, the more numerous the rattlesnakes became; and at the very top, he was forced to trod upon them. However, none struck back at him, and he found a ladder at the very peak and descended into the heart of the mountain.

Once inside, he found himself surrounded by Rattlesnake People. One of them, a guard, greeted him with surprise. "You are a man," he said. "No person of your kind has ever entered our home."

The youth answered, "I do not think that I am a man. Yet, surely, you are!"

The rattlesnake guard was pleased to hear this, and he passed a smoke to the youth, who took it gladly and smoked deeply. After he was done, he said, "I was sent here by Shell Woman; she said to ask your aid in getting home."

*Buffalo Dance at Hano. 1904.*

"We cannot grant this, for we are merely the guardians of our chief, who is below."

Then the youth was allowed to pass down another ladder into yet another kiva. There he saw Rattlesnake Chief, sitting alone. "How is it that you have come here?" the chief demanded when the youth entered into his private room.

"I have come to ask you for help."

Rattlesnake Chief regarded the youth and then said, "You must be a man!"

"I do not think that I am a man," the youth returned. "But I do know that I must find some food. I have come to you for help."

Then the chief, pleased with these words, taught the youth the Snake Ceremony and all the songs that accompany it, and he gave him a girl who would help him on his journey home. Together, they went northward, the girl carrying a bundle of food on her head. However, when this food gave out, she removed her belt and shook it, and more good things to eat fell on the ground. (This is because the Rattlesnake People have food hidden under each overlapping scale of their bodies.)

After years of traveling, they reached Tokonabi, and in due time the girl gave birth to many little rattlesnakes. The people were fond of them, despite the fact they were snakes; but one day, some of their children stepped upon them and were bitten, and this made the people move on, farther southward. Wherever they stopped to camp on their journey, however, they did the Snake Ceremony and sang for rain. And the rain always came.

*The Reed Clan* — In the underworld, Elder and Younger Brother lived with their grandmother, Spider Woman. They stayed near the people, yet apart from them. When the Reed People emerged upon the earth, these three went with them, and the people said, "Why don't we all travel together, and help one another?" And it was decided that they would.

After a time, the brothers climbed Snow Mountain High Place, which we call now the San Francisco Peaks. From there, they saw the basin of the Little Colorado covered with pools of stagnant

*Nato — The Goat Man. Hopi Pueblo. 1906.*

water. When the people heard of this, they asked the brothers to get rid of that water. So the brothers journeyed into the Grand Canyon, and there they met with two brothers, like themselves, and yet another Spider Woman. Together, they made a bowl of medicine water and looked into it to see what should be done.

Then they made six arrows, the feathers of which were taken from a bluebird, a roadrunner, a chicken hawk, an eagle, a small parrot, and a large yellow bird. With these, the two brothers journeyed back to Snow Mountain High Place. From the southside, they shot the arrows, one by one, into the sides of the mountains, making small holes through which the mountain water might run off.

However, the holes were too small and the arrows too weak.

Once again, they journeyed down into the Grand Canyon and gazed into a medicine-water bowl. This time, flying through the water, they saw

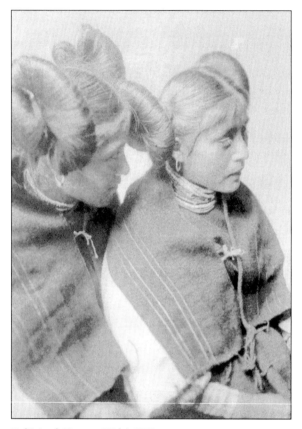

*Puliini and Koyame. Walpi. 1921.*

a condor. Shooting their arrows at the bird in the bowl, there came a sound of fluttering and falling overhead. Out of the sky, a great condor fell, landing dead at their feet. With the feathers of the condor, they tipped four arrow shafts of pine, oak, spruce, and syringa. They now fired their arrows into the rocky walls of the great canyon; a huge hole was made, and water rushed out of it. As the gushing water pounded free, it made what is now the canyon of the Little Colorado. After all the water drained off, the ground was still too soft to support the weight of a man, so the brothers ground

up hard shells and stones and turned them into dust, which they sifted over the soft earth. Soon, this hardened and became the canyon floor we know today. Then the brothers returned to the people, who got ready to journey on again.

On Middle Mesa, the people made a town of stone houses on top of a small butte, looking toward Walpi. Then the two brothers told the people they must leave, and together with Spider Woman, they went to Salt Lake, where they still dwell.

While the Reed People lived in their stone houses, there were others who made a town on the side of the mesa now marked by the ruin of Old Mishongnovi. The two peoples, thereafter, joined up as one to hunt rabbits and have ceremonial dances. Now it happened that one of the Reed People had a pet cat. At night, while the man slept, the cat went out and caught rats, and sometimes rabbits. Yellow Bird Boy, the son of Crier Chief, saw this admirable pet and wanted one for himself. "Where are such animals to be found?" he asked his father, who replied, "They live far to the east on Shell Mountain [in the range to the east of Albuquerque.]" "In four days, I go," said the youth. "Let my sister grind corn and make *piki.*"

On the third day, Crier Chief bound up a bundle of *piki*, and at sunrise the next morning, Yellow Bird Boy started off. Many days later, he reached his journey's end, near the mountaintop in the east. There he saw Weasel, a mountain guardian, who was prepared to attack him. "Be calm," the youth said, offering Weasel a *paho*, which he accepted, and then became friendly. Next, he met Cougar and Bear, both of whom he placated with *pahos*. Finally, he arrived at the very top of the mountain, where he saw the entryway of the Dog People. Before the entrance, coiled in the sun, was Great Snake. "Where are you going?" he asked. "To the home of the Dog People," said the youth, and added, "I have come far just to give you this offering," and he extended his *paho* to Great Snake, who accepted it.

Then Yellow Bird Boy was allowed to pass down into the mountain on the rungs of a sacred ladder. Downward, he saw human beings, who invited him to descend. The ladder as he lowered himself, rung by rung, was completely surrounded

*Nampeyo Decorating Pottery. Hopi Pueblo. 1900.*

by walls of glimmering water. However, though the walls shivered and glowed, they did not touch him. He descended, dry, and met an old man, who straightaway offered him a pipe. Thankfully, Yellow Bird Boy accepted the smoke, and after he had puffed four times, he said to the old one, "Father." And the old man responded, "My son." Then the youth filled his own pipe and offered it to his host. After this, a meal of meat and *piki* was presented to Yellow Bird Boy. He ate to his satisfaction, and when he had finished, the old man inquired, "Well, my son, what is it to be?"

"I have come a long way," Yellow Bird Boy said.

"I can see that."

"And all for the sake of obtaining a pet."

"Ahh," said the old man, smiling. "Then you shall have a dog. First, we dance. Then you shall choose a pair, a male and a female."

He danced in the kiva room, whose walls were covered in dog skins. The moment the drum began to beat, the people put the skins on and became dogs themselves. As they danced, the young man sat by the fire and watched. He chose two, the smallest in the party. The moment he made his choice, the dancing stopped; the dancers hung up their skins and gathered round their visitor. The old man approached him, saying, "Remember this well, my son. Take good care of these dogs; do not mistreat them. Whoever mistreats them will have rheumatism in the knees: That is the way dogs defend themselves." Yellow Bird Boy listened well to this counsel; then he tied a cord around his waist, and in the folds of his robe, he stored the two puppies. Then he left Shell Mountain and headed home.

In the evening when he camped, he always fed the dogs before he ate. Close to home, he put them down so they could follow him. But when they cried out with weariness, he picked them up and carried them. At last, he arrived home, and the people greeted him with respect. He himself was proud of his dogs, who, in time, would learn to hunt rabbits for him. Also, it was not long before the female became pregnant and bore a litter of puppies. At night, when they cried, the mother sought food for her children, often slipping over to

*The Plaza at Walpi. 1921.*

Mishongnovi and stealing the food that was set out in the little open windows. One night, she was discovered; the next night, the villagers set a watch, and when the dog entered Mishongnovi, the guards killed her.

Then the Reed People were very upset; they felt like leaving that place. Yellow Bird Boy told his father that in four days they would all depart, and he, being Crier Chief, made the announcement. During the time that followed, the people ate as much as they could, so they would not have to leave any food behind. Before sunrise on the fifth morning—in the place where the

*Picking Up the Snakes. 1906.*

mission now stands—they placed a long row of bowls containing cooked food, and, returning to the village, they took up their packs and left. As they passed the dishes, each person took a bit of food from each bowl, thus offering a prayer that the food might accompany them in spirit.

When the people of Mishongnovi discovered the Reed People had gone away, they sent messengers after them. "It is best that you return," the messengers said. But the Reed People were resolute: "Once begun, the journey must be completed." So the messengers begged some man's medicine (the Reed People control the Warrior Brotherhood) from them. This, the people gave, but a puff of wind swept it off into the dust. The messengers begged for more; the Reed People refused. However, the Reed People's chief did give them an ear of sacred corn, for it is well known that their corn grows more readily than that of Mishongnovi. In the course of time, a juniper tree grew up where the bit of man's medicine had fallen, and in later times, when the Mishongnovi warriors were readying themselves for battle, they came to this place and planted *pahos*. After many wanderings, the Reed People were permitted to join the village on the mesa at Walpi. "What have you to offer us?" the Bear Chief of Walpi asked. The Reed chief replied, "We have man's medicine," and they were

let in, and thus the Reed People found a new home.

*The Badger Clan*—After coming out of the underworld with all other human beings, the Badger Clan, who were not named yet, wandered about the earth. At last, they settled at Siu-va, by the sacred spring that is the dwelling place of the kachinas. It was at this place that they saw a badger come out of its burrow, and they then began to call themselves Badger People. At the same time, they saw a porcupine, but they did not take him for a blood relation. Porcupine said, "I wish to be your clan totem; therefore, I will show you something." Then he ate piñon gum, and defecated blue paint. He ate skunk-brush berries, and vomited red paint. He ate flowers of rabbitbrush, and defecated yellow paint. The people recognized the powerful gifts of Porcupine, and took him in as their relative.

Some of the people also took in Butterfly, and one day he was sent to seek a new country. He fluttered over the valley and came to the village of Oraibi. When the people heard about this village,

*Guarding the Snake Kiva. 1907.*

they moved toward it. However, as they were not let into it yet, they camped at the foot of the mesa. Then they went on down the valley for about three miles. The time of year then was autumn.

One winter's day, the son of the Crier Chief of Oraibi was out hunting. He pursued a rabbit far down the valley. It finally disappeared in a clump of bushes. The youth was searching around there, without success, when he heard a voice say, "I am here." There, in the thicket of thatch, he saw a circular hole in the earth. The voice spoke to him from within: "Come in," it said.

He answered, "Will there be harm in doing so?"

"There will be no harm. Come," the voice said.

So the youth passed into the hole, and found himself in a kiva with a number of people. The rabbit, he was told, was one of the girls who sat there with him. They gave him food and a smoke. When he was finished, they asked him to watch some of the girls weave a picture. He did this, pleased to find that the image pictured in cloth was that of Wiyakote, uncle of the kachinas. "From watching carefully, you can learn," one of the girls said, "how to make ceremonial sashes for the kachina dances." However, she then added, "You must remain here with us all night." That night they performed the kachina dances, which he duly took note of, and then in the morning, they sent him back home to his village.

In time, after the youth told of his adventure, his father, who was the Crier Chief said, "Ah, this is the medicine that is needed for admittance at Oraibi." There was much rejoicing among the Badger People when they were told that they would be allowed to come to the village, but they expressed the desire to enter it at night. When they reached Oraibi in two parties, wearing their kachina masks, they split up into two groups and distributed the food they had brought for gifts. At sunrise they ran about on the roofs of the houses. The people who had gathered there to watch the dances fled in terror. While they were hiding, the Badger People ran to the north side of the plaza, removed their masks, and revealed themselves as ordinary human beings. It was in that part of the village, exactly where they stood, that the Badger Clan made their

home in Oraibi. There was, sometime later, a woman who married a man from Walpi, and thus started a Badger Clan there. But that tale, which tells of the founding of Sichomovi—to relieve the overcrowding at Walpi—is not for this time, but for another.

*Flute Boys, Priests, and Maidens. 1921.*

*Flute Dancers Returning to Walpi. 1905.*

*Pima and Yuma History*

The Indians of Piman and Yuman origin reside within the limits of Arizona but extend into the Mexican state of Sonora and into eastern California. The Yuma and the Mohave, whose homes are on the banks of the Colorado, are large-boned, strongly built, and clear-skinned. Within a short distance of them, in the high altitudes, live the Walapai, of the same family. They are the direct opposite of the river Indians— hardy mountain types, physically and mentally quick of action, for their rugged mountain home has always demanded a hard fight for existence.

Adjoining the Walapai, in Cataract Canyon of the Colorado, are the Havasupai, also of the Yuman family. These wiry mountain people cultivate their canyon home, growing fruit and vegetables, but they are also very capable hunters. The Maricopa, another Yuman tribe, who have lived long in the valley of the

*Maricopa Girl. 1907.*

Gila, are another river people. The Pima from earliest tradition have dwelt within the Gila drainage in southern Arizona. They are industrious, keen of mind, friendly to outsiders. The Papago are so closely allied with them that it is not easy to differentiate. One part of the Papago is sedentary, like the Pima; the other shifts from place to place over a limited area as the abundance or lack of water necessitates. The Qahatika, also of Piman stock, live in five villages in the heart of the desert south of the Gila. A stranger to their land would regard it as a sandy waste, yet they manage to draw sustenance from the barrenness that surrounds them.

These various tribes have been broadly termed, with the Pueblos, the sedentary Indians of the Southwest. Most of them came in direct contact with Spanish missionaries, who after two centuries of zealous effort have done little to draw them away from their own gods. As a rule, the extent of their Christianization has been a willingness to add another god to their pantheon.

The Pima are particularly fortunate in having an abundance of desert foods on which to live. There are deer, rabbits, quail, doves, and fish; the country also holds a diversity of vegetables and fruits. The giant cactus, *hasen*, bears a fruit about the size of a pear, which is gathered in great quantities by means of a long pole with a sharp wooden blade at the end. This is stewed into a preserve and stored for future use, or is preserved by drying, while large quantities are converted into syrup and a sort of wine. Eaten fresh, the fruit has the flavor of figs, though it is sweeter.

The fruit of the tuna, or prickly pear cactus, is eaten both fresh and cooked and is used as well for making a beverage called *navait*. The cholla cactus is also a staple. The fruit is gathered with wooden pincers, brushed about in a basket to remove the spines, and then cooked in a pit lined with hot stones and brush. After twelve or fifteen hours, it is taken out and laid on cloths to dry, when it is ready to be stored for winter use. Usually, this product is ground, mixed with wheat flour, and boiled into a thick mush. It is, however, also cooked without grinding, and flavored with herbs.

Formerly, mesquite beans were another part of the desert diet of the Pima. These were crushed in a large mortar, and, using an arrow-brush sieve, the seeds were separated from the pulp. Next the pulp was placed in a circular hole and sprinkled with water. This hardened into a sugary mass, about which a rough storage basket was woven.

Like most tribes of the Southwest, the Pima have always been an agricultural people. From their earliest history, they have grown crops by irrigation, conveying the water from the rivers in canals—which then watered the crops through a dipping and hand-carrying process. Under this system, their farms produced corn, squash, beans, and cotton; but all of these were grown in small quantities. Since the coming of the Spanish, the Pima have learned to irrigate by flooding, and they now have much larger harvests than in the old days.

From the earliest times, the Apache were the hereditary foes of the Pima, who lived, it is said, in

*Hso-Man-Hai. Maricopa. 1907.*

constant fear of sudden attack. The Pima, however, learned that the Apache were early sleepers as well as early risers. Thus, in retaliation, they would often strike a sleeping camp before the waning moon had risen. Afterward, they would retreat before the Apache could rally in the streaking light of dawn.

Perhaps because of the enmity for the Apache, the Pima did not seem to resent the coming of the first white people. Early California emigrants met no resistance when passing through Pima country. On the contrary, refuge from marauding Apache and Yuma Indians was always to be found in the Pima *rancherías*. However, when the Apache raided a cross-country wagon train and livestock were loose, the Pima appropriated them.

Accounts of internal strife constitute a large part of Pima tradition. Feuds often broke out between two neighboring villages, or between groups of villages. Blood feuds frequently involved a number of villages in internecine war. This may, perhaps, account for the presence of the Qahatika, who live about forty miles due south of the Pima reservation.

When or why the Qahatika separated from their Pima kindred on the Gila and wandered into the inhospitable desert, no one seems to know. Many years ago, some say, the Pima were living at Akichinh, near the Picacho, when a large party of Apache made war on them and drove them away. The greater part went to the Gila and established the settlement at Sacaton; others, the ancestors of the Qahatika, went into the desert and made their homes there.

One wonders how human beings can wrest the necessities of life from such barrenness. Yet they do. Fortunately, it is a land of constant sun and warmth, requiring little clothing. In the old days, the men wore only a loincloth and the women a short skirt of yucca fiber. They

*Harvesting Cactus Fruit. Maricopa. 1907.*

gleaned from the bright sands both plant and animal patrons, and from these made their desolate surroundings into a home. When asked why they do not go to the river valleys, where they might have good farms and live in plenty, their answer is that their home is best; and they say that they do not have sickness, as do their brothers who live by the rivers.

However, the never-ending struggle with the hostile desert seems to have left its mark on these people, for they are as thorny as the plants they feed upon. Not only is this noticeable to the visitor but it is recognizable by the kindred tribes, and is accounted for by the Papago in their creation myth.

Although they depend largely on the natural food supply, such as mesquite pods and cactus fruits, the Qahatika also use the technique of dry farming. If there is no natural rise of ground about their little fields, a low embankment is thrown up to retain the rush of winter rains. The soft, loose soil absorbs moisture to a great depth, and a few heavy winter rains afford the people of a fair crop. They plant wheat in December and harvest in May or June. It is cut with the sickle and threshed in the Southwestern mode, by driving horses over the loose grain spread on the ground.

One cannot help wondering how these Indians would have managed if nature had made the giant cactus with a solid trunk. These middesert people depend solely on the woody ribs of the giant cactus for their building material. When the tree dies, the pulpy interior tissue desiccates, leaving a bundle of sun-bleached bones, which, in turn,

*A Pima Home. 1907.*

become poles for house building. Here, in the rock-strewn desert that allows only a little to grow, the giant cactus flourishes, and alongside it, the Qahatika.

The Pima, the Papago, and the Qahatika each have their version of the creation myth, and every storyteller offers his own particular vision of it. According to legend, there were many primal creations before the final, and most recent, one. The others were, for various reasons, unsatisfactory. Therefore, the first origin people were destroyed by all sorts of cataclysms. It is said that one race of people were ill-formed and another multiplied too rapidly, causing overpopulation. Five times, they say, the people were wiped out, for one reason or another. And yet they survived, and, some say, prospered.

The legend tells that the earliest people settled in the Salt and Gila valleys and made their homes there. They built extensive irrigation canals and massive houses. Suuhu, the ruler of these people, committed many crimes, and the people tried to kill him five times to punish him, but always he escaped. In the end, he turned traitor and sought other people and other ways with which he might wreak his vengeance.

In the east lived Chuwutumaka with his warlike hoard. Sujuhbu enlisted his aid, and they returned with an army that devastated the land and annihilated all of the people. According to the myth, these invaders were the ancestors of the present Pima tribe.

*Qahatika Maiden. 1907.*

*Czele/Marie (Schoolgirl). Pima. 1907.*

### The Pima Creation Myth

*Chuwutumaka and Suuhu, Creators and Destroyers*—Before the beginning of time, there was nothing but space—space without limit, darkness blacker than night. For ages, a tiny seed, feathered with downy filament, drifted through this deep space. And as it flitted and fell through endless night of the ages, it grew, and once grown, it became a being of human form. This being is now known as Chuwutumaka, Earth Doctor, the creator.

Chuwutumaka rubbed his fingers upon his chest and drew forth a bit of matter, which he then rolled into a ball and placed in the air before him. However, the ball did not stay still; it began moving toward the west. Three times it went that way; each time Chuwutumaka tried to make it settle in

*Qahatika Child. 1907.*

the air. But it was intent on traveling ever westward. Finally, the fourth time of its journey, it remained still, and so Chuwutumaka knew that here, at last, was his own resting place, where, he thought, I can continue to create without being disturbed.

Chuwutumaka's first creation was a greasewood bush, to which he brought forth many ants, so that they would carry grease into the branches and make it dry properly. Then he made screwworms, and they bore into the ball, loosening the texture of it, drying it well before he stood upon it. After this, he stepped upon it and started to sing the sixteen songs, resting between every fourth one. And as he sang, he danced; and as he danced, the round ball began to grow and soon became the earth, with hills, valleys, canyons, and mountains.

*Maricopa Water Girl. 1907.*

Now the earth was not still; it twisted and turned and rolled so much that Chuwutumaka put the great sky over it. Then he made a big spider, which spun ropes that held the earth in place. When the spider was done, all was still. And yet, all around was darkness, endless darkness. Sure, Chuwutumaka thought, there should be light, that my beings may see. So he fashioned a clay bowl and filled it with water, which he allowed to become hard. Then he tossed the contents of the bowl into the sky, and it became the sun. In like manner, he made the moon and, finally, the stars, which he drew forth by spraying water from his mouth into the sky. Having finished that which was above, Chuwutumaka turned his attention again to earth, which he made beautiful by giving life to all things green and fruitful. The sky came down then and met the earth, and from their union a god was born, Suuhu, Elder Brother. Then came Coyote, child of Sun and Moon. These two deities had divine powers, and they soon made use of them.

The first thing they did was try to make people.

*Qahatika Man. 1907.*

Chuwutumaka faced east, Suuhu faced south, and Coyote sat with his face to the west; all three were back-to-back, so that their creations might remain a secret until the appropriate time. And thus were Chuwutumaka's people fashioned in his own image, and therefore were beautifully formed. Suuhu's people, though, were reptiles that creep upon the ground; and Coyote's, as it turned out, were strange-looking animals with great ears and little hands and feet. Now, when Chuwutumaka saw the creations of Suuhu, he chastised him, saying, "Surely these beings will torment the people I have made." Then he upbraided Coyote's people, ordering that they be taken far away to the west.

Coyote did as he was told, but Suuhu became angry, and soon a great quarrel ensued. To save himself from being the first one to spill blood upon the earth, Chuwutumaka caused the ground to

*Stone Maze. 1907.*

open up and swallow him. However, before he disappeared, Suuhu raked him with his long fingernails, staining his hands with blood. This he washed off in a nearby lake, and thus disease and disaffection were brought into the world.

Suuhu, still angry, sought out the handsomest man on earth and told him this: "You will marry as many women as you meet, and bring forth as many children as you can; and all will be subject to my will." This was done, as ordered, yet when the handsomest man met, at last, the handsomest woman, she withdrew from him and did not want to bear his child. In the end, he won, but the child born of this union wept great tears, and these became the rivers and waters of desolation.

A great flood then swept across the land, drowning all things that lived on it. Suuhu made a water jar of greasewood, which launched and drifted about on the surface of the flood. Coyote took refuge in a hollow reed. These two were saved; all the rest of the people were drowned. After a while, they ended up on top of Black Moun-

tain. The flood receded and left the land bare and brown. Then came Chuwutumaka, out of the earth, and he bade Suuhu and Coyote to sit down with him and make the people all over again, which they did; but this time, all three made creatures of comely form. However, Suuhu soon grew bored and began to transform Chuwutumaka's people into stone. Once again, as a result, Chuwutumaka descended into the earth, taking his people with him. On leaving, he caused another great flood to devastate the land.

Chuwutumaka's people, under the earth, thrived. One day, he opened the entrance of a gopher hole and, widening it greatly, let his people out upon the earth. Quickly, they swarmed the villages that were populated by Suuhu's people; in the end, not one of these subjects lived to tell of the awful destruction. The victors prospered in the land of the fallen, and Chuwutumaka, once again, descended into the earth. He lives there now, and his subjects, the Pima, have stayed in the very place where he left them.

# APACHE AND NAVAJO

**Apache History**

Since their early history, the bands of the Apache had occupied the mountains and plains of southern Arizona and New Mexico, northern Sonora and Chihuahua, and western Texas. This area is greater than that of the states of New York, Pennsylvania, New Jersey, Connecticut, Massachusetts, Vermont, Maine, Ohio, North Carolina, South Carolina, and West Virginia. They were feared among Indian and white alike. An admission of fear is hard to elicit from any Indian, but all who lived within raiding distance of the Apache, save the Navajo, their Athapaskan cousins, freely admit that for generations the Apache were regarded with trepidation.

Constant pillaging against Mexican settlements earned a cruel indictment for the Apache. In 1837, the Mexican states of Sonora and Chihuahua offered a bounty for Apache scalps. The horror of this policy lay in the fact that the scalp of a friendly Indian brought the

*The Lookout. Navajo. 1904.*

same reward as that of the fiercest warrior; worse still, no exception was made of women or children. Nothing could have been more effective than this scalp bounty in arousing all Apache wrath. Both Mexico and the United States paid dearly in lives for every Apache scalp taken under this barbarous system. Predatory warfare continued unabated during the next forty years in spite of all the Mexican government could do. With the consummation of the treaty of Guadalupe Hidalgo in 1848, the Apache problem became one to be solved by the United States as well.

In 1864, under Gen. James H. Carleton, the "war of extermination" was begun in a most systematic manner. On April 20 this officer communicated a proposal of cooperation to Don Ignacio Pesqueira, governor of Sonora, saying, "If Your Excellency will put a few hundred men into the field on the first day of next June, and keep them in hot pursuit of the Apaches of Sonora, say for sixty or ninety days, we will either exterminate the

*Apache Dancers. 1906.*

Indians or so diminish their numbers that they will cease their murdering and robbing propensities and live at peace."

This request was met. The settlers in Arizona, under agreement, placed a force in the field, provisioned with army supplies. Several hundred Pima, Papago, and Maricopa Indians also were supplied with guns, ammunition, and clothing and pressed into service; but a year's effort netted the combined forces little gain. Although two hundred Apache were killed and many head of stolen stock recovered, practically no advance toward the termination of hostilities was accomplished.

In April 1865, Inspector General Davis arranged a conference at the Copper Mines in New Mexico. Present were Victorio, Nane, Acosta, and other chiefs, including the sons of Mangas Coloradas. The U.S. Government had adopted a policy of removal by which the Arizona Apache desiring peace had to join the Mescaleros at the Bosque Redondo in New Mexico. To this, they flatly refused to agree, and the warfare continued.

Practically all the Apache were assembled in Arizona in 1865, and they waged hostilities with renewed energy for the next five years, being joined by the Walapai in 1868. The close of this period found the situation quite as unsettled as ever.

On June 4, 1871, Gen. George Crook was placed in command. Crook was not an exterminator. In the fall of the same year, he said:

"I think that the Apache is painted in darker colors than he deserves, and that his villainies arise more from a misconception of facts than from his being worse than other Indians. Living in a country the natural products of which will not support him, he has either to cultivate the soil or steal, and as our vacillating policy satisfies him we are afraid of him, he chooses the latter, also as requiring less labor and being more congenial to his natural instincts. I am satisfied that a sharp, active campaign against him would not only make him one of the best Indians in the country, but it would also save millions of dollars to the Treasury, and the lives of many innocent whites and Indians."

Crook's policy was one of peace, but he made it plain to the Indians that if they did not agree to peace when liberal terms were offered, they could expect a campaign against them of unequaled vigor. It was thus that by 1873, the Tontos, Coyoteros, and Apache-Mohave were subdued and the backbone of Apache resistance broken.

The Apache-Mohave and the Tontos were placed on a reservation on the Rio Verde; the Coyoteros were taken to the White Mountain district near Fort Apache; the Piñalenos and parts of other bands surrendered and were established at San Carols. In all, approximately three thousand Apache had been brought under control. About one thousand hostiles yet remained in the mountains, but by 1874 they had become so nearly subjugated as to make it seem advisable to transfer the Arizona reservations from the War Department to the Office of Indian Affairs, which was done. The policy of the Indian Office from the beginning had been to concentrate the various bands upon one reservation at San Carlos. Disaffection arose between different bands, until this became a despicable place to nearly all, while continued adherence to the removal policy drove the Chiricahua, who had been at peace for years, from their southern Arizona reservation to seek refuge with the Ojo Caliente Apache in southwestern New Mexico. In 1877 these Chiricahua and the Ojo Caliente band were forcibly removed to San Carlos, but while en route, Victorio and a party of forty warriors made their escape. In September of the same year, three hundred more fled from San Carlos. As a result, many settlers were murdered. In February 1878, Victorio and his band surrendered at Ojo Caliente. But they said they would die fighting before submitting to removal to San Carlos. The major portion of the three hundred Chiricahua, who had left San Carlos, surrendered at Fort Wingate, New Mexico. All these were taken to the Mescalero reservation in New Mexico.

Haunted by the dread of removal to San Carlos, the appearance of a party of Grant County officials at the Mescalero agency on a hunting tour a few months later caused Victorio and his band to flee with a number of Chiricahua and Mescaleros to the mountains of southern New Mexico.

For two years, until he met his death at the hands of Mexican troops in the fall of 1880, Victo-

rio spread carnage throughout Texas, New Mexico, and Arizona. He enlisted the aid of every willing renegade or refugee of whatever band or tribe in that area. After him, Nane, Chato, Juh, Geronimo, and other warriors carried the fighting and raiding along until June 1883. Then Crook, reassigned to Arizona, followed Geronimo into the Sierra Madre. There he brought them back, broken and ready to accept offers of peace. The captives were placed upon the San Carlos and White Mountain reservations. Under military surveillance, and with Crook in control, they took up farming. But in 1885 Crook's authority was curtailed, and through some cause, never quite clear, Geronimo, with many Chiricahua followers, again took the warpath. Crook being relieved at his own request, Gen. Nelson A. Miles was assigned the task of finally subduing the Apache. This was accomplished with the recapture of Geronimo in the Sierra Madre in September 1886. The last of the fighting Apache were taken as prisoners to Florida,

*Ndee-San Gochonh-Thunder Apache. 1903.*

later to Alabama, and then to Fort Sill, Oklahoma, where, numbering 298, they remain at this writing. They continue as farmers, in peace and quiet, but still under the control of the military authorities.

One of the last hostile movements of note was the so-called Cibicu fight in 1882. In the spring of that year, an old medicine man, Nabakelti, Attacking the Enemy, better known as Doklini, started a "medicine" craze in the valley of the Cibicu on the White Mountain reservation. He had already a considerable following, and now claimed divine revelation and dictated forms of procedure in bringing the dead to life. He made sixty large medicine wheels of wood, painted symbolically. There were also twelve sacred sticks, one of which, in the form of a cross, he designated "chief of sticks." Then with sixty men, he commenced his dance.

One morning at dawn, Nabakelti went to the grave of a man who had been prominent in the tribe and who had recently died. He and his followers danced about the grave and then dug up the bones, around which they danced four times in a circle. The dancing occupied the entire morning. Early in the afternoon, they went to another grave, where the performance was repeated. In each instance, the bones were left exposed; but later, four men, specially delegated, went to the graves and erected a brush hut over the remains.

Nabakelti told the people that they must pray each morning for four days, at the end of which time the bleached bones would be found clothed with flesh and live again. By the end of the second day, the Apache band on the Cibicu grew very excited. They watched the little grave-houses constantly, gathering in groups about the other graves.

Some of the Apache employed as scouts with the detachment stationed at Fort Apache heard of the craze and obtained leave of absence to investigate. They returned and informed the commanding officer, then acting as agent, that their people were going mad. A number of scouts and troopers were sent to learn the cause of the trouble and to ask Nabakelti to go to the fort for an interview. Though angered by the message, the old man agreed to go in two days. Meanwhile, he had the little brush houses over the bones tightly sealed to keep out preying animals and curious Indians. He then ex-

*Yenin Guy. Apache. 1903.*

plained to his people that, owing to the interruption by the whites, it was probable that the bones would not come to life at the end of four days, as predicted, but that he would make a new dance later and prove the efficacy of his creed.

Then he started for the fort with his entire band of dancers, sixty-two in number, each with his "sacred medicine"—wheels, sticks, and drums. They journeyed afoot, stopping occasionally to dance, and reached the grounds of the fort late in the afternoon of the second day. On they passed, dancing. They camped that night on the flat a little above the fort, where they waited for someone to come over to interview them. The agent did not send for Nabakelti that night, so at daybreak He started up White River with his band, passing by the present agency site, and crossing into Bear Springs Valley. They took the trail toward the Cibicu again, reaching the *carrizo* in the evening. There they camped for the night and did another dance. The following morning they took the trail for their home, which they reached rather early in the day.

As soon as the band had reached its destination, another summons was delivered to Nabakelti

*An Ostoho Cowboy. Apache. 1903.*

to appear before the agent at the fort. This time the old man sent back word that he would not come: He had gone once, and if any had wished to see him, they had had their chance.

On receipt of this reply, sixty mounted soldiers, armed and provisioned, were sent over to the Cibicu to put a stop to the dancing. Apache scouts had been stationed to watch the maneuvers of the Indians and to keep the officials informed. They met the troopers, who made a night ride to the stream, and informed them where the old medicine man was encamped. Early in the

*An Apache Girl. 1903.*

morning, the soldiers reached the Cibicu at a point about two miles above Nabakelti's camp. A detachment was dispatched to arrest the medicine man and bring him to the place where headquarters were being established.

Nabakelti yielded to the demands of the soldiers and forthwith rode up to headquarters. Everything seemed very quiet. There was no demonstration against the soldiers, who stacked their arms and unloaded the pack trains. The mules were hobbled and turned loose and the cavalry horses tethered and fed.

While this apparently peaceful condition prevailed, a brother of the medicine man, angered because of the arrest, dashed into camp on a pony and shot and killed the captain in command. Instantly, hardly realizing where the shot had come from, one of the troopers struck Nabakelti on the head and killed him. The soldiers then went to higher ground, a short distance back, where they made preparations for an attack.

On learning that Nabakelti had been killed, and deeming the soldiers wholly to blame, a small party of Apache attacked the troopers. Six cavalrymen were killed, the mules stampeded, and the provisions burned, all in a short time. The Apache then made their escape and left the valley.

The U.S. government probably never lost money faster in an Indian campaign than it did as a

result of its interference with Nabakelti's harmless medicine craze. Had he been left alone, his inevitable failure, already at hand, to bring the dead to life would have lost him his following, and in all probability his ill-success would have cost his life at the hands of one of his tribesmen. As it was, the hostilities that followed extended over several months, costing many lives and a vast sum of money.

For nearly three hundred years, the Apaches threatened all colonists who dared to settle within their boundaries; thus, the Apaches of Arizona and New Mexico occupied a region that became terra incognita, while the inner life of the people was a closed book. There is little wonder, then, that much of what we know about the Apache and their customs was originally given to us by army officers; there-

*Apache Girl and Papoose. 1903.*

fore, this study was entered into with special interest. Much patience was consumed before the confidence of elders was gained and our work was finally completed. The creation story that follows was related by medicine men. Afterward, it was repeated and verified until no doubt of its accuracy remained.

Linguistically, the Apache belong to the great Athapaskan family, which had its origin in the far north, where many tribes of the family still live. Judging by the similarity in language, the Apache and the Navajo, in prehistoric times, were as nearly a single group as the present bands of Apache are; and, likewise, there is sufficient similarity in the underlying principles of their mythology to argue a common tribal origin. Several of the mythic characters are identical in both tribes, as, for example, the war gods, Nayenezgani and Tobadzischini. These miracle-performing twins, in each case, are the sons of Mother Earth.

*At the Ford. Apache. 1905.*

However, there are differences in the mythology as well as consistent similarities. The Apache story of their creation portrays human beings in their present form, while in the Navajo genesis myth, there is the evolution of the lower animals through successive underworlds until the present world is reached. The beautiful genesis myth of the Apache is complete; it does not reflect an incipient primitive culture, but one that has arrived fully developed.

The Apache is devoutly religious; his life is completely molded by his religious beliefs. From his morning prayer to the rising sun, through the hours, the days, and months—through life itself—every act has some religious significance. Animals, elements, every observable thing of the solar system, all natural phenomena, are deified and revered. The Apache, even if willing, could not directly impart their religious beliefs or their philosophy. It is only by study of their myths, myth songs, and medicine practices, and by close observation of their life, that a comprehensive idea of such beliefs can be gained.

## The Apache Creation Myth

*Kuterastan, The One Who Lives Above*—There was a time when nothing existed—no earth, no sky, no sun or moon to break the illimitable darkness. But as time rolled on, a spot, a thin circular disk no larger than your hand—yellow on one side, white on the other—appeared in midair. Inside the disk, there sat a bearded man, who was the same size as a frog. The man was named Kuterastan, the One Who Lives Above. But some call him Yuadistan, Sky Man.

Kuterastan, as if waking from a long sleep, sat up and rubbed his face and eyes with his hands. Then, bending forward, he looked up into the endless darkness. Light appeared everywhere above him, and all below became a sea of light. A glance to the east created yellow streaks of dawn. Another glance—to the west—made the saffron tints of dusk. And, as he looked all around him, in all directions, clouds of many hues were born of his gaze.

Now, once again, he rubbed his face and eyes. And from the sweat of his face, as he rubbed his palms together and shook them with a quick downward fling, there appeared a little girl the size of a doll. She sat upon a shining, vaporless, miragelike cloud.

*Alchise. Apache. 1906.*

Kuterastan directed her to stand up, but she did not answer him. Clearing his vision once more with his hands, he offered his right hand to the girl, whose name was Stenatliha, Woman Without Parents. Now she took hold of his hand and asked him, "Where did you come from?"

He replied with a question of his own: "Where did you come from?" Then, he added, "Look to the east; it is light! There will be light in the south, in the west, and in the north."

The girl, Stenatliha, looked and saw that it was so.

And Kuterastan stepped, then, upon the cloud. "Where is the earth?" she asked.

Kuterastan replied by asking, "Where is the sky?"

Then, asking not to be disturbed, he began to sing: "I am thinking, thinking, thinking what I shall do next."

Four times he sang this.

At the end of the fourth time, he brushed his face with his hands, after which he again rubbed them briskly together and parted them quickly.

And there stood before him Chuganaai, the Sun.

Then he raised his left hand to his brow. And from the sweat that was gathered there, which he rolled between his palms, there came forth a small person, Hadintin Skhin, who is also known as Pollen Boy.

The four sat upon the still cloud for a time as if in a reverie. The first to break the silence was the one who had started the creation, Kuterastan.

"What shall we do next?" he asked. Then he said, "I do not like this cloud to live upon, but we must stay together. . . ."

And then he set to work, making Nacholecho, the Tarantula, who, later on, helped to complete the making of the earth.

Kuterastan further made the Big Dipper, whose duty it was to guide and befriend; and he made the Wind, Lightning Maker, Lightning Rumbler. However, after this, he turned to the girl, Stenatliha, and said, "Truly this is not a fit place to live; let us now make the earth."

And so saying, he at once began to sing: "I am thinking of the earth," which he repeated four times. When he finished singing, the other three took his hands, so that the sweat of theirs adhered to his.

Now, when Kuterastan began rubbing his hands together again, there slipped from between them a small brown body, no bigger than a bean. Kuterastan kicked it, and it expanded; he kicked it again, and the body grew some more.

Chuganaai, the Sun, gave it a severe blow with his foot, and it became larger still. Hadintin Skhin, Pollen Boy, kicked it, and so the body grew again.

Now Kuterastan told the Wind to go inside the body and blow outward in all directions. This he did, greatly expanding it, so that they could hardly see its edge.

*Tsahizn Tsah. Apache. 1906.*

to sing a song, which she did: "The world is made and will soon sit still."

Kuterastan and Stenatliha stood and faced Chuganaai and Hadintin Skhin. Into their midst came Nilchidilhkizn, who dashed away to the cardinal points with the four posts. These he placed under the sides of the earth. And the earth rested upon them and did not move. This pleased Kuterastan and he sang a song, repeating the words over and over: "The world is now made and sits still."

### Jicarilla Apache History

The Jicarilla Apache occupy a reservation of nearly 450 square miles of mountainous country in northern New Mexico. Linguistically they are of the same stock as the Apache of Arizona, but here the relationship

Lightning was next directed to exert his strength, and with a terrific flash and roar, he penetrated the body to its center, and it grew much larger all around.

Then Tarantula was called on to assist, and accordingly, he started off to the east, spinning a strong black cord, on which he pulled with all his might. Another cord of blue he spun out to the south, a third of yellow to the west, and a fourth of glistening white to the north. A mighty pull on each of these stretched the surface of that dark brown body to almost immeasurable size.

At last, Kuterastan told all to cover their eyes with their hands. When they opened them, a moment later, they beheld Nigostun, the Earth. No hills or mountains were yet in sight, nothing but a smooth, treeless, reddish brown plain.

Nilchidilhkizn, the Wind, scratched his chest and rubbed his fingers together. And out of his fingers flew Datilye, the Hummingbird. Datilye was told to make a circuit of the earth and report what he saw. He started off toward the east, circled south, west, north, and back from the east. All was well; the earth was most beautiful, very smooth, and covered with water on the western side.

But the earth was not still; it kept shifting and rolling and dancing up and down. So Kuterastan made four great posts—black, blue, yellow, and white—to support it. Then he directed Stenatliha

*Apache Maiden. 1906.*

ends. Each, according to their respective genesis myths, had their origin in the general region in which they live today. However, the Jicarillas—in dialect, mythology, legends, and medicine rites—resemble the Navajo more than any of their own Apache groups.

The Jicarillas are a particularly interesting tribe because of their composite nature. Small in number, they have been influenced by other nearby tribes—the buffalo hunters of the Great Plains, as well as the peaceful Pueblo of Taos.

As mentioned above, Jicarilla medicine rites are much like those of the Navajo, but when a comparison is made between the two, the life of the Jicarilla seems almost lacking in ceremony. And yet, when contrasted with the various Yuman tribes on the Colorado and Gila Rivers of Arizona, it appears fairly rich.

In terms of their medicine ways, the Jicarilla

*Jicarilla. 1905.*

believe the souls of the dead rise skyward. In one portion of the sky, so they tell, among vast herds of buffalo, all those who have met death in battle are gathered together, rich and happy. In another part of the sky, it is explained, are those who have succumbed to sickness and old age.

Evil ones—those who have practiced witchcraft—have a place apart from the rest. This place, separated from the other portions of the sky by a high rock wall, is where the evil ones are condemned to dig for eternity; they dig to reach a happier home. Spirits, the Jicarilla say, can work only in darkness. Thus, the work of the night is forever brought to naught by the coming of the day.

## The Jicarilla Creation Myth

*The People Emerge from the Underworld*—In the beginning, all people, birds, and beasts were far beneath this earth, somewhere in the darkness.

There was no sun or moon. And it was not a good place to live, because of the darkness.

After a time, there came Chuganaai, the Sun, and Klenaai, the Moon. They directed the people to leave the world of darkness, showing the way, which was through a rift in the sky. But the sky was so far above that the people knew of no way to reach it. So they made a pile of sand in the form of a mountain. They painted the east side white, the south blue, the west yellow, and the north side all colors.

Then they gathered seeds from all the plants they knew and placed them inside the little mountain. Chunnaai sent back his messenger, Anltsistn, the Whirlwind, to instruct them how to make the mountain grow larger.

Then all gathered about it, and they danced and sang. And after four days, the seeds sprouted and the mountain began to grow up and all around. This continued for four days, at the end of which time the mountain seemed almost to reach the sky; but suddenly, it stopped growing, and none knew the cause.

From Chunnaai, then, came Whirlwind. And

he told the people there gathered of how two of their maidens had entered the sacred space on the mountaintop and had wantonly broken and destroyed plants and fruits. This, they said, was why the mountain had stopped growing.

Out of two long poles and four buffalo horns, the people made a ladder, which, when placed on the mountaintop, reached the sky. Great Whirlwinds, Nlchitso, went up to see what this new place was like. Peering through the opening in the sky, he saw that the world was covered with water. Then he descended the ladder.

Next, the four Whirlwinds went up: White Wind rolled the water to the east, Blue Wind rolled it to the south, Yellow Wind blew it away to the west, and Many-Colored Wind blew what was left of the water off to the north.

Then the Whirlwinds blew over the earth for four days to dry it, but they left some of the water, which flowed along in streams.

When they returned and told what they had

*Jicarilla Cowboy. 1904.*

*Visitors at Jicarilla. 1905.*

done, the people sent Kage, the Crow, who was wise, to regard the land. They waited long, but Kage did not return. So they sent Little Whirl-wind, who found Kage perched upon some dead bodies. He was plucking out their eyes. Now, because of his wickedness in forgetting the people in their time of need, his feathers—once white—now turned black.

After a while, Nagaschitn, the Badger, was sent to see if the land was good. But just as soon as he had crawled through, he sank in the black mud and could go no farther. To this day, Badger's legs are black.

Skunk, who was light in weight, was sent up next. But even he sank in the mud and blackened his legs. So the people sent Cha, the Beaver, who traveled about for a long time. He found all the wa-

*Jicarilla Type. 1905.*

*Jicarilla Girl in Feast Dress. 1905.*

*Chief Garfield. Jicarilla. 1905.*

ter running away in streams, so he built dams, and this made many lakes. But he came and told the people the land was good to live in, and this pleased them greatly.

Presently, they started up the ladder. Now, when the last person passed over, the buffalo horns bowed from the weight, and that is why they have since been curved.

During the first days, the sun did not rise above the horizon. This was because of the web made by

*Lone Tree Lodge. Jicarilla. 1904.*

Masche, the Spider; he had woven it in the east and held the sun back. But the people succeeded in tearing the web away. And from that time, the sun, each day, has traveled across the whole sky.

On emerging from the underworld, the people began moving in a great circle, traveling from north to east, and then to the south and the west. When they found a place that pleased them, they stayed; and Chunnaai and Klenaai gave them a language of their own.

Four times the land was thus encircled, but each time the circle grew smaller. When, for the last time, the people came to the north, Haisndayin, the Jicarillas, found their home in the mountains near the Rio Chama.

### Navajo History

The Navajos have never had a tribal chief, so called, and so their leaders have never commanded more than a small following. Manuelito, who was acclaimed head chief in 1855, probably had a greater following than any other Navajo in historic times. However, even he could not rely on the majority of warriors of his widely scattered tribe.

Although divided into many bands, like the Apache, the Navajo, unlike them, were not engaged in ceaseless depredation. Their sporadic raids were conducted by small parties, quite independent of any organized tribal movement. They preferred, rather, to follow a pastoral life. However, if they had possessed the Apache's insatiable desire for war and a galvanizing political cohesion, the Navajos might have ruled the Southwest.

For a long time prior to New Mexico becoming a territory, Navajos had been in the habit of making raids on Indian pueblos. Later, they attacked Spanish settlements along the Rio Grande, mainly to steal livestock. But both Indians and Mexicans were captured and enslaved. The Mexicans lost no opportunity to retaliate, with the result that scattered throughout their villages in the valley of the Rio Grande there were more captives of Navajo blood than there were Mexican prisoners among the Navajo tribe.

However, in the matter of sheep, cattle, and horses, the Navajo were far ahead in the game of thievery. They even boasted that they could easily have exterminated the Mexicans had they not needed them as herders of their stolen flocks. In consequence, bitter enmity arose between the Mexicans and the Navajo. This reached its height about the time Col. Stephen W. Kearney took possession of the territory in behalf of the United States in 1846.

Kearney was sent at that time to Navajo country for the purpose of making a treaty of peace. The treaty, like several others that followed, was soon broken, and the raids continued as before. In 1858 the troubles arising from the plundering became especially severe and led to several other expeditions, but with little result. The problem became a serious one in 1861, when the Civil War caused the withdrawal of troops from the frontier. The way was thus open to the devastation of the country by the Navajo and the Mescaleros. General Carleton, however, formulated a policy of extermination. Early in 1864, Col. Kit Carson traveled to Canon de Chelly, the Navajo stronghold. There he succeeded in killing, capturing, and compelling the Navajos to surrender. The backbone of hostility was now broken, and before the beginning of 1865, some eight thousand Navajo were under military control within the new reservation at Bosque Redondo, New Mexico. In 1868, after a punishing term of incarceration, those Navajos who had not died of disease arrived at Fort Wingate on the way to their old home, the so-called four corners region of New Mexico, Arizona, Colorado, and Utah.

There they have lived and flourished ever since.

Traditionally, the Navajo are a seminomadic people, whose reservation of more than fourteen thousand square miles is the desert plateau region of northern Arizona and New Mexico. Between the mesas and low mountains, the Navajo drive their flocks of sheep and goats. Year in and year out, the flocks slowly drift back and forth from plain to mesa and from mesa to mountain.

It is contended by some that the early Spanish missionaries taught the Navajo to weave—but why should the white man be credited with this art? The mummies found in the prehistoric cliff ruins of the Navajo country are wrapped in cloth finer than any ever produced with a Navajo loom. No doubt now remains that Pueblo people were incorporated by the Navajo in ancient times.

From the Spanish, it is certain, however, that the Navajo learned the fine art of silversmithing; Mexican coins, especially the peso, are the principal source of the art. Buttons and beads are made from American dimes and twenty-five-cent pieces. The silver and shell bead jewelry of the Navajo is his savings bank. During times of prosperity, he becomes the possessor of all the jewelry he can afford. When poor crops or long winters threaten distress, he then pawns it at a trader's.

Most Navajo ceremonies are conducted, at least primarily, for the purpose of healing disease; and while designated healing ceremonies, they are, in fact, ritualistic prayers. The component ritual prayers of some ceremonies number in the hundreds. The principal ceremonies are those that require nine days and nine nights in their performance.

*A Navajo. 1904.*

Of the ones known, the names of nine are given here: Night Chant, Mountain Chant, Happiness Chant, Shooting Chant, Water Chant, Feather Chant, Bead Chant, Evil-Spirit Chant, Coyote Chant. Each is based on a mythic story, taken from the overall story of creation, and each has four dry paintings, or so-called altars. Besides these nine-day ceremonies, there are others whose performance require four days, and many simpler ones requiring only a single day, each with its own dry painting.

The most elaborate ceremonies are conducted between the first frost of autumn and the second moon following the winter solstice. While primarily designed to restore the health of an individual, they are intended also to benefit the entire tribe, many of the prayers being offered for the general welfare of the people rather than for the patient under immediate treatment.

*An Oasis. Navajo. 1904.*

### The Navajo Creation Myth

*The Separation of the Sexes and the Great Flood* — In the world below, there was no sun and no moon, and therefore no light. There was, however, vegetation, and the animal people thrived. Among the latter were Gray Wolf people, Nakletso; Mountain Lion, Nashtuitso; Badger, Naaschid; Locust, Woneschidi; Pine Squirrel, Klozeslskai and Klozeslzhini; Blue Fox, Mai-Dotlishi; Yellow Fox, Mai-Iltsoi; Owl, Nascha; Crow, Gage; Buzzard, Jesho; four different varieties of Hawk people, and many others.

Their world was small. At its eastern rim stood a large white mountain, and at the south a blue one. These formed the home of Astse Hastin, First Man. A yellow mountain in the west and a black one in the north harbored Astse Estsan, First Woman.

Near the mountain in the east, a large river had its source and flowed to the south. Along its western bank, the people lived in peace and plenty. There was game in abundance, much corn, and many edible fruits and nuts. All were happy. The younger women ground corn while the boys sang songs and played on flutes of the sunflower stalk.

The men and the women each had eight chiefs, four living toward each cardinal point. The chiefs of the men lived in the east and south; the women chiefs lived in the west and north. The eastern chiefs took precedence over the southern chiefs, and those of the west came before those of the north.

One day, led by their eight chiefs, all of the men went off on a hunt. When they had gone but a short while, the head chief dispatched the youngest of the four chiefs of the south to return to camp and tell the women to clean the camp thoroughly and bake a quantity of bread while the men were away.

Instead of doing as bidden, the young man visited with the head chief's wife. The hunters were gone four days. They returned laden with much game, weary and hungry. To their surprise, they found the camp unkempt; also, no bread had been baked in their absence.

Immediately, the head chief called for his young messenger and asked what had happened. He explained that he told the woman chief what

*Hatali Nez. Navajo. 1905.*

*Navajo Girl. 1904.*

was expected but that she hadn't listened to him. Then the head chief called upon his wife and demanded to know why she had refused to obey his wishes.

She curtly replied that it was her business, not his. Further, she explained that the women did more work than the men. They tilled the fields, made the clothing, cared for the children, and did the cooking. The men, she said bitterly, did practically nothing. So if the women took some time off to do as they pleased, that was their affair.

*Navajo Medicine Man. 1904.*

The head chief thus became very angry. However, his wife said that should he—and all the other men—wish to leave, they might do so, for the women could get along better without them.

Now the argument between them went on, and was unresolved. In the end, the head chief decided to test the women's will. The following morning, he told the men to depart, and they crossed the great river flowing from the east on cottonwood rafts, which they used as ferries.

All food supplies, clothing, and utensils were left with the women. The men took only a small amount of seed corn. Four *nulti*, "hermaphrodites," protested that they didn't want to leave the women, but, as they were needed to care for the male infants, their protests were ignored. Four old cripples, too weak to move, were left behind, but other than these, no male inhabitant remained in the old village.

As soon as they landed on the opposite bank of the river, the men began to make their new camp. Houses were built, game caught, skins tanned, and fields made ready for crops. But, that first winter, the men suffered from want of the things they had left behind. However, the women had bountiful crops, and through the late fall and winter, they feasted and danced. The singing that they danced to was done by the four old crippled men.

The following fall, the men were better off than before, but the women were less fortunate. Having none but themselves to provide for, they had emptied their granaries and let their fields grow fallow. By the end of the second year, their clothing was worn to rags.

The men, though, had grown more prosperous. Their well-tended farms yielded much corn for the winter; the pelts of deer and antelope furnished warm clothing and bedding. The third year, therefore, found the men living at ease, while the women had been reduced to absolute want. They called across the river, begging the men for a pardon.

Then it was that the youngest of the eight male chiefs confessed his guilt. He admitted that he was

*The Blanket Maker. Navajo. 1904.*

*Giving the Medicine. Navajo. 1905.*

the meadows, where there was neither current nor riverbanks. Coyote, being a meddler and troublemaker, spied them one day, and thinking they were very pretty, he stole them, tucking them under the folds of his coat.

At this time, there was no sun, moon, or stars to give light. But in the east, every morning, there appeared White Dawn, four fingers high. The midday was lighted by Blue Dawn in the south. The late afternoon was lit by Yellow Dawn in the west. The north, however, always remained dark.

responsible for the stance taken by the head chief's wife. This, however, did not soften the head chief, but served only to renew his anger. He merely expressed his regret, saying that the first seeds of wrong should not have been sown.

With starvation staring at them, the women, at the end of the fourth year, tried to swim across the river of separation. But these attempts resulted in death, for the river was much too swift to ford. Four times, then, was the head chief asked for help by the women. And on the fourth plea, he gave orders to loose the rafts and bring the women over.

A miserable lot they were — unclad, wan, and wasted. Yet a return to the old life commenced at once, and soon the women returned to their former selves; and peace, happiness, and prosperity reigned again.

Now the broad river that flowed from the east had its source in two springs: a male spring and a female spring. At the heart of each of these lived two large Water Monsters. Their children, two Water Monster babies, delighted in swimming from the depths of the spring, out across

On the morning following Coyote's return from his trip to the east — he was sent to discover the source of the dawn — the head chief noticed that White Dawn was not as broad as usual. It was only three fingers high, with a dark streak beneath. This was because of Coyote's theft of Water Monster's babies.

A Wolf Man was sent to learn what was wrong. He hurried off, returning at nightfall with the report that all was well in the east. The next morning, though, White Dawn was narrower still and the darkness beneath was larger.

Now a Mountain Lion messenger was dispatched to seek the cause. He reported that all was well. But those in camp noticed deer in the distance, traveling westward at a quickened pace.

The third morning, the belt of darkness was wider than White Dawn, which gave off an alarmingly dim light.

The head chief then sent White Hawk to determine the trouble. His report, like that of each of the other messengers, was that nothing unusual appeared in the east. But now ante-

*Pike Hodiklad. Navajo. 1907.*

*Navajo Belle. 1904.*

*Many Goats Son. Navajo. 1904.*

*Tobadzischini. Navajo. 1904.*

*Nayenzgani. Navajo. 1904.*

lope and other game were running westward in fearful numbers.

On the fourth morning, White Dawn was entirely obscured; nothing but darkness appeared in the east. Sparrow Hawk sped away. He returned quickly with the news that water was fast rising in the two springs at the head of the river. Soon, he said, a great devastating wave was going to come and spread westward.

The camp then became a scene of wild commotion. Quickly gathering the corn and other seeds they could carry, the

*Tonenili. Navajo. 1905.*

people fled for White Mountain, in the east.

On reaching the top, they saw the waters climbing rapidly up the eastern slope. So they descended and ran to Blue Mountain, in the south. They took with them handfuls of earth from its crest, and from its base a reed with twelve sections, which a Wolf Man carried.

From the top of Blue Mountain, the great wave of water was fast approaching. Snatching the earth from the mountain, they hurried on to Yellow Mountain, in the west. Again, the great wave seemed higher than ever, so they snatched up some more earth and ran on to Black Mountain, in the north. A Mountain Lion, this time, was entrusted with another reed.

Once there, the water surrounded them and crept up the sides of the mountain. The female reed from the west was planted on the western side, near the top. The male reed from the east was planted on the eastern slope. At once, both began to shoot up into the sky.

Into the twelve internodes of the female reed climbed all the women, while the men made haste to get into theirs. Turkey, being the last to get in, had his tail caught by the foamy waters, whitening the tips of the feathers, which are so to this day.

The reeds grew very rapidly, but equally fast rose the waters around them. For four days, the reeds grew thus, meeting at the sky at the end of the fourth day. This seemed an impenetrable barrier, but Locust had taken with him his bow of darkness and sacred arrows. With these, he made a hole in the sky, and the people passed on into the world above—the present earth.

*Lynx Cap. Navajo. 1905.*

# II—The Plains

Edward S. Curtis is best known for his definitive photography of the Plains people, those tribes who inhabited the vast expanse from the Missouri River in North Dakota, to the southern plains and upper waters of the North Platte and Arkansas Rivers in Colorado, Wyoming, and Nebraska, to the high mountains of Canada and the Teton region to the south. Wherever the tall grass grew and the mountains cast their shadow, the people of the plains could be found.

Curtis identified deeply with the plight of the Plains Indians and with their bold former history as nomadic warriors. It is, therefore, not surprising to find a passionate spiritual presence in his writing about these tribes. He staunchly defends the Cheyenne, with whom he identified greatly, and protests their despicable treatment by the U.S. Government. And of the dwindling, disease-reduced Mandan, he presents some of his most interesting mythology. It is certainly not widely known that the Mandan council fires once burned at the mouth of "the great water," the Mississippi, and that their original home, as spoken by their elders, was a land where birds sang all winter long and the trees remained green.

The Arikara, Curtis informs, were once a part of the Pawnee, while the Atsina, or "big-bellied Indians," the French-named Gros Ventres, were a branch of the Arapaho tribe. Curtis shows the myths of the Arapaho as having "a deep and abiding faith in the mystery of life," and his transcription of the coming of the buffalo is a worthy tale, a summation of the Plains people's economy, spirituality, and the intricate structure of their society.

At the close of this section, the chapter on Cheyenne, Piegan, Crow, and Sioux, one particular tale stands out as a shining example of how similar some European myths are to Native American ones. Specifically, this is the story of Corn Silk, the rhapsodic Crow myth, which bears amazing resemblance to that of Snow White and the Seven Dwarfs.

However, it is with the Teton Sioux that Curtis penetrates the unity of all the Plains tribes, discovering in Wakan Tanka, the Great Mystery, a rationale for all life.

The Sioux, he explains, are so gracious in their love of "the Mystery" that they even attribute the loss of the buffalo herds, the magnificent beasts "swept from the earth as in a twinkling," as a sign of *wakan,* "mysterious." So it is that holiness is "a white buffalo cow moving gracefully over the prairie," and though their life is destroyed by the white man, nothing, Curtis comments, can take away the visionary power of the Sioux. And thus the Mystery remains—forever.

*Mandan
History*

Mandan tradition tells of a gradual migration up the Missouri "from the place where the river flows into the great water." Their stories speak of the land to the south, where the green of the trees never faded and the birds were always singing. One can hardly doubt, therefore, that the Mandan dwelt originally in the warm Gulf region near the mouth of the Mississippi. Indeed, it is now known that several tribes belonging to the same linguistic family as the Mandan, Hidatsa, and Apsaroke lived in the Gulf region during the historical period, and remnants of some of the tribes still reside there.

The earliest village site definitely located by their traditions is on the Missouri, a short distance below Cannonball River in North Dakota. It was there they lost one of the sacred turtle drums, as narrated in the origin myth, and the village is now referred to as Turtle Goes Home into Water.

The Mandan migrated up the

*Prayer to the Great Mystery. (Slow Bull. Sioux.) 1907.*

Missouri, their course lying to the west, and four miles below Knife River formed two villages. This was about 1783. Here they were visited by the party of Lewis and Clark, who wintered near there. Traders from Canada and French interpreters had already established themselves in the villages. Toussaint Charbonneau (the husband of the celebrated Sacajawea, or Bird Woman, the Shoshoni captive), who became an interpreter for the expedition, had been living among the Hidatsa from 1796. In 1832 steamboat traffic between St. Louis and the upper Missouri was begun, and the Mandan villages were thus made readily accessible to travelers and traders.

In 1837 came the terrible scourge of smallpox. Out of a total population of sixteen hundred, fifty-three males about fourteen years of age escaped. Probably 150 is a fair estimate of the number of survivors in the two Mandan towns. The deserted houses were plundered by the Arikara,

*Buffalo Dance Costume. Mandan. 1908.*

now occupy a reservation of nearly fourteen hundred square miles, mostly on the north side of the Missouri River in western North Dakota. Of these, only about a score can lay claim to being of pure blood.

When observed by Lewis and Clark, Catlin, and Maximilian von Wied-Neuwied, the Mandan were a vigorous people, living in lodges that were not only spacious but provided with comforts unknown to the roving tribes. They had crops for their immediate needs and a surplus for barter. Like all their neighbors, they depended chiefly on the buffalo for their meat supply.

Today there is scarcely a shadow of their former greatness—the six populous villages and thousands of warriors. Now, scarcely a hardy full-blood is left, only a few feeble old men and women bemoaning the fact that they did not die before the hopelessness of the present came upon them. But from these ancients, we have gathered enough lore to restore the life that has passed. A few years more, and the knowledge in the memories of these old ones will have departed with them.

Compared with neighboring Indians, the Mandan were not a warrior people and their fighting was mostly defensive, not predatory. Certainly they were not the equal of their foe, the Sioux, and it was owing only to their well-built stockades that they were saved from extermination. The Sioux, after reaching the Missouri, harassed them so often that it was even necessary for the women, when going out to gather berries and roots, to be guarded by the men. It was a common occurrence for buffalo hunters to be attacked by small bands of Sioux invaders, and only at harvest time, when their enemies came to barter for corn, was there an occasional truce.

Corn was the chief staple of the Mandan, and it was grown in considerable quantities. The fields consisted of small patches of rich alluvial land cleared of trees and shrubs; the ground was worked with a wooden dibble and with a hoe bladed with a buffalo scapula. Each family's garden was divided into three to seven beds of six rows each. An unusually large plot was about eighty yards in length. As with many tribes, the work of preparing the soil and tending the crop

who had just come up from the south and now decided to remain; with them, the remnant of the Mandan made their homes.

The Mandan, Hidatsa, and Apsaroke made a treaty of friendship with the United States at a council at Knife River on July 30, 1825. They signed the Treaty of Fort Laramie in 1851, by which the limits of the territories dominated by various northwestern tribes were established. A reservation, including the site of the village at Fort Berthold, was created in 1870, but its dimensions were reduced in 1886. With the Hidatsa and the Arikara, the 250 descendants of the thousands who once lived at Heart River in the midst of plenty

was a task of the women, the men meanwhile performing the duty of keeping sharp lookout for Sioux and others. In addition to maize, they raised, in small quantities, beans, squashes, and sunflower seeds, a mixture of which with corn and buffalo fat made the "four-mixture" so often mentioned in ceremony and myth.

No tradition of the Mandan alludes to a time when they did not cultivate corn, and it enters into a great many of their myths, as in that of the contest between Kahonhe, Waving Corn, and the Sun:

Waving Corn was always in her cornfield, in which she built a strong scaffold to live and watch her corn. The Sun, falling in love with her, came down and sat by her side, saying, "I love you better than I love any other woman." She refused him, but the next day the Sun returned and sat beside her on the scaffold. Still she refused him, and sent him away three times.

"Very well, if you will not have me, you shall never taste of this fine field of corn!" the Sun said angrily.

"I will eat the corn; that is why I planted it," cried Waving Corn.

After that, the Sun shone so hot that the corn withered and sank to the ground. When darkness came, Waving Corn went over the field, wondering how to defeat the Sun. Suddenly, the corn rose up and was green as before. In the morning, a heavy fog covered the earth, but at noon it walked away and the Sun shone hot on the land, and the cornstalks were dry and rattly. Again, as night came, Kahonhe walked forth and, as she touched it, the seared and wilted corn rose up. Four times this was done. At last, the Sun gave up and the corn prospered and was gathered and stored.

## The Mandan Creation Myth

*Numak-mahana, One Man*— Numak-mahana, One Man, wore the robe of a gray wolf; his moccasins and anklets were of jackrabbit skin. On his back, inside his robe and going up above his head, was a staff decorated with raven wings and an eagle feather. In the crook of his left arm, he carried a pipe.

As he looked at the earth, he thought, This is not good. The ground is not solid to walk on. I see nothing anywhere except myself. Looking behind him, he saw his tracks, and thought, Perhaps if I go back, I may discover where I came from. So he went back and at last came to a clump of weeds. Crawling up one of the stalks was a very large grasshopper. One Man stood looking at the weeds and the grasshopper, and thought, I wonder which one of you is my mother? But he did not speak.

He then turned away and hurried on, and after a while, he met another man, Ki-numakshi, He Becomes Chief.

"Ho, Younger Brother!" was his greeting.

*Mandan Earthen Lodge. 1908.*

"This is the first time I have been called Younger Brother," responded Ki-numakshi. "It seems to me that I should be called Elder Brother."

Then followed a dispute as to which one should have the honor of being Elder Brother.

"Let us stand here," said Ki-numakshi. "The one who lasts the longer shall be Elder Brother."

"No, my little brother," spoke Numak-mahana, "that would not be fair, since I am so much stronger than you."

"I know you are strong, but we will decide it that way," answered the other.

So Numak-mahana took his staff in his hand, made three motions toward the earth, and then thrust it deep in the ground, saying, "This will stand for me."

Ki-numakshi shook himself and became a sleek, finely formed coyote, which, after turning around four times as if making a bed, lay down beside the pole.

Numak-mahana went away, looking thoughtfully at the earth and considering its unfinished condition. In the course of time, he forgot all about Ki-numakshi, but one day, longing for a companion, he remembered, and his heart was sad that he had not made a friend of him. "Now," he said, "he

*Good Bear and Family. Hidatsa. 1908.*

is dead. But it was not my fault, for he said he was Elder Brother. I shall go back to the place and see what is there." He found only a pile of whitened bones to remind him of the coyote, and his staff had rotted half away. Again he went wandering over the world, and after a long time he returned once more. This time, there was no trace of the coyote, but over the spot where the bones had lain, a dark patch of grass was growing thickly. His staff had rotted away until only a stub was left.

He said to himself, sorrowfully, "Well, you would be Elder Brother, and now you are dead!" He pulled up the rotting staff, and it became as it was in the beginning. At the same instant, there appeared standing before him a sleek coyote, which immediately became a man.

"Now you see that I am the elder," he cried, exulting over Numak-mahana, who was compelled to yield him the honor of being Elder Brother.

They separated, and after a long time they met again in the east where the soft sand was bordered by water.

"Elder Brother," said Numak-mahana, "let us make this earth good with rivers, lakes, springs, hills, and trees."

"I have just found that thought. Let us do this," was the answer.

So Numak-mahana stretched forth his staff and there was the river flowing into the great water. Then he said, "Elder Brother, you go north of the river and I shall work on the south, and let us make a good land." So it was divided between them.

When their work was done, Numak-mahana went to see what Ki-numakshi had accomplished, and he was displeased with the flat, unbroken surface of the land to the north.

"It is just the way I wanted it," declared its maker. "It is smooth and easy to walk on." He then returned with Numak-mahana to the south and was greatly pleased with the varied appearance of the country, its streams and lakes, green hills, and rolling prairies.

Again they separated. As he went, Numak-mahana looked at himself and wondered about his origin and why he was carrying the pipe and staff. Soon he came upon a buffalo bull lying on the ground.

"Why do you lie there, brother?" he asked.

"I do not know," was the answer. "I eat this grass, but I do not know who made me. What is that you are carrying?"

"I do not know," said Numak-mahana. "There is a hole, but nothing to put into it."

"I will make you something to put into it," Buffalo said.

So he pawed the earth and made a little soft wallow. Then he told Numak-mahana to go away and to return when he heard the earth rumbling. Numak-mahana departed, and after a time he heard the earth rumbling and felt it shake beneath his feet. "What is that for?" he asked of himself. He pondered long, and when he remembered what Buffalo had told him, he returned. There in the wallow, he saw a fine growth of beautiful plants in bloom; butterflies were fluttering about and alighting on the blossoms.

"Pick a handful of these tobacco leaves and blossoms," Buffalo suggested. Then he rolled over, leaving a blanket of his hair on the ground. "Dry your leaves on that," he said.

When the tobacco was dry, Numak-mahana asked, "What am I to do with this?"

Buffalo sent him to a man whose body was painted red.

"Get a dry buffalo chip," the man said, and Numak-mahana brought the chip and received fire from the man whose name was Fire That Burns

*Crow's Heart. Mandan. 1908.*

*Scattered Corn Woman. Mandan. 1908.*

lowing them. The next day, the chief was on the roof and the boys came along. Again he noticed the buffalo calf, but suddenly it turned into a boy. The chief knew that here was a remarkable being, and he asked him to come to his house and eat with him. They had corn soup and four-mixture—corn, beans, dried squash, sunflower seeds, and buffalo fat. The boy ate the whole of it, and the chief thought, This is a buffalo turned into a boy; for the buffalo were very fond of corn. Many times after that, the chief asked the boy to visit him, and at length the wonderful youth began to tell him of the coming of the great herds of buffalo. Little by little, the people learned of his mysterious power. Finally, when he became a young man, it was known that he was Numak-mahana.

After he grew up, Numak-mahana said that he was going away, for he had lived long with them, eating the same food, drinking the same water, laughing when they laughed, sorrowing when they sorrowed. He told them that when they were in need of food, they should pray to the turtle, and buffalo would be sent to them. When they were in danger, they should call his name, One Man, and help would come; and if ever the Mandan dwindled to only a few people, who wished to die together, then they should turn the turtles on their backs, sing a song, which he now gave them, and strike the drums once. Numak-mahana then went away to the south.

Now the people moved up the river, and they arrived, at last, near the Cannonball. Here one day, they brought out the turtles to decorate them, as was the custom. Three they adorned with black eagle feathers, but the fourth they gave a spotted feather. Angry with jealousy, the fourth turtle rushed down to the river, and though many laid hold of him, they were not strong enough to prevent him from disappearing into the watery depths. Fearing the consequences of losing this sacred turtle, the people called for Numak-mahana. He came, and when he was told of what had happened, he held his staff over the river and the water drew back and revealed the turtle lying at the bottom.

"Why did you run away from these people?" Numak-mahana asked.

"They gave the others eagle feathers, but to me

in the Ground. Afterward, Buffalo and Numak-mahana smoked a pipe together.

In time, Numak-mahana wandered off to see if there were others like himself. Not finding any, he decided to make some at the place where the river met the great water. There, he took the lower rib from each side of his body; of the right he formed a man, and of the left a woman. Numak-mahana then left them for a while, and on his return, he found a man-child and a woman-child. These were a pair of human beings. They lived together and were the first Mandan.

Numak-mahana went away, promising to return, but a long, long time passed before he did. One day, a chief sat on his housetop, scanning his village. Some boys were sliding down a hill and into a hollow; just behind was a buffalo calf, fol-

only a snowbird feather," was the turtle's reply.

Numak-mahana explained in vain that the feather they had given him was that of a spotted eagle, which was the best. But the turtle replied, "I am here now, and I will not go back."

After that, the people kept calling on Numak-mahana for help in lesser troubles, and after coming many times, he said, "This time when I go away, I shall not return. But when a gentle breeze blows from the south, that will be my spirit."

Afterward, when the people were being attacked by a powerful enemy, many medicine men tried to call Numak-mahana back, but without success. So the people made a great heap of buffalo robes, and they gave the skin of a white buffalo calf to an old medicine man, who wrapped the white skin about him. Sitting on the robes, he chanted, "I am going; I shall return! I am gone; I have returned!" Then throwing off the skin, he sat, covered with sweat, as if he had been running a long way. He cried, "He is coming!" The people looked to the south and saw Numak-mahana running, as he always did, the sunlight glinting on his skin. And as he waved his dazzling staff, the enemy of the Mandan collapsed where they stood and lay upon the ground, dead. That was the last time Numak-mahana was ever seen, but they say he is always present in the south breeze, for he is the one who drives away the cold north wind of winter.

*Numak-mahana. Mandan. 1908.*

spelling, Arickaree. Although the earliest known region of this group was within the southern alluvial stretches of the Mississippi, it is apparent that their wanderings covered a vast range of territory. Any influence that a southern habitat may have had on them was worn away by their long residence on the plains and by contact with the Mandan and Hidatsa. The Arikara are an offshoot of the Pawnee, and, more directly, of the Skidi band of that tribe. As to why they separated from their brothers, tradition is not clear.

In their northward movements, the Arikara established villages along the Missouri and near the mouth of the Platte. It is hard to believe that a people could have traveled so far in such a short time and built so many villages designed for permanent occupancy. In 1770 the Arikara were below the mouth of Cheyenne River; Lewis and Clark in 1804 found them above the Cannonball; Catlin visited them in 1833 at Grand River; and after the Mandan had been nearly exterminated by the smallpox epidemic of 1837, the Arikara joined the remnant of the tribe below Knife River. After close to a century of northward wandering, they came into conflict with the U.S. Government's policy of Manifest Destiny, the westward expansion movement. By 1833 they traveled southward and rejoined the Pawnee in Nebraska, but they soon exhausted their welcome. At the end of two years, they were forced by their hosts to return to the Missouri.

History shows that at the time of their separation from the Pawnee, the Arikara were a large tribe with ten subdivisions. War and disease must have dealt harshly with them, for when visited by Lewis and Clark, they had three villages at the

## Arikara History

The Arikara were popularly termed Rees from the abbreviated form of the incorrect

mouth of Grand River and they then numbered about 2,600. By 1871 they were a little more than half that; in 1888 they were but 500, and in 1907 they had dwindled to 389.

The tribal enemies of the Arikara, following the separation and during their migration northward were the Wichita, Comanche, Kiowa, Cheyenne, Apsaroke, and, of course, the Sioux. At times they were on peaceful terms with the Mandan and the Hidatsa, but more often at war. They say that prior to the establishment of final peace with these two sedentary tribes, they could not claim a friend or an ally—every man, Indian and white, was their enemy. Masters of discord, the Arikara have been most unfortunate in their dealings with the white race. Rival fur companies used them as pawns, a policy that in 1823 culminated in their attack on a trading party of one of these companies, and the resulting unfriendliness continued throughout the succeeding decade.

The first treaty with the Arikara was that of 1825, and in 1851 at the general treaty making at Fort Laramie, an agreement with them and with other tribes was made. The first reservation boundaries of the Arikara, Mandan, and Hidatsa were established in 1870, but these were withdrawn ten years later; in 1891 the reservation was again diminished in area, but in the following year a comparatively small tract was added. In 1887 their lands were divided, and by the peculiar law under which this was effected, they became citizens of the United States with the right of franchise. Though cursed in 1820 by rival fur companies, they became even more heavily burdened in 1887 by being purchased and then thrown into dissension by rival politicians.

## Arikara Creation Myth

*Packs Wolf as Numak-mahana. Mandan. 1908.*

**The Medicine Elk**—Red Wolf was very handsome and strong, but he was quite poor, and his only family was an aged grandmother. Despite his poverty and lowly rank, he loved the chief's beautiful daughter, Grass Singing, and knowing that she had refused many suitors who had wooed her with rich gifts, he resolved to put his chances to the test.

So he stationed himself outside her father's lodge, and in the twilight he saw her slender figure in the doorway, then she glided down the trail that led to the stream. Quickly, he followed, and a moment later, emerging silently from the trees, he saw her standing at the water's edge. The dipper hung listlessly from her hand, and her eyes gazed vacantly into the lapping water. This was his opportunity. He stepped swiftly to her side, threw a part of his robe over her shoulders, and put his arm around her.

Grass Singing did not move away. "What do you want?" she asked. He said that though he had nothing to give for her, he loved her and had come to ask her to run away with him and be his wife. She thought for a moment, then said: "When do you wish it?"

"Tonight," he answered.

Grass Singing pleaded for another day, so on the following evening they met outside the village, she with her bag containing awl and sinew thread and he with bow and arrows. All night they traveled, and all day, and at sunset they arrived at the border of the badlands. They had eaten nothing.

Back in the village, the chief's family had been searching far and near for the missing girl, but having learned that Red Wolf was also gone, they decided that she had eloped. Then they covered their faces in shame, for she was the daughter of a chief, and beautiful, and should have been won with many robes and eagle tails.

In the morning, Red Wolf went out with bow and arrows, and soon returned, staggering under the meat and hide of a black-tailed deer. They ate and were happy.

Of the stomach of the deer, he made a water vessel, then together they constructed a shelter of brush over a framework of poles and thatched it with grass.

*The Sacred Turtles. Mandan. 1908.*

"Stay here for a while," said Red Wolf, "and I will hunt."

So he hunted and killed many deer, and his wife dried the meat and tanned the hides. The season was autumn, and the skins were good. One evening, Red Wolf said, "I think we have enough meat and skins now. Tomorrow we shall fix an old eagle pit that I have found." In the afternoon, they went to the old pit, repaired it, and gathered brush to make the covering. Red Wolf stuffed a deer hide and fastened fresh meat at the shoulders. On the following day, the wind changed and came straight from the west, and as the omen was favorable, Red Wolf said that he would hunt eagles that day, adding, "But I will not leave you here alone. Go with me, and midway, I shall leave you in the thick cedars. There you must stay. If my luck is good, I will be gone for a while, but if the eagles do not come soon, I shall return quickly."

So it was planned, and so they did, and by midday he had caught four eagles. They journeyed homeward then, happy because they loved each other and the spirits had been kind.

The next day, as the wind still blew from the west, they went a second time to the pit, and again Red Wolf caught four eagles. A third time the eagle pit was visited and the usual number of birds captured, and as they returned, Red Wolf said, "We have enough eagles. Tomorrow I shall seek fresh meat."

"I will remain here," Grass Singing said on the following day, "and finish the tanning of this last hide; then I will come to the place in the cedars. Wait there if I am late."

So he set out and she began her work. After a time, she heard the sound of someone clearing his throat, and as she turned quickly, her eyes fell upon a wonderfully handsome man. An eagle feather was in his hair, a string of bear claws around his neck. For an instant, she gazed, fascinated, then ran into the lodge to prepare food. Glancing out to see if the stranger was waiting, she saw that he had turned away and was walking toward the west. An overpowering curiosity to see where he was going came upon her, and she at once followed. He passed around a hill, and she caught a glimpse of him before he disappeared behind another.

In this manner, she kept up, until finally, the mysterious man vanished into a clump of cedars. The young woman paused at the edge of the trees, but a voice invited her: "Come in!" She pushed her way through the thick growth and soon reached a lodge, which she entered. There sat many women, all young and pretty, and all of different tribes; and at the side of the room sat the man.

In the meantime, Red Wolf had reached their meeting place and gone on, thinking that his young wife must have decided to stay at home. Fearfully, he ran to the water, searched all the trails their feet had worn. He called and wept, but there was no

*Arikara Medicine Ceremony. Night Men Dancing. 1908.*

The green leaves still fluttered from its tip and about its entire length there wound a green vine. Red Wolf was eager to start at once on their quest, but his deliverer told him that he must rest for four days. However, after this time had passed, the stranger said, "Someone near here has your wife, but you shall recover her and take all that he has. Now, you must prepare yourself, for that man is ferocious. My son, how old do you wish to be?"

Not understanding, Red Wolf looked blankly at his benefactor, who went outside the lodge and reappeared as a broad-horned elk.

"This is what I meant," he said. "How old do you wish to be? You must change yourself into what I am."

"I should like to be your age," answered Red Wolf.

"My son," returned the elk, "I am not yet strong. Say again how old you would like to be."

"I wish to be middle-aged," said Red Wolf, "neither too old nor too young."

"That is right. Now take the things I was wearing when you first saw me and put them on just as I did. When you reach the place where your wife is being held, you must act quickly, for her captor is very clever."

They started, Red Wolf leading, and from the top of a hill the elk nodded and said, "Your wife is among those cedars. Raise your whistle and blow; then lower it, turn to the right, and walk, and do not look back. When your wife comes, I will tell you."

So Red Wolf turned and walked away, blowing upon his whistle, while the elk remained on the hilltop. Through the trees appeared a line of women running toward the sound of the elk whistle.

"Your wife is coming," called the elk. Red Wolf, looking back, was filled with joy to see Grass Singing running toward him. But there was no time to speak—the elk told Red Wolf to move hastily. As the women went over the brow of the hill, a warrior came rushing out from the edge of the woods. He stopped and shot an arrow at Red Wolf.

"Roll on the ground," cried the elk. Red Wolf did as he was told and, as he rolled in the prairie grass, he became a powerful elk. Then the warrior

trace of Grass Singing. In the end, suspecting that something bad had happened, he fell into deep despair and started mourning. Then he neither ate nor drank, and on the fourth day, so weak that he could scarcely stand, he staggered to the stream. There he threw himself down among the willows, thinking, I may as well die here.

Suddenly, he felt someone touch his foot.

"My friend, if you are still alive, rise," said a voice. "I know why you are mourning."

Red Wolf rolled over, facing the sky. A few drops of water trickled into his parched mouth and over his face. He opened his eyes and saw a man bending over him. The stranger offered another handful of water, and Red Wolf took a drink.

"I know," the man said, "that you are starving yourself on account of your wife. But she is not far away; you shall see her soon. Can you get up?"

Red Wolf struggled to his feet, and together they went slowly to the lodge, where the man prepared food. Once strengthened, Red Wolf noticed that his new friend wore a necklace and wristlets of elk toes, and two eagle feathers in his hair, one at each side. He saw that his robe was yellow and that he carried a long willow whistle painted yellow.

rolled and became a bear. Blood gushed from his mouth, and as he prepared to rush in, Red Wolf stood fast, facing him. The bear charged, but Red Wolf lowered his head and pressed his horns into the bear's shoulders. However, the bear was very powerful and threw him off.

Now, Red Wolf's benefactor, the elk, joined the fight. Using his own horns, he forced the angry bear back down again, and the red medicine ran from the bear's mouth, and he grew weak. Red Wolf once again attacked his head and shoulders, while the elk locked up against his legs. Then, with a great moan, the bear breathed his last breath, and died.

The victors turned once more into men and walked wearily back to the nearby lodge. Above the body of the bear, though, a cloud of fog rose up and spread over the land; the fog was so dense, the two could not see their way. They were forced to crawl on their hands and knees. Finally, they found the lodge and the women awaiting them.

"My son," said the elk-man, "you must not think it necessary to give me anything." And then he rolled on the ground and turned back into an elk.

"Father," Red Wolf answered, "for your kindness, I must give you something."

Then, out of his bundle, Red Wolf took some of the eagle tails, from one of his wife's deerskins, he cut narrow strips. A feather and a thong were given to each woman, and then Red Wolf said, "Father, all of these women are now yours."

The women came out, one by one, and tied their feathers to the elk's horns.

"My son," he said, "I am well satisfied with these women. Now, I will give you a gift. All that I was wearing when you first saw me now belongs to you. When you fight, in war, you shall do things without being harmed, and in this way, you will become a great man. But one thing you must remember: Your wife, Grass Singing, must remain with you for life. Now, go back to your people."

Then the elk turned toward the wooded stream, lowered his head until his nose almost touched the ground, and whistled. Then he went off at a swift trot, and the warrior's women followed him into the shadow of the trees.

Red Wolf and Grass Singing gathered up all they could carry, and at sunset they began their

*Crow Ghost. Arikara. 1908.*

*The Bear Emerges. Arikara. 1908.*

journey. All night and all the next day they traveled, and in the darkness of the second night, they
entered the village of their people. They had decided that he should return to the lodge of his
grandmother, while she, with the bundle of eagle
tails and skins, would go to her own family.

Grass Singing was received in silence, for the
sight of her brought back afresh the feeling that
she had disgraced the family by going away with
so poor a man as Red Wolf. She, on her part, uttered not a word, but after a while, she opened her
bundle.

Then the disgrace was forgotten, replaced with
admiration for the rare eagle tails and soft deer and
mountain-sheep skins. Feathers were distributed
among the men of the family, and skins among the
women, but so many remained in the bundle that
people even came to trade for them. In the end, the
chief and his wife received more gifts than if their
daughter had accepted one of the tribe's richest
suitors. Then Red Wolf's brothers-in-law sent for
him, and around his bed were piled many gifts.

Red Wolf became prosperous and honored just
as the elk had promised. The day that he tried his
elk medicine, he found it was successful. He could
not be harmed in battle, and so he became reckless
and took whatever women he desired, including
the wives of others.
This disgraced the
village, for whenever
Red Wolf blew on his
elk whistle, the women
came readily to his bed.

Time passed and,
at last, the men held
a secret council, in
which it was decided
to kill Red Wolf. They
went up against him
and he made no effort
to defend himself.
Wrapped in his yellow
robe, he was safe; their
arrows were unable to
pierce his body.

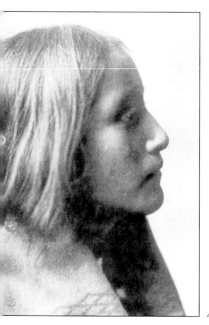

*Arikara Maiden. 1908.*

"At the Water's Edge." 1908

In the end, Red Wolf had no regard for the
rights of anyone. He became wild with power—
relentless and lascivious. One day, however, a
young woman whom his medicine had drawn away
from her husband, obtained from him the secret of
his strength. This she quickly imparted to his
tribesmen. They made incense of elk horn and hair
and passed their arrows through it. Then all the village, intent on killing Red Wolf, went searching for
him.

They found him out on the prairie, sitting
alone. He knew that something was about to happen, and when their arrows, filled with the magic
of elk medicine, passed through his body, Red
Wolf fell. Then, lest life return to him, the people
cast his bones into a great fire; and thus was Red
Wolf finally consumed, his great magic divided
among the people so that they, too, might share the
power of the elk.

# ARAPAHO AND ATSINA

*Arapaho History*

The Arapaho have primarily been known to us since the beginning of the nineteenth century. During that time, they roamed over the southern plains, near the upper waters of the North Platte and the Arkansas; they also lived beside the streams flowing into the Yellowstone to the north and the Rio Grande to the south. Little is known of their history before their arrival in this region, but they are believed to have migrated from the northeast, where they lived in western Minnesota and raised corn prior to crossing the Missouri.

Exploring the Saskatchewan country in 1789, Alexander Mackenzie observed that, next to the Blackfeet, and extending "to the confluence of the South and North branch, are the Fall, or Big-bellied Indians, who may amount to about six hundred warrior. . . . The Fall, or Big-bellied Indians, are from the South-Eastward also, and of a people who inhabit the plains from the North bane of the last-mentioned river [Missouri], latitude 47.32. North, longitude 101.25. West, to the south bend of the Assiniboine River, to the number of seven hundred men." The Fall Indians were the Atsina, or Gros Ventres of the prairies, who originally formed a part of the Arapaho, and it thus appears that the latter tribe in 1789 occupied the plains from the Missouri at about the site of old Fort Stevenson in North Dakota northward to the Assiniboine River in southwestern Manitoba, a distance of about 150 miles. That they were even then not newcomers in the region is indicated by the letter of Saint Pierre, written in 1751 at Fort de la Reine, on the Assiniboine, in which he speaks of the war made by surrounding tribes on the Gros Ventres.

It was probably not later than the beginning of the eighteenth century that the Arapaho crossed the Red River of the north into the plains, at about the same time that the Cheyenne established themselves on the

*Arapahoe Camp. 1910.*

western fork of that river. The tribe was
then composed of five divisions, speaking fairly distinct dialects, but all, of
course, mutually intelligible. These,
passing from north to south, as they
camped, were: Aaninena, nicknamed by
the modern Arapaho as Hitounena, Beggars; Baasawunena, Brush-Lodge Men;
Nakasinena, Sagebrush Men; Hana-
hawunena, Rock Men; and Nawathi-
neha, Southerners. The last named are
the present-day Southern Arapaho; the
Sagebrush Men are the Northern Arapaho; the Beggars are the Atsina. The
other two divisions have been absorbed
by the Northern and the Southern Arapaho.

According to Mackenzie's estimate,
the entire tribe must have numbered between four and five thousand. The
northernmost band, the Atsina, with
nearly half the population of the tribe,
pushed northwestward beyond the
South Saskatchewan, and the remainder crossed
the Missouri and moved in a generally southward
direction. De Smet, the Jesuit missionary, concluded from native testimony that the Atsina "separated from the nation a century and a half ago, on
account of differences between the chiefs." The
date thus indicated, 1713, appears to be too early,
as we have seen that they were on the lower
Assiniboine as late as 1751. The crossing of the
Missouri by the Arapaho occurred probably not
long after 1789, the date of Mackenzie's observation, for Lewis and Clark in 1806 reported them, to
the number of fifteen hundred, on the headwaters
of Loup River in what is now central Nebraska.

The explorers called them variously Kanina-
visch (a corruption of the Ojibwa name), Gens des
Vach, and Blue Beads. They were described as on
the defensive against the Sioux but at peace with
others. It was also remarked that they exchanged
horses and leather for the goods that the Mandan
obtained from British traders. Ten years later,
Stephen Harriman Long was informed that the
Arapaho "wander in the extensive plains of the
Arkansas and Red Rivers, have always great num-

*Traveling. Atsina. 1908.*

bers of horses, which they rear with much less difficulty than the Shiennes, whose country is cold
and barren."

In 1818 the Atsina, having committed depredations on a post of the Hudson's Bay Company, fled
to the south and found refuge with their kindred,
who were then camping at the head of Powder
River, in the present Wyoming. In 1823, when the
Atsina returned to the country north of the Missouri, the Arapaho were on the North Platte. It is
improbable that the same people were roving the
plains of the Red River at one season and camping
a thousand miles northward on Powder River at
the next. The facts seem to prove that at the date of
Long's observation, the division into a Northern
and a Southern band was in existence, and indeed
since from the first there were five dialectic groups,
it is probable that there was a more or less distinct
line of division from the moment the Arapaho
crossed the Missouri.

In 1862 the two bands were noted by Ferdi-
nand V. Hayden as quite distinct. "The first portion
call themselves na-ka-si-nin, 'People of the Sage,'
and number one hundred and eighty lodges. They

wander about the sources of the South Platte and the region of Pike's Peak, also northward to the Red Buttes on the North Platte. Sometimes they extend their journeyings in search of buffalo along the foot of the Big-horn Mountains. . . . They spent a large portion of the winter of 1859 and '60 on the branches of Powder River, near the base of the Big-horn Mountains. The second band call themselves na-wuth-i-ni-han. . . . They number two hundred lodges, and range along the Arkansas River and its tributaries. . . . It would seem from 'Long's Expedition to the Rocky Mountains' that the Arapahos occupied nearly their present district in 1819 and '20."

The Arapaho were hostile to Shoshoni, Ute, Comanche, Kiowa, Pawnee, Apsaroke, and Sioux. From the Shoshoni, their traditions say, they captured their first horses, and with the Ute, whom they regarded as their bravest enemies, they fought most frequently. In 1841 they joined the Cheyenne in making peace with the Sioux, the Kiowa, and the Comanche. Since the earliest times, they have been closely allied with the Cheyenne, and since the date last named, this friendship has included the Teton Sioux, particularly the Oglala. With the Cheyenne, they participated in the series of uprisings beginning in 1856, and though the Southern band gave up the struggle in 1868, the Northern Arapaho were implicated with the Oglala Sioux and the Northern Cheyenne in raids along the frontier; also in several engagements with the troops, notably in the annihilation of Custer's command in 1876. In 1869 the Southern band was placed upon a reservation in Oklahoma, which they shared with the Southern Cheyenne, and in 1878 the Northern band was finally brought under military escort from the Pine Ridge Reservation of the Oglala and settled on the Wind River Reservation, Wyoming, along with the Shoshoni, with whom for several years they had been at peace. Estimated in 1862 at, respectively, 2,000 and 800, the two bands in 1890 numbered, according to census, 1,272 and 885, respectively. Their present numbers are 892 and 861.

The sacred artifact most valued by the Arapaho is the Flat Pipe. This object, held by a family of the Northern band, consists of a wooden stem about two feet long, inserted into a cylindrical bowl of black steatite, which is inlaid with a whitish stone. Carefully concealed in a mass of skin wrappings, the pipe is kept in a ceremonially painted lodge and placed on a stand supported by four sticks driven into the ground.

The lodge of the keeper of the pipe is just inside the camp circle, and opposite the entrance of the camp. Like the priest of the Lakota Calf Pipe, the pipe-keeper always rode in front of the moving column; however, unlike the Lakota, the Arapaho keeper was a man rather than a young maiden.

The sacred pipe was shown only to those favored few who could afford the expense attendant upon the ceremony. On such occasions, those present smoked the pipe and prayed for health and

*On Little Powder River. Arapahoe. 1910.*

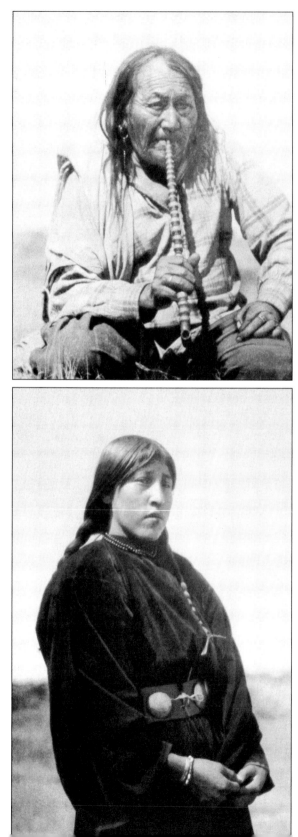

*A Smoke. Arapahoe. 1910.*

prosperity as well as other things they desired. The keeper then related the story of the pipe's origin. But this was not a simple myth of creation, for it began with the manner in which the pipe came into the possession of the people and continued with a mythical history of the first people. From several descriptions by Arapaho who have heard it, the myth of the pipe-keeper is a combination of folk-tales, social traditions, ceremonial customs — in short, the basis of Arapaho moral life. The lore of the pipe is a sort of oral bible of the Arapaho. It can be recited only when the pipe is uncovered — and only by the pipe-keeper. Four nights are passed in the telling.

When the pipe-keeper, Weasel Bear, died in 1908, he had no male heir of mature age, and the sacred bundle was given, without mythological instruction, to his daughter, a young woman. There is no one now alive able to repeat the myth in its entirety, but its beginning is told in the following incident:

There was once a raft of four logs floating on the water that covered the earth. On the raft was the Flat Pipe. There was also a person, the Father. Besides these two, there was nothing visible except water.

The Father called all the waterfowl and the creatures under the water. When they came flocking about him, he said that he wished them to search for the land, for there was nothing on which the pipe could rest.

One by one, the fowl dived, but they failed to find anything. The turtle asked to try. He remained under the water four days and four nights, but he brought to the surface mud from the bottom of the water.

The Father took the mud from the turtle's belly, worked it in his hands until it became dust, and blew it to the four quarters of the world. Land appeared in every direction, and while it was still soft and moist, the Father took some of the earth and formed two images, into which he put life. These were the first Arapaho, a man and a woman.

*Arapahoe Maiden. 1910.*

While the Southern Arapaho revered the Flat Pipe and its custodian no less than the members of the Northern band, few were able to make the long journey to the northern country, hence, in recent years, they have paid much attention to the Sacred Wheel. It occupies a place exactly similar to that held by the pipe—its possession is hereditary; it is kept, swathed in wrappings, in the back of the owner's lodge and is opened only at the request of one who wishes to offer special supplication. When anyone desires a great favor of the deities, he may vow to "wrap the wheel." He then takes food and skins (now cloth) to the lodge of the custodian, where, after much smoking and praying and the unwrapping of the wheel, he places his offerings upon it for a new covering. The wheel is about twenty inches in diameter and is formed of a square withe, one end of which is carved into a snake's head. It is ornamented with eagle feathers and with symbolized markings, and is the type of wheel used in the game of hoop-and-pole.

How deeply the Arapaho are immersed in their religion is seen in the ceremonial adornment of robes and lodges. Robes were ornamented with several, sometimes with numerous, bands of quill-work. This embroidery, as well as the work of painting a lodge to conform to a vision, could be performed only under the supervision of a woman who owned one of seven medicine bags. These contained the necessary instruments and materials for embroidery and painting, and were transmitted either by inheritance or by purchase. A woman who desired the right to ornament robes would invite one of the old women who owned the sacred bags to her lodge. The latter, accompanied by helpers, came, and with a minutely elaborate ritual, she instructed the novice in every act and movement of the work. One complete band was laid on each day until the robe was finished, but the old woman presided only on the first day.

Corresponding to these medicine bags of the women are an equal number in possession of the seven old men who constitute the highest of the age societies. Their rites are performed in a sweat lodge constructed at the center of the camp, and their position is that of a tribal priesthood. They, or some of them, preside as instructors at each cere-

*Mother and Child. Arapahoe. 1910.*

monial performance of the societies and at the Sun Dance, and their sweat bath typifies the purification of the tribe.

The power of the supernatural was sought by the Arapaho in a manner universal among the Indians—namely, by fasting in lonely places. In this phase of life, they differed from the majority of Plains tribes in that the fast was commonly not undertaken at the age of puberty, but after maturity had been reached. The conception of sexual knowledge as a bar to communion with the supernatural powers, so frequently encountered, is entirely foreign to Arapaho thought.

Men fasted, and had visions, even after passing middle age. To the faster, "if the powers pitied him," there appeared the spirit of some animal in human form, whence it was called, as also by the Piegan, "unreal person." The peculiarities of its dress and adornment were to be carefully noted by the faster and adopted as his own for use on ceremonial or other important occasions.

When the spirit animal sang, the faster listened attentively so that he might use the same songs to secure the aid of this helper. When it directed him to gather leaves, roots, bark, earth, which were to be used for healing mind and body, the faster listened well, and remembered. Finally, when the spirit resolved itself into an animal form and disappeared, the vision quest was complete. The period of fasting varied from a day to seven days, with four days and four nights as the norm.

After awaking from his trance, the faster returned home. As soon as possible, he obtained the

*"Beside the Stream." 1908.*

things demanded by his vision. These constituted the contents of his medicine bag, which was, as a rule, the skin, or a part of it, of the animal spirit with whom he had had communion. Since the supernatural being of the vision became the faster's tutelary spirit, men fasted not once, but many times, in the hope of obtaining many spirit helpers. But medicine power was not only acquired through fasting; it was also inherited or purchased.

In addition to the medicine bags, which were made by direct command of the spirits, there were also objects that, casually obtained, worked "sympathetic magic." Some of these were true fetishes; that is, objects seemingly endowed with life and capable of exerting supernatural influence. However, many were talismans, which, though not held to be conscious entities, did possess some power—if imagined—of their own. Thus, a man cherished the hoof of an antelope, that his horse might win the race; or he kept a special bullet so that the guns of his enemies might miss their mark; or he had a sacred stone so that his body might be impenetrable to missiles. In any case, it is clear that the Arapaho's spiritual belief system was as complex as it was simply based upon his deep and abiding faith in the mystery of life.

### Arapaho Creation Myth

*The Buffalo Lodge*—Once, long ago, there was a warrior by the name of Blue Bird. He had a good life and two wives, who treated him with respect. However, one of them, Buffalo Woman, was not happy with her husband. He did not care for her as much as he cared for his other wife. One day, feeling that her husband would never love her, she decided to run away and to take with her their son, whose name was Calf Standing.

They sought the home of the Buffalo People and arrived there in four days. A little after that, Blue Bird decided to follow them, and he came to the great buffalo camp just as the buffalo were preparing to do their dance.

"I have come," Blue Bird announced, "for my

wife and son, who have run away from me."

Buffalo Chief said, "If she is truly your wife and he is truly your son, you may take them. But first you will have to prove to us that you are the great warrior we have heard about. Otherwise, we cannot know if you are who you say you are."

Blue Bird agreed to the tests that Buffalo Chief put him through, the first of which was to find his son in a gathering of calves. "This is my son," he said with certainty; and so it was, and his son was given to him.

Next he was asked to race against a herd of young bulls. This he did also, winning by a length.

The final ordeal, Buffalo Chief told him, was that he had to stay

*Atsina Camp Scene. 1908.*

awake four days and four nights. During this time, the Buffalo People were going to tell stories. In the other trials, Calf Standing had assisted his father, but there was no way he could sleep for him; in the end, after the third night, Blue Bird nodded off and fell sound asleep. As soon as his eyes shut tight, the Buffalo People began to dance, round and round, trampling the body of Blue Bird, grinding it into the earth.

Now, before setting out on his quest, Blue Bird had told his brother, Magpie, that if any harm came to him while he was among the Buffalo People, a great column of dust would ascend to the sky. So, when the Buffalo People danced over his body, the dust rose in an immense cloud. Magpie saw this and said to Blue Bird's first wife, Elk Woman, "What my brother told me has happened. Prepare a sweat lodge, and I will search for a piece of his body."

Then he flew toward the cloud of dust, and when he came upon it, he heard some groaning. He followed the sound and at last discovered a tiny bit of feather lying in the many hoofprints. "Blue Bird wore this feather on his head," Magpie said to himself, and with it he hastened homeward.

The sweat lodge built by Elk Woman was ready for him when he got there. Magpie crouched

in the southeast corner of the lodge, holding the piece of feather, and cried, "O Father, I have brought back my brother!"

Then he shot a black arrow straight into the sky and called out, "Look, brother, the arrow will strike you!" He shot another black arrow at the southwest corner; a red one at each of the two remaining corners. Each time he released his shaft, he uttered his warning.

Now the fourth time he shouted, "Look, brother, the arrow will strike you!" the willow wood of the lodge sprang apart and Blue Bird stepped forth. "I have much to tell you," he said, "but first we must do something—the buffalo will soon be here, and they will be very angry."

Elk Woman, who was overjoyed at the return of her husband, came up with a plan. Using four different kinds of sacred bark, she wove a circlet that would bring the buffalo to the ground. Chokecherry, red willow, cottonwood, and alder— four hoops, in all, she placed about the camp.

Soon the buffalo came, thundering.

Heads lowered, they came wildly snorting.

But the hoops held, and the Buffalo People broke through them; some lost their horns and others became entangled. And as soon as they fell, stumbling, Blue Bird's people let loose a fierce rain of arrows, which stopped them in their tracks.

At the fourth hoop, the last to guard the camp, Buffalo Woman herself appeared out of the haze of dust. Vengeful, she tore up the hoop and ground it under her feet. However, at that very moment, Elk Woman, who was once her lodge sister, saw who she was and recognized her fury. Placing an arrow in her bow, Elk Woman fired; the arrow went straight through Buffalo Woman's heart. She staggered, dropped in a heap, and died.

So it was that when the dust cleared and settled, the buffalo became food for the people. And so, too, was the first buffalo lodge built by Blue Bird; and the people sang and danced in honor of their friend and food and their onetime foe, the great-horned wanderers, the buffalo.

### Atsina History

The Atsina, commonly called Gros Ventres, are a branch of the Arapaho. Their name for themselves is Aaninen, Atsina being their Blackfoot name. The Atsina believe they once dwelt toward the south, where they left the main tribe on account of a quarrel over a buffalo carcass.

Running Fisher's account of the subsequent migration from the north is that in an autumn of long ago a terrible plague came upon the people, destroying more than half their number. Fearing a revisitation, they began a southeast journey from the far Northwest. All through the winter, they drifted, and as spring drew near, they came to a large river flowing eastward, which Running Fisher believes to have been the Saskatchewan.

The ice was strong enough to cross, so the tribe started over it. A third of the people made it safely and another third were yet on the ice. The remainder waited patiently on the northern bank. Among those still crossing over was an old woman leading her grandson, who, seeing a horn protruding through the ice, asked his grandmother to cut it off for him. The woman at first paid no attention, but the boy's plea was so insistent that she turned back and began to chop off the horn. As she cut, blood commenced to flow, and suddenly a great monster heaved itself out of the water and glittering ice and drowned all of the people.

Those of the tribe who had already crossed now continued on their journey to the southeast.

*Atsina War Party. 1908.*

However, those who had waited on the opposite shore were so terrified by the disaster that they turned back. This narration, based on myth, probably has its share of truth as well.

Whether the Atsina came to northern Montana before the Blackfeet is hard to answer. They were, however, in the Blackfoot country in the middle of the eighteenth century. In Lewis and Clark's time (1805–1806) the Atsina roved between the Missouri and the Askaw, or Bad River, a branch of the Saskatchewan. The narrations of their tribal wars give the best idea of their movements following their arrival in Montana.

The earliest intertribal battle, according to their own reckoning, happened four generations ago. At that time, they say, the area now occupied by the Atsina and Blackfeet was Shoshoni country, and this battle was one of invasion into Shoshoni territory. The ground on which they fought was a rocky butte some distance north of the Bearpaw Mountains, in Montana, but south of Milk River. The Shoshoni greatly outnumbered the Atsina, who held their own for a time through the great bravery of a man named Dirty-Eyed Bird, but, notwithstanding his prowess, they were on the verge of defeat when an Atsina, with the first and only gun in possession of the tribe, rushed forward and, at close range, shot one of the enemy.

The Shoshoni, strangers to firearms, looked upon the mysterious killing in amazement. They believed it was due to some spiritual power, and so they fled in terror. This battle occurred before the Atsina acquired their first horses. We are given a hint of the date by the fact that the Dakota obtained their first guns during the closing years of the eighteenth century.

The next recorded battle was engaged a generation later, after the Atsina had obtained a few horses. This also was against the Shoshoni, and was fought between the Marias River and the site of Fort Benton. The Atsina greatly outnumbered the Shoshoni and almost annihilated them. The survivors fled south, forever abandoning the region as their home. The name of no chief taking part in this battle can now be recalled.

Next came a battle that occurred at a time when a war party of Piegan and Atsina, led by White Owl, found the Sioux camped at the mouth of the Yellowstone. They charged the camp but were driven back, and to protect themselves, they built a breastwork of logs. Here in the depth of winter, they held off the superior Dakota force

*Moving Camp. Atsina. 1908.*

*Running Fisher. Atsina. 1908.*

for ten days, subsisting on their dogs, which they ate raw, having no means for building fires. Finally, imminent starvation forced them to attempt an escape at night. But few of this war party reached home. It is believed that this siege took place in the latter part of the eighteenth century.

Perhaps a generation after the last fight with the Shoshoni, a young Atsina brave ran away to the south with the young wife of the tribal chief, Old Bald Eagle. The husband was so filled with longing for her that he induced the whole tribe to go in search of his fickle spouse. At length, they found the runaway pair living among the Arapaho. This is probably the visit to that tribe (around the year 1820), often referred to as the return to their people. The location of the Arapaho at that time is not known to the Atsina, except that it was somewhere near the Platte River.

After recovering his wife, the chief started to lead his people back to their northern home. On this journey, while camping on Rosebud River, Montana, they were attacked by a large party of Sioux and so severely beaten that they fled, leaving half their women prisoners among the enemy. The Sioux, however, must have been oversupplied with wives just at that time, for in a few days they provided the captives with food and clothing and sent them to overtake their people. The women traveled constantly and reached the Atsina camp on the Musselshell in two days and two nights. The chief lived to return with his young wife to their former camping ground, but his people had become greatly weakened in numbers after years of wandering among hostile tribes.

A year after the battle with the Sioux on the Rosebud, another fight occurred with the same relentless enemy. The scene was south of the Missouri, on Wolf Creek, which empties into the Judith, in central Montana. The Sioux forces were stronger than the Atsina, and for a time the battle was in their favor.

The hero of this occasion was a poor young man who had won no honors and was even without a horse to ride. He painted and dressed according to the vision he had received while fasting, and forcibly taking a splendid pinto pony from a chief's wife, who was guarding it, he rode into the fight.

The bravery of this warrior was that of a madman. He was everywhere at once, striking the Sioux down on all sides and spreading terror in their ranks. His actions so greatly encouraged his tribesmen that they rallied and won the day. The Sioux afterward sent word to the Atsina that they should take good care of such a valiant warrior, and stories and songs of his wonderful deeds on that day are still heard in Dakota camps.

Sitting Woman, the first chief of that name, was leader of the previously mentioned party. It was during his lifetime that a hunting party of thirty lodges in the sweet-grass hills were beset by Sioux, and all but two of the men were killed or captured. The two escaped by riding the famous pinto horse which had saved the day once before.

The next battle was in the Bearpaw Mountains of northern Montana, where a large party of Sioux made a fierce assault on the Atsina camp while the men were out hunting buffalo. However, they heard the noise of attack and rushed for the Dakota, as men do who must fight to protect their women and children. This hand-to-hand fight ended in defeat for the Sioux. But the loss to the Atsina was heavy, and to add further to their grief, their wonderful pinto warhorse was wounded.

According to Running Fisher: "The reason of that was that when Sitting Woman was killed in the previous battle they trimmed the pinto's tail; that weakened his spirit-power, and besides that someone thoughtlessly loaded him with buffalo-meat after a hunt. On account of that the enemy were able to hit him with a bullet. He died in a few days, and the whole camp mourned as if a chief had fallen."

Then followed, according to the narration, a battle near Fort Benton, at about the time of its establishment as a trading post. A party of Atsina and Bloods, coming to trade, encountered a party of Sioux, who were planning to attack the fort. The Dakota were the victors, and all but four of the Bloods and Atsina were killed. Comes in Sight Yellow, Flies This Way, Sacred Plume, and Not Liked by His Parents escaped, and afterward they became great warriors and chiefs.

Under the leadership of an unknown chief of the Bloods, a combined party of that tribe and the Atsina went south in search of the Apsaroke and found their camp near Lodgegrass Creek, in south-central Montana. The Apsaroke scouts had watched their coming and, knowing their strength, had prepared for the conflict by digging pits for the women and children. The battle was bitterly fought throughout the day, and although the Apsaroke were practically defeated, the attacking war party withdrew under cover of night.

Again, a large war party under the father of Running Fisher went against the Apsaroke, meeting the enemy near Owl Hill Butte, north of the Musselshell. This affair proved to be little more than a game of charge and countercharge, with few killed on either side. The expedition was to punish the Mountain Crows for an earlier attack on the Atsina camp. In that encounter, the Atsina swam across the Yellowstone to escape. In doing so, their ammunition and bowstrings got wet, and the Apsaroke found them an easy prey, killing every person except two small boys. The fighting strength of the Atsina in this engagement was forty warriors.

After these last two fights, an enduring truce was solidified between the Atsina and the Apsaroke. The Mountain Crows held themselves somewhat aloof in the same superior manner they assumed toward their kindred, but the River Crows became quite friendly with the new allies. So strong was the friendship, indeed, that it threatened to end in the permanent withdrawal of the River Crows, and their more powerful tribesmen

sent word that unless they returned to the Crow country by a specified time, they would be treated as enemies. The alacrity with which they heeded the warning and returned to their old haunts has assumed the nature of a tribal joke.

The reminiscences of the present generation of warriors are replete with stories of strife against their former allies, the Blackfeet, following the severance of their friendly relations in 1862. Once when Running Fisher and White and Yellow Cow were boys, their people were encamped on both sides of Beaver Creek, east of the Little Rockies. The encampment was attacked by a party of Bloods and Piegan. The assault was so furious that the Atsina became demoralized, and all the people on one side of the creek were slaughtered. Many of the invaders were killed, but the victory

*Three White Cows. Atsina. 1908.*

was with them. A little later, in 1866, some three hundred Atsina were slain by the Blackfeet in a single engagement, which instilled such fear in the survivors that in the following year they refused to go to Fort Benton for their share of the supplies then being distributed among the Montana Indians.

In 1867, a few years after peace had been effected between the Apsaroke and the Atsina, a large party of both tribes were dwelling close together near the Cypress Mountains in northern Montana. In the camp were three great war leaders, the Atsina Sitting Woman, the second of that name, and Twists His Tail and Lone Tree of the Apsaroke. A small returning war party reported that they had seen thirty lodges of Blackfeet some distance away. Great excitement spread around in the camp of the allies, for here was an opportunity to win easy victory over their enemy. Sitting Woman, whose medicine was the sun, called all the chiefs and warriors into his lodge, where he made medicine in preparation for the coming battle. For a long time, he sang and talked to his fetishes. Then he told the watching warriors that it was good, that they would have an easy victory. Twists His Tail opened his sacred bundle. He held up a hoop and, looking through it, gazed into the land of the unknown.

Then Lone Tree, whose medicine was the eagle, was asked to make his own medicine. When he did so, it was in his own lodge, the flaps of which were closed tightly. No women were permitted in

*Atsina Scalp Dance. 1908.*

or near it, and only old warriors and medicine men were allowed within. All around the lodge were gathered warriors, waiting for his vision.

Lone Tree made incense of ground cedar; then, wrapped in a buffalo robe with the fur side outward, and wearing an eagle skin on his head, he sat close to the rising smoke.

After a while, he began to move about like an eagle, whistling, singing, and staring sharply. He continued singing for a long time. Then, at last, he came out of his trance and turned to the expectant men. "Sitting Woman," he said, "your father is the Sun; he is able to see everywhere, even the smallest insects in the thick grass. Why does he deceive you? I see the blood of our people flowing toward us from the camp of the enemy, and the bird refuses to drink it." Throughout the camp ran the unexpressed fear of impending danger, but the Atsina chiefs would not heed the warning of Lone Tree, and on the following day the greatest war party that ever set out from an Atsina camp started off, led by the proud Sitting Woman and Twists His Tail. Scouts soon returned with word that the thirty lodges were decoys and that beyond were large camps of the enemy. Still the chiefs would not heed the warning.

The Apsaroke held a parley among themselves and expressed their belief that the enemy were too strong to be successfully assailed. The majority of the Atsina had forced them into this undertaking against their better judgment. They therefore planned to proceed to the attack, make one swift rush, gather as many horses as they could, and, if the odds seemed to be against them, retreat at once. The attack was splendid, but from the timber back of the decoy camp came such a horde of Bloods, Piegan, and Sarsi as they had never met before. The wily Crows followed their plan and escaped with slight loss; the Atsina, however, were not equally fortunate, suffering so greatly that the story of this battle will pass through the generations as the worst defeat in the history of the tribe.

According to Running Fisher, when he was a young man the tribe had fifteen hundred lodges. This would give them a population, during the closing years of their tribal life, of five to seven thousand people. It is difficult to reconcile this statement with that of Lewis and Clark, who estimated the "Fall Indians" at 260 lodges, or 2,500 souls. It should be remembered, however, that the explorers did not, in this instance, write with the authority of actual observation. In fact, they never saw the Atsina tribe.

The Atsina have been mentioned comparatively little in history, partly, no doubt, because of their isolation. But they have also shown less hostility toward advancing civilization as their neighbors. It would seem almost a habit with many writers to speak slightingly of the Atsina. Yet the record of their tribal wars shows no indication of deficiency in courage. The Apsaroke say of them that they were a fine people, not given to quarreling, and reasonable in discussion and argument. The pleasure of the writer's experience with them was unmarred; indeed, the Atsina have been one of the most agreeable and tractable tribes he ever met.

*Atsina Creation Myth*

*The Spider Trickster*—Spider was a restless fellow who could never stay in one place very long; he was always making little excursions about the country. One day as he was walking down the riverbank, he saw Bear on the opposite side, and wishing to have some fun with him, he shouted across, "Ho, Bear!" Bear raised himself and looked all around.

"How ridiculous you are!" called Spider. "Your eyes are small and squinty, and the hair is dark around them!"

At this, Bear became very angry, and splashing into the river, he swam across to punish his tormentor. However, Spider ran away quickly. Bear pursued with bristling hair and wide open mouth. Spider, as he ran, tried to think of a way to escape. He was speeding along when he came to a pile of stones. Stopping, he said to them, "Brothers, let us make a sweat lodge here."

The lodge appeared as he spoke, and some of the stones piled themselves around the edge of the

*Atsina Maiden. 1908.*

cover, while a few went inside. Spider entered and Bear came up right behind him.

"Brother, what is wrong?" Spider called out from within the darkness. "Who are you chasing?"

Bear growled, "I am trying to catch Spider, the trickster."

"He was running by," Spider said. "No doubt he was up to some mischief! Anyway, there is no use running yourself to death. Why not come in and take a sweat?"

Bear agreed, and went in. Then Spider hopped out and pulled the flap down, whispering to the stones, "Brothers, sit on this flap and do not let him out!"

In the meantime, Bear had been pouring water on the heated stones inside, and the steam was getting very hot. Soon he had enough, and cried, "Brother, open the door!"

Spider whispered to the stones, "Hold fast, brothers! Don't let him out!" Then, club in hand, Spider walked around the lodge. Every time Bear's head showed against the cover, he dealt him a hard blow. Bear roared in rage, but there was nothing he could do.

"Now." Spider chuckled, and he put all his strength into one powerful swing. And that was the end of Bear.

Next, he skinned him and cut up the meat. Coyote joined him, and said, "Brother, give the entrails to me; I am very hungry!"

But Spider answered impatiently, "Leave me alone! You are always putting your nose where it doesn't belong."

Coyote pleaded until he was told to take some entrails to the river and wash them; for doing this, he would have some for himself. Coyote went to the river, but instead of washing the entrails, he ate them. Then he came back with a doleful story of how Fish had snatched them out of his paws. Spider offered him the rest, but as soon as Coyote was out of sight, he followed him. Creeping up to the riverbank, he saw Coyote devouring the last morsel. Then, without a word, Spider ran back to the swamp, where he awaited the thief.

Presently, Coyote came up, whining, "Fish has robbed me again!"

But Spider had a large stone in his hand. "Robbed again, huh?" And he banged Coyote on the head and knocked him down. Then he told him to go to their grandmother and borrow her cooking pot. Coyote went out to a patch of brush, and shouted, "Grandmother, we want to use your cooking pot!" Soon the vessel came rolling down out of the bushes, and Spider commanded it to fill itself with water and sit on the fire, all of which the magic pot did. Spider now finished cutting up Bear, and he put the meat in the pot and stirred up a hot fire. When the meat was cooked, he spread it out on the grass, and shouted, "Spider is inviting everything that lives to come and eat with him!" All the animal people came and swarmed around him. He told them to sit in rows, and then he seated himself on a nearby stone, with Coyote beside him.

"I am going to eat first," Spider announced. "After I'm full, I'll feed the rest of you." He started to reach for the food, but he was stuck to his seat and could not move.

"Brother," he said to Stone, "don't do that; don't hold me like that." But Stone said, "But I always stay in one place four years."

Not knowing that Coyote had told Stone to play this trick, Spider appealed to him to move the meat closer. However, Coyote chuckled and said, "Hey, you animals, seize the meat and eat it quickly! Brother Spider is stuck to his seat and cannot get up!"

The animal people fell upon the food and it was soon gone. Spider pleaded that a little should be left for him. But they laughed at him; then they went away and Stone released him. Here and there, at the edge of the fire, Spider gathered up the little pieces they had overlooked. Suddenly, a spark flew out and struck his belly, burning him so badly that he jumped back, spilling his scraps into the fire. This aggravated his ill temper, and remembering the trick played upon him by Stone, he called to the sticks that were scattered around: "Brothers, come into the fire!" So they all came and threw themselves on it. Stone viewed these preparations with alarm. "Let me go!" he begged, but Spider said, "Let's see if you can remain in one place four years!" He placed Stone in the hot fire and Stone crumbled into pieces. Spider was a bit scorched himself, but having had his revenge, he did not care.

"Brother," he said, "hereafter when someone puts you into the hot flames, you will break." And this is why stones crack today when they are placed in a roaring fire.

Sometime after this, Spider visited a lake where there was a large flock of ducks. He was still hungry, and he tried to devise a plan to catch them. Stripping off his clothes, he painted his body with white clay. Then he cut his hair short, as if he was in mourning. Lastly, he walked round and round the water's edge, crying. Whenever he came close to the ducks, they would swim away, warning each other: "Look out for Spider! He is a trickster." However, Spider kept crying pitifully, and after a while, the ducks felt sorry for him, and they swam up to the shore to ask what was the matter.

"My brothers," said the trickster, "a war party came and killed my wife and children. Come with me and we will find the enemy." The ducks agreed, and Spider told them to sit in rows that he might choose the bravest. Then passing along, he ran his hands over their bodies, and whenever he found one whose breast was fat, he cried out, "Here is a brave man! Step over there, my friend," and the foolish fowl, flattered at being called brave, would obey.

When Spider had selected all the fattest, and sent the skinny ones away, he announced, "Now we will dance before going on the warpath. Keep your eyes shut while we are dancing, for anyone opening his eyes will be killed by the enemy. Stand in a circle and I will sing." Then passing behind them as he danced, Spider wrung their necks, one by one.

Loon, who had been watching, shouted, "Look out! Spider is killing you!" Squawking in terror, the ducks flew away. Spider, gathering up the dead, scowled at Loon, who had stopped a short distance out in the lake.

"For this," he said, "you shall hatch your young last of all the waterfowl, and your home shall always be the water."

Coyote, thin and lame, now appeared and stood

*Incense. Atsina. 1908.*

watching the trickster as he picked and cleaned the birds.

"Brother, won't you give me the refuse?" he asked.

"Bring me the pot," answered Spider, "and you may have it all."

Coyote went away and soon returned. The vessel rolled up and was told to take its place on the fire. Then Spider made a proposal: "Brother, while the food is cooking, we will race around the lake. The winner will take all."

"But I am lame and cannot run," answered Coyote. "You ought to give me something, anyway."

Spider insisted that Coyote race with him. Finally, Coyote consented, saying that he did it only to be agreeable. They had started out and gone for some distance when Spider, far in the lead, called back, "Why can't you run? I thought you were racing with me!"

So Coyote rolled on the ground and passed by Spider and rolled all the way to the fire, where he quickly pillaged the pot.

"Brother, brother!" shouted Spider. "Save some for me!" But Coyote devoured the last morsel and then slipped out of sight. Spider came up to the fire and sat down.

"I wonder why it is that I always get something good to eat and then I never have a chance to eat it." Shaking his head sadly, he walked home.

On one of his expeditions down the river, Spider came to a fine pool in which were a number of pretty girls bathing.

"Come, and we will comb your hair," they called, and he, not unwilling, accepted the invitation, for he was very tired. They gathered about him, and under the soothing touch of their soft fingers, Spider began to doze. But as soon as he was asleep, the girls became burdock burrs. He awoke, and finding his hair matted and tangled with burrs, he was furious. What was he to do? It was impossible to pull them out, so he was forced, in the end, to cut his hair short.

In this condition, he started home, wondering what he was going to say to his wife. At last, a plan occurred to him, and as soon as he arrived in sight of the lodge, he began to weep and wail. This attracted Spider Woman, who came out to see what was the matter with her husband. When she saw him, she was angry at the change in his looks, and said sharply, "Fool, why have you cut your hair? What mischief have you been up to now?"

Spider answered, "Is it you, my wife? I thought you were dead, because a little while ago I passed some men who told me that you had died in my absence. That is why I was mourning, and that is why I cut my hair!"

Flattered at this evidence of her husband's affection, Spider Woman took him into the lodge, where for many days he enjoyed an unusual respite from her constant scolding.

*Cheyenne History*

To date, the earliest American reference to the Cheyenne is contained in a letter of La Salle, written in 1680. He refers to them as Chaa, the French spelling of the Sioux name for them, Shahiyela. A group of Cheyenne, La Salle mentions, came down on a trading mission from their home on the headwaters of the Mississippi, to his fort on the Illinois. In 1806, a century and a quarter later, Lewis and Clark also mention the Cheyenne. A portion of their tribe had journeyed from their new home in the Black Hills to the Missouri River. They urged the explorers, as their forefathers had urged the Frenchmen, to send traders to them. Their country, they said, "was full of beaver," and "if the white people would come amongst them they would become acquainted," and the white people "would learn how to take the beaver."

*Ben Long Ear. Crow. 1905.*

According to Lewis and Clark, the new village of the Chien, or Dog, Indians was "about 15 miles below the mouth of Warricunne Creek." This is, in fact, Beaver Creek, which joins the Missouri at Emmonsburg, North Dakota. The journal entry for the Cheyenne, dated 1804, describes them as being haunted by their old enemies, the Sioux. The metamorphosis of the Cheyenne from agriculturists among the woods and lakes of Minnesota to roving hunters on the Great Plains was accomplished, in part, by the Sioux (specifically, the Teton branch) themselves.

Along with their neighbors, the Sotaia and the Arapaho, the Cheyenne were, by turns, at peace and at war. The general condition seems to have been one of peace. However, this was not the case with the Sioux and the Assiniboin, although the Cheyenne did have intervals of amity with them, as well. They raided the Spanish settlements in the Southwest, bringing away horses and mules; and they traded often with the Arikara, and occasionally with the Mandan and Hidatsa.

In 1840, according to the Sioux calendar, a permanent peace with the Cheyenne was established. Thereafter, the two tribes were allied against native enemies, as well as with the American troops, to such a degree that "Sioux and Cheyenne" became a set phrase. It was in 1833, though, that a large part of the Cheyenne took up residence on the Arkansas River near Bent's Fort in southeastern Colorado. The rest of the tribe remained in Wyoming. The separation was not yet a permanent one, for the two bands frequently met, camped in a large circle, hunted and made war together, and in fact regarded themselves as one. A clearly defined division begins to be evident in 1851. At that time, at Fort Laramie, Wyoming, treaties were concluded

with the Sioux, Cheyenne, Arapaho, Apsaroke, Assiniboin, Hidatsa, Mandan, and Arikara. The Southern Cheyenne and the Arapaho were treated jointly.

The Treaty of Fort Laramie gave to the Cheyenne and Arapaho a reservation covering about half of Colorado, the southeastern corner of Wyoming, the southwestern corner of Nebraska, and a large area in western Kansas. This was made necessary by the great tide of western emigration that began about 1846 and reached its height in the California gold rush of 1846. The document that the Indians signed assured to them, in addition to the reserve, an annuity of fifty thousand dollars for fifty years. The Senate, without consulting the Indians, curtailed the period to ten years. The government also disregarded the third article of the compact, which bound the nation to protect its

*Gray Dawn. Cheyenne. 1910.*

wards' territory. The fact that the reservation was literally being possessed by settlers, and substantial cities established there, shows how well the government fulfilled its obligations.

The friction continued to increase. In 1857 troops went into the field, and thus began the era that shows that, excepting the Sioux, no tribe has made a more stubborn resistance against their foredoomed extinction as a "primitive people." Perhaps the most shameful record of the government's subjection of the Cheyenne occurred at Sand Creek in 1864. Five hundred Cheyenne, gathered at the solicitation of the government, and under its protection, were encamped in Colorado. Col. J. M. Chivington attacked them at daylight, while over Chief Black Kettle's lodge there floated a United States flag, and a white one, as well, on the same pole.

*A Favorite Cheyenne Costume. 1911.*

It is certain that Chivington had been begged by men in his own command not to attack the friendly Cheyenne. However, he ordered them to kill large and small, men and women, insisting that no prisoners were wanted. There can be no question that he and the officers under him had full knowledge of the barbarities of the massacre. The evidence is conclusive that all those killed were scalped; that women were so mutilated as to render description unprintable; that hours after the attack, when there was not a militant Indian within miles of the camp, children were used as targets. Not satisfied with the savagery of the "battlefield," the troops attended, en masse, a theatrical performance in a Denver opera house, and there brandished fifty freshly taken scalps.

During the coming years, the disgrace and annihilation of the American Indian was directed also at his chief food source, the buffalo. Between 1872 and 1874 at least five million buffalo were slaughtered for their hides alone. In addition, in 1875 the cry of gold in the Black Hills sent prospectors and miners flocking into Indian country, with the result that the Cheyenne and the Sioux joined forces to keep them out. In 1876, immediately following the combined Sioux and Cheyenne attack on General Crook on the Rosebud in Montana, Gen. George Armstrong Custer crossed the divide between the Rosebud and the Little Bighorn. Seven days after the Crook affair and twelve miles from its scene, there occurred the infamous "Custer engagement." While it is considered today mainly a conflict with the Sioux, the Northern Cheyenne were well represented.

The seventeen years of conflict with the Cheyenne, which cost untold lives and untold millions, were unquestionably a governmental disaster and a deliberate disregard for Indian rights. Secretary of the Interior O. H. Browning, in his 1868 report, states: "It is believed that peaceful relations would have been maintained to this hour had Congress, in accordance with the estimates submitted, made the necessary appropriations to enable this department to perform engagements for which the public was pledged."

Spilled water and spilled blood were the order of the day; madman and manacle prevailed, with lunacy on both sides, and reason was abandoned to the winds, which cried for justice. In the end, the bitterest of winters stopped the Cheyenne conflict, and it is doubtful whether anything else would have ended their intransigence—certainly not bullets, nor treaties signed in falsehood, nor reservations promised and rescinded. Poverty and want have largely been the portion of the Cheyenne on the discouragingly sterile reservation on the Tongue River of Montana. Hopefully, better days will come for this handful of people who so stubbornly held out for a tithe of what they rightly thought their own.

*Two Cheyenne Migration Myths*

*The Migration*—While in an external way the Cheyenne resemble the Sioux and other Plains Indians, there is a subtlety of spirit, an independence that is characteristically their own. Their resentment of ill treatment through the disregarded treaties and promises is one thing, quite separate from the recognition of their own ferocity, which occurs in the following myth.

There was a man whose family lived quite apart from the tribe. He had two children, and he spent his days hunting. Before starting out, he would paint his wife's face, and when he returned, he would always find her face unpainted. One day he went away as usual, but he came back almost at once. He then saw a water monster come and take the paint off his wife's face.

So, he thought, my wife has been deceiving me.

Then he killed the woman and the water monster. He cut up her body and took the meat into the lodge. His two children ate the flesh, and the younger one knew that he was devouring his own mother. This is why the Cheyenne have grown fierce.

There is, in this story, a mere hint of the Cheyenne's early habitat among the lakes and forests of the East. Usually their myths tell of the long days on the prairie, but occasionally some fragment appears that gives a glimpse of the lost past. It is like the wind blowing across the meadows of childhood, so vaguely that it seems to be a dream. One of these fragments is the story of the waterfall.

In the earliest times, the people lived beside a lake, which turned into a stream, which soon plunged over a precipice and became a lofty waterfall. Some players were gathered there, playing the game of rolling wheel. Two of them, men, suddenly looked at each other, and saw that they were dressed and painted exactly alike.

One said, "You appear to be imitating me."

The other protested, "This is my way of dressing and painting. How do you know this way?"

"I got it from the old woman under the waterfall," was the answer.

"It is true, what you say," said the other. "We both must have this from the same spirit."

*Devotees en Route. Cheyenne. 1910.*

They came to a good understanding, these two; and later on, they moved their camp down to the river. "Let us consult the old woman of the water once again," one of them said, and the other nodded agreement.

Then, before the eyes of all who were gathered, the two disappeared. They swam, underwater, toward the great waterfall. Back of the falling water, which was thunderous in their ears, the two men came into a cave, where an old woman was sitting. She greeted them in the customary way and then gave them dried buffalo meat, corn, beans, and seeds of the squash. "These are gifts," she explained. "Gifts for the people." They took them gratefully, and bidding good-bye to the old woman, they dived under the sheet of falling water and emerged on the other side of the spray.

What they held in their hands was more than enough food to feed the entire village. The people were much impressed. And that was the beginning of the use of buffalo for food and of the planting of seeds in the earth to grow corn, beans, and squash.

This myth, the growth of it, and subsequent changing provide a good example of the history of the people and their life cycle, from eastern mountain to southern and northern plain. For instance, there is a faint reminiscence, perhaps, of Cheyenne life near the Falls of St. Anthony. And since it is highly probable that the tribe once inhabited the Algonquian territory of eastern Canada, there may be a hint of Niagara here as well. In any case, we have an ideal illustration of the growth of a myth.

In various versions of the same tale, we are told that the seeds were brought out of a lofty waterfall, or from the depths of a spring flowing from a hillside; or that the heroes went into a butte and got them; and, finally, that the butte was on the eastern margin of the Black Hills. Here we have, in effect, a panorama of the changing environment of the people as they moved from lake, river, and cataract to the semiarid plains west of the Missouri. Thus the great waterfall loses its immensity; it becomes a spring within a hill. Then it changes again and becomes the hill itself. After this, it is localized to the earliest-known home of the narrator. A man who has lived all his days on the prairies of Dakota finds a bold butte an easier feat of the imagination than a roaring mountain of water.

*The Sacred Arrow*—A young woman of long ago knew that she was approaching motherhood, but only after four years had passed was the child born. The people said, "This boy must be a Holy One." When he reached the age at which boys begin to wear robes, a calfskin was given to him, and he immediately began to wear it with the furry side exposed. Shamen wore their robes so, and, one day, the boy entered the lodge of these old men and sat down beside their chief.

As it happened, each of the shamen was exhibiting his greatest powers. After a time, it was the boy's turn to prove his right to sit beside these men of magic power. First, the boy made incense of sweet grass and purified a bowstring in the smoke. Then, after two of the men had encircled his neck with the bowstring, he covered himself with his robe and commanded them to pull on both ends of the string with all their strength. They obeyed, and his head was severed from his body and it rolled noisily upon the ground. The two shamen placed it under the robe with the body. Shortly after, they removed the robe.

Where the boy had lain, mutilated, there was now an old man lying curled up. Over him they replaced the robe, and when they raised it again, a human skeleton was revealed. Now they covered the bones and once more removed the robe, to find they had disappeared. Finally, the shamen threw the robe over the spot of bare ground. This time, when they removed it, the boy was sitting in the same position as when he had joined them. This was magic that none of the other shamen possessed, and thenceforth they regarded the boy as having the greatest of supernatural powers.

Now the boy grew into a youth, and one day, after a hunt, as he bent down to remove the skin of a buffalo cow, an old man came up to him with his pack dogs. According to custom, the old one had the right to take any portion of a hunter's buffalo; however, this rude old man demanded it all.

*Beginning of the Altar. Cheyenne. 1911.*

"Take the meat, Grandfather," said the youth, "but leave me the hide, for I wish to have a robe made."

"I will take both," cackled the old man, "for I need both." Then he shoved the youth aside and began to cut up the carcass.

The youth, not knowing how to respond, shrugged; but when he returned to his work, he was pushed away. A sudden anger overcame him then, and he passed round behind the old man, raised a heavy buffalo bone, and struck the elder a hard blow on the head. The old man fell, lifeless. The youth finished his work and returned with the hide to his grandmother's lodge.

Now, when it became known that the old man was dead at the hands of the youth, the warriors surrounded the lodge of his grandmother. They had decided to kill him, for the old man was one of their chiefs. So, with weapons ready, they rushed the lodge. However, the clever youth heard them coming and he quickly overturned a cooking pot, which made a column of smoke rise from the hissing fire. From this cloudy vapor, he arose in the form of an owl and passed through the smoke hole. A few days later he returned, secretly. Once again, the warriors tried to take him, but he assumed the form of a grass snake and slipped away from them. Five times in succession, the magic youth eluded the warriors, and each time he turned into a different animal—once, a wolf; another time, a prairie dog—but always he was too quick to catch.

After the fifth time, the youth left the people and wandered among the hills. At length, he came to a butte that was higher than any other. In the side of the butte, there appeared a door. He entered and the door closed behind him. Now he found himself in a tepee-shaped cave. In a circle, as if in a lodge, there were gathered many aged men. Each one had a medicine bundle and each was from a different tribe. The circle was complete, except in one place, and that was where the youth sat down. Beside him was a medicine bundle wrapped in a fox skin.

One after another, the old ones opened their medicine bundles, and songs and prayers came to their mouths and gave voice to their visions. At last the bundle wrapped in fox skin was opened by the old man who sat near the youth. Inside were four arrows, whose stone points were wrapped in eagle down.

So it happened that the youth learned the songs of the medicine arrows, and he remained within the butte for four years, learning the secrets of the old men's medicine. All during this time, the people were starving, for his power had taken all the animals from their country and kept them hidden among the hills. At the end of his four-year instruction, however, he returned to the people, a changed man.

It was then that two hungry boys, wandering far from the camp in search of roots, were met by a strange man carrying something wrapped in a fox skin. "Gather some dry buffalo chips," the man

*Offering the Pipe to the Earth. Cheyenne. 1910.*

commanded them, and they did so. Later, when they brought forth the chips, the man touched them and they became sticks of jerky. The hungry boys ate their fill, and then the man said, "I am called Sweet Medicine. Take some of this meat to your fathers and say that the one whom they drove away has now returned. Tell them to pitch the camp in a new place and make a double lodge in the center. Have four good men meet me there with pipes of smoke."

The boys hastened homeward, and they made sure the man's words were obeyed. On the following day, he came to them as he had said

*Dancing. Cheyenne. 1911.*

he would, and he taught four shamen the rites of the sacred arrow. At the end of his teachings, the whole camp shuddered, and the earth moved. The men looked out of the lodge and saw something that no one would ever forget: As far as the eye could see, there were buffalo, great-shouldered and two-horned. And thus the famine of the Cheyenne ended.

### Piegan History

The Piegan, the Bloods, and the Blackfeet are so closely related that they have been designated collectively as Blackfeet. Originally, they were forest people of Algonquian stock, whose migrations from the Atlantic seaboard moved slowly westward until they reached the buffalo plains of Alberta and Montana. There they became prairie Indians, the last of the woodland Algonquian tribes to migrate to the western prairies of the United States.

Tearing Lodge of the Piegan spoke of his people's migration before 1800:

"Our three tribes came southward out of the wooded country to the north of Bow River. We began to make short trips to the south, finding it a better game country with much less snow. Finally we gave up our old home. This happened in my grandfather's time. We call that former home 'In-the-Brush.' Now the Piegans led and were followed by the Bloods, and later the Blackfeet. We all hunted in the plains between Milk River and the Yellowstone. The Piegan wintered on the Musselshell or the Upper Missouri; the Bloods stayed on the Belly River; the Blackfeet on Bow River, or its tributary, High River."

Sometime before the beginning of the nineteenth century, then, the Piegan made their southerly migration, meeting with the Kutenai, with whom they procured their first horses. After the Piegan had begun to make short trips into the prairies, they met some white people for the first time and traded with them. Mackenzie, who saw the Piegans in 1789, was probably the first explorer to note their population; he estimated that he saw around 8,500 people.

The smallpox plague, which nearly eliminated the Mandan in 1837, had already struck the three tribes, and their numbers were reduced by about one-third. They suffered again from smallpox in 1838, and also in 1845. In the winter of 1864, the three tribes lost about 1,780 due to measles. The Indian agent reported that the Bloods alone left five hundred standing death lodges as silent monuments of the winter's devastation. The people attributed this disease to the malevolence of the white men, saying that it was sent to them in the yearly goods they had received.

Disease was the white man's first bequest to these tribes; quickly following, as a fit ally in the distribution of death, came whiskey sellers. The usual procedure was that when the Indians went to trade their furs, they were given just the right amount of liquor to induce a favorable trade. By the time they recovered from this trickery, their furs were in the possession of the traders.

Fate, apparently not content with the darkness it had dispensed to the Blackfeet tribes, dealt them another blow in the winter of 1883–1884, when more than one-fourth of the Piegan died of starvation—six hundred was the exact number recorded. There were, however, many other deaths in isolated camps, of which no record was made. The winter of misery and death was the result of American policy stupidity; this was coupled with the "disappearance" of the buffalo.

A study of the Piegan conflict with white people, either citizens or soldiers, proves they were the

*Joe Russell. Piegan. 1910.*

most harmless of tribes. It is true that in the press the name Blackfoot or Piegan was continually associated with massacre, outrage, and treachery. In truth, such crime as they were guilty of was usually the direct result of drink, for which "civilization" was wholly responsible. Few tribes have been so unfortunate in this respect as the Blackfoot group. They dwelt partially in the United States and partially in Canada, and the traders and traffickers under each government vied with one another in wrecking them. Each side with whom they dealt in their international existence did all it could to

*Camp in the Foothills. Piegan. 1905.*

incite the Indians to attack the other government. The average Indian (who has but one people and one government with which to contend) is deserving of much empathy. However, when he is the victim of two governments and their subjects, he is unfortunate indeed. And this, sadly, is what befell the Blackfoot brotherhood.

In life and manners, the Piegan differed little from the other hunting tribes of the plains region. The buffalo furnished their food, and its skin, horn, and bones, with the addition of the skins of antelope, elk, and deer, supplied dwelling, clothing, and implements.

The author first saw the Piegan during the summer of 1898 at the season of their medicine lodge ceremony. They were in camp on a depressed stretch of prairie, which was nonetheless well concealed from anyone approaching. The camp was combined of Piegan, Blood, and Blackfeet— perhaps some 230 lodges. If this poor remnant of a once-powerful tribe was an inspiring sight, what must it have been at the height of their existence? Red Plume of the Piegan describes the camp of his people when he was a youth as a circle a mile or more in diameter and, in some places, sixteen lodges deep. To have seen such a camp would have been worth long privation and hardship. Traditionally, the lodges were of buffalo skin, and later of canvas, in the common tepee form. A distinctive feature of the Piegan lodge was the characteristic decoration of the inner lining. They often painted their lodges to indicate either the coups of the owner, his medicine, or both. In the Piegan camp, a man was expected to have more than one wife. However, it was the first wife who sat by the husband's side, the others being in a measure servants of the first. Younger sisters of this wife were potential wives of her husband, but he was not compelled to take them.

In arranging a marriage, the young man presented to the girl's father as many horses and blankets as he and his family could afford. The greater the number of presents, the prouder the girl. To be taken as a wife with scant exchange of presents was no honor. To elope was a disgrace to all parties concerned. The rules governing a wife's conduct were strict, and the punishment for transgres-

*Reuben Black Boy and Family. Piegan. 1910.*

*Spotted Eagle, Heavy Gun, Calf Robe. Piegan. 1910*

sion most severe. If an unfaithful wife was not killed, she would be mutilated, an object lesson to others. The guilty man was also likely to be killed by the wronged husband, or he could escape such punishment by sending horses and other presents.

Life in an old Piegan camp centered around the hunt, and the greatest of these was the buffalo. In autumn the tribe separated into bands, meeting again in the spring for the great communal hunting party. No individual hunting was allowed. The

*A Child's Lodge. 1911.*

dramatic chase on horseback was under the leadership of a chief, or chiefs, and attended by various religious rites.

The white buffalo, as with other tribes, was sacred, and to take one in the hunt was a matter of great importance. When shot, they say, the buffalo would fall with its head to the east, toward the rising sun. Then, without dismounting, the hunter called to another man in the party, and said to him, "I give you this white buffalo."

If the man thus called had in his possession a very fine horse, he said, "I accept it." The hunter then rode away. The man who had been given the white buffalo dismounted and set fire to some buffalo chips, one of which he laid at the animal's nose, another at the tail, another at the feet, a fourth at the back. On each burning chip, he placed sage, and with a bunch of sage, he wiped the blood from the buffalo's wounds. Next, he carefully skinned it, removing every particle of skin from the face to the edge of the hooves. Leaving the meat, he wrapped the skin in a robe, mounted his horse, and rode to his home.

There he ordered his best horse to be brought and tied in front of his tepee. After this, he took the skin inside and laid the bundle before the place of honor. Food was prepared and an invitation given to the man who had killed the buffalo. After feasting and smoking, the tepee's owner said, "There is your horse outside." The white buffalo hide was dressed, the head skin and tail still attached, and the owner wore it only on sacred occasions.

Now, after keeping the hide for a year or two, the man prepared a feast. The sacred skin was put in the place of honor once again. Some presents were put beside it and a fine horse was tied in front of his tepee. Then a medicine man who knew all the sweat-lodge songs was called, and when he came, the owner of the skin gave him a pipe and said, "That horse outside is yours. I would like you to sing the songs of the sweat lodge, for I am going to give this skin to the sun."

*Medicine Bags. 1911.*

The medicine man sang the songs, seven of them. He sang them once, and began to sing them again. While he sang, he painted the skin: a black half hoop showing the course of the sun, then a circle for the moon, another for the morning star, and, at the sides, two straight lines for the sun dogs. The medicine man finished the song just as the seventh song was sung the second time. "Take this skin," he said to the owner of it. "Place it in a tree on a high

*Red Plume. Piegan. 1910.*

hill." And the owner obeyed, singing songs to the sun and asking the sun's blessing, in exchange for the gift of a sacred white buffalo robe.

## Four Piegan Creation Myths

*The Dance of the Sun* — There was an orphan boy named Poor, who was always lonely. One day as he sat by the river, crying, a handsome youth came out of the brush and stood before him. "Why are you weeping?" he asked.

"I have no family, no friends," said Poor.

"Well, then," said the handsome stranger, "I will be your friend."

Poor did not know that his new friend was Morning Star. They played together that day, and when Poor was hungry, Morning Star disappeared into the forest, returning with food for them to eat. In the days that followed, they spent their time constructing a miniature sweat lodge of a hundred willows, making a round lodge of poles, and singing the songs that Morning Star knew.

After a time, Poor's only sister became concerned about him. He no longer took any meals with them, and she wondered how he fed himself. One day, her husband went down by the stream where the two were playing. He saw what they did; there was something extraordinary about it, and so when he returned to his lodge, he said nothing to his wife.

When Poor had grown into a man, however, his brother-in-law asked him about the strange playing by the river. "I believe what I saw you do was sacred medicine," he remarked.

Poor said, "I could perform what I once practiced as a boy, but my sister would have to help in the ceremony. Also she would have to declare to the whole village that she was a virtuous woman." His sister declared herself ready and able to do this, and under the direction of Poor, the first Sun Dance was held.

*The Medicine of the Sweat Lodge* — In times gone by, there was a girl of great beauty, Pretty Willow, who was the daughter of a chief. Although sought by many, she showed favor to none. Now, there was also a young man whose face was badly scarred; his name was Scarface, and he, too, had fallen in love with Pretty Willow. However, when he asked her to be his wife, she laughed at him so

*Piegan War Bonnet and Coup-stick. 1909.*

Star, the Sun said, "Go and fetch a coal from our fire."

Morning Star brought the coal on a forked stick, and the Sun took a piece of sweet grass and placed it on the coal. As the incense began to arise, sweet-smelling, he started to sing: "Old man is coming with his body; it is sacred."

The Sun passed his hands through the smoke, rubbing them over Scarface's left arm and side and face, then he did this over his right arm and side and face. And the odor of earthly people was taken away, and thus was Scarface purified in three more sweat lodges in the same way. And then, afterward, his body gave off a yellow light.

Finally, the Sun lightly brushed his face with a feather, and his scar went away. With a final touch to the youth's head, he turned his hair to gleaming gold, exactly like Morning Star's. After this was done, he took the two youths into his lodge and presented them to his wife. "Which," he asked, "is our son?"

She pointed to the one who was named Scarface.

"Old woman," he said, "that is not our son. We shall call him Mistaken for Morning Star."

When the people heard that the poor disfigured youth they had named Scarface had returned, all golden and lovely like a star, they thronged to see him. "I have been in the sky," he told them. "Morning Star looks just like this." The people admired him very much, especially the beautiful girl, Pretty Willow. Then the handsome one, glowing in the sunlight, explained how the Sun had given him some special things that he could teach them. "First," he said, "he taught me of the sweat lodge, then of the coal and the sweet grass, and how to cleanse myself." He showed them these things, how it was done, and the people learned sweat medicine, and they practiced it, in honor of the sun.

*The Wife of Morning Star* — Two girls were lying on the ground under the stars, for it was too hot to sleep in the lodge. After a time, they saw the rising of Morning Star, and one of the girls cried, "I wish I could marry that bright star!"

The following day, as she stooped over her

scornfully that he left the camp and went southward.

For many days, he traveled, hungry and alone. At last, mourning his hard lot in life, he fell to the hard ground, and soon he fell fast asleep.

Now Morning Star looked down, and pitying the young man, he said to his father, the Sun, and his mother, the Moon, "There is a poor young man upon the earth, whom I must help." His parents approved. "Go and get him," they said.

So Morning Star took Scarface up into the sky. His father, the Sun, said, "Do not bring him into the lodge yet, for he smells bad. Build four sweat lodges first." This was done, and the Sun led Scarface into the first sweat lodge. To Morning

bundle of wood, a handsome young man stood before her: "I am that bright star you wished to marry," he said. "I have come for you."

So she went with him up into the sky, and she became the wife of Morning Star.

"There is one thing I must ask of you," he said.

"What is that?" she questioned.

"You must never dig up the large turnip that grows in front of our lodge."

She agreed to this, but one day her curiosity got the better of her and she tried to dig it up. But the turnip was so deeply rooted in the ground that she could not budge it. "What is wrong with my digging stick?" she wondered. Just then two cranes flew across the sky, and she called to them to help her.

The woman crane alighted, and said, "Because I have been a true wife, I can offer you my aid." And she then taught Morning Star's wife the songs that accompany the digging stick. After which, she thrust her bill into the ground and pulled out the

*Flint Smoker's Daughter. Piegan. 1910.*

stick and the turnip, both of which Morning Star's wife carried home with her.

Now, because she had looked down through the hole left by the root and seen her old home, Morning Star knew that his wife would now be homesick. So without delay, he summoned Spider, whose silken rope was lowered down through the hole to the earth. Morning Star's wife slid down the rope and joined the people. And she brought the sacred turnip from the sky, and with her root digger, she became the first medicine woman in the ceremony of the Sun Dance.

*The Gift of the Longtime Pipe*—Once heavy clouds hung over the earth; thunder rolled and a great storm threatened. The people were filled with fear. But then a beautiful daughter of a chief said to the sky, "Thunder, take away the storm and I will marry you." Immediately, the thunder stopped, the clouds passed, and the sky grew clear.

A short time later, the girl was off in the forest, picking berries, when a tall man appeared before her. "I am the man you promised to marry," he told her. The girl, remembering her promise, bowed her head in acknowledgment. Then he took her away with him into the sky. She lived there with him for

*Running Rabbit. Blackfoot. 1900.*

*Bull Shoe's Children. Piegan. 1910.*

a long time, but the day came when she longed to be with her father and the people once again. Thunder understood this, and he allowed her to return, giving her a sacred pipe as a present for her father. This was the Longtime Pipe of the Piegan.

## Crow History

The rigors of Apsaroke, or Crow, life made the women as strong as the men; and women who could carry a quarter of a buffalo, ride all day and all night with a raiding party, or travel afoot 250 miles across an unmarked wilderness in four days and nights were not ones to have weak children. Hence, the Crows were among the strongest of the Plains Indians.

They were and are the proudest of Indians, and although comparatively few (they now number only 1,787, and are constantly decreasing), they rarely allied themselves with other tribes for purposes of defense. For probably two and a half centuries, they were the enemy of every tribe that came within striking distance, and for a goodly part of this time they were virtually surrounded by hostile bands with a common hatred against this mountain tribe that likened itself to a pack of wolves. The western Sioux, aided by the Cheyenne and Arapaho, tried to force them westward. The powerful Blackfeet invaded their territory from the north and northwest; Flatheads and Nez Percés were worthy foes from the west; and the wily Shoshoni pressed in from the south. Yet the Apsaroke were ever ready to repel invasion from whatever direction it might come.

There were, however, brief intervals of peace with the different tribes. With the Sioux, their bitterest foe, they sometimes smoked the pipe and negotiated peace for a year. Such truces so seriously made in many smokes were often quickly broken by some irresponsible young man stealing a horse or a woman. Then, in a moment, peace was at an end and war raged once again. As a rule, however, these periods of tranquillity lasted long enough to permit discussion of previous fights and a general comparison of the honors therein won.

The country that the Apsaroke ranged and claimed as their own was an extensive one for so small a tribe. In area it may be compared, east and west, with the distance from Boston to Buffalo, and north to south, from Montreal to Washington—certainly a vast region to be dominated by a tribe never numbering more than fifteen hundred warriors. The borders of their range were, roughly, a line extending from the mouth of the Yellowstone southward through the Black Hills, thence westward to the crest of the Wind River Mountains, northwestward through Yellowstone Park to the site of Helena, thence to the junction of the Musselshell and the Missouri, and down the latter stream to the mouth of the Yellowstone. This region is the veritable Eden of the Northwest. With beautiful broad valleys and abundant wooded streams, no part of the country was more favorable for buffalo, while its wild forested mountains made it almost unequaled for elk and other highland game.

The Apsaroke enjoyed the climax of their existence during the scant century following the acquisition of horses. Previous to that event, their life had not known the fullness that was theirs when they had herds of horses, and when firearms replaced arrows and lances. Notwithstanding their aggressive, warlike disposition, they never were in serious conflict with our government, nor did they commit many depredations against white settlers, who, although regarded by them as trespassers, were rarely molested. The Indians captured many horses from early hunters and trappers, but this was to them a legitimate procedure, for these men were intruders on their lands, taking their game; consequently, all captures of livestock were regarded as just compensation.

In the old times, the Apsaroke, during a large part of the year, were constantly on the move. One day they would be quietly encamped on one of their favorite streams, the next traveling in quest of buffalo or solely for the mere pleasure of going. Their customary camps were along the mountain streams, where the lodges were commonly placed in a circle, but at times, where the valley was narrow, they were close together, paralleling the wooded watercourse.

The larger camps were always the scene of great activity. Horses were tethered everywhere close at hand; on the slopes far and near, thousands were grazing, while on the nearby hilltops, groups of people were outlined against the sky. Here are chiefs and councillors in quiet discussion of tribal affairs. As they pass the pipe from man to man and look down upon the village with its hundreds of lodges, their eyes are glad, for the picture is one of plenty, and the murmur of the camp speaks only of happiness. Close by are laughing children, their skin gleaming in the sunlight, and the old men reflecting: "It is well that their bodies know the heat and the cold; it will make strong warriors and mothers."

In the camp itself, there is a panorama of activities, confusion of sounds. Women are stretching the drying hides and filling great drying racks with long, thin strips of rich red buffalo meat. In the lodges, others are tanning skins, and on many sides can be heard the thud of the wooden tray as

women gamble with plum-seed dice. In other lodges, men are shouting a wild song as they engage in the hand gambling game, while in the open, another group is playing at hoop-and-pole, and others the game of the arrows. The sick and the wounded are being cared for by medicine men, who accompany their incantation with rattle and drum. Men and women, old and young, are constantly passing from lodge to lodge for a word or a smoke, and good is always placed before them.

As evening approaches, the people begin to gather around the lodge fires, and with the arrival of men laden with meat of the hunt, the village assumes an even livelier air. Heralds of the chiefs are shouting invitations to the feasts, and as night falls, the lodges glow in the darkness. If the weather is at all cool, the evening is spent mostly indoors, where on soft skins and furs, heaped in profusion, the people lounge in full contentment. From many

*The Eagle Catcher. 1908.*

dwellings echo the muffled beat of the drum and the droning song of men and women, and occasionally is heard the note of a flute as someone serenades his sweetheart.

Early in the morning, the village is astir, for the counsel of the men who have thoughts is: "Do not follow the sleep to the end, but waken when it requires determination; be up and alive to what is going on about you!" As soon as the family awaken, they throw blankets around their bodies and go to the river for their morning bath. If the water is icy cold, so much the better, for it requires a strong heart to plunge in, and it inures the body to cold and heat. Husband and wife and small children go together, each family a group of itself. Probably not ten yards away is another family, and so on for a mile or more, many hundreds bathing at the same time. At other hours of the day, it would be the height of impropriety for a woman to expose any part of her body, but at the morning bath there is no embarrassment, "for this is our custom," they say.

When the chief decides that camp is to be moved, his crier goes through the village in the evening, crying out, "Prepare, prepare! Tomorrow we move!" And again at the first blush of day, he rides from end to end of the village, calling, "Hunhunheeeeeee! Today the chief says we move toward the buffalo! Men, bring in the horses; women, throw down the lodges!" As all have known from the previous announcement that they are to move, the morning meal is finished before daylight appears. Soon all the herds of horses come trotting in and the women are running about

*On the Custer Outlook. Crow. (Curtis with Crow Scouts.) 1908.*

among them, throwing ropes over the necks of the old, gentle pack animals. Others are at work on the lodges, the covers of which come rattling down, soon making of the camp a skeleton of bare poles. From the middle of each framework, a column of smoke curls skyward; sleepy children still in their blankets are rolled out as their mothers pull the robes from under them in the work of packing. The youngsters whimper for something to eat and are thrown a hard, dry piece of meat for their breakfast. Soon the horses are packed with high bundles of robes and clothing, and the lodge poles tied at the sides, usually six to a side, two horses being required for each lodge. Here and there, horses break away and go galloping through the camp before their packs are secured, scattering their loads and causing great excitement and confusion. Women call; children cry; grandmothers mumble.

The chief rides off a short distance in the direction they are to go, and some of his old men sit about him smoking and talking. Then they move forward a distance and halt while the people complete their preparations for the march. Now the line begins to form—first the chiefs and the old men; then a band of arrogant, gaily dressed warriors, with newly stolen wives riding behind and carrying their husbands' shields and lances; next a body of clansmen with a group of proud young wives bedecked in all their finery. Behind them, the column continues to form, family by family, each driving its herd of horses, until at length come straggling by those who have been slow in packing. A moving column of six hundred lodges is miles in length and of a width determined by the groups of families or by the nature of the country traversed. When they near the place the chief has designated for the night's camp, many of the grandfathers ride ahead and select spots for their own lodges, clear the ground, and gather dry wood. As the irregular line drags in, they stand beside their chosen places, calling out to their wives where to come. If the weather is cold, they already have kindled small fires and now take down the little children from the tops of the packs and hold them in the warmth of the leaping flames.

One summer, nine hundred lodges of Apsaroke

*Winter Camp. Apsaroke. 1908.*

went to the Yellowstone, intending to cross. As the water was very high and the river nearly half a mile in width, the Kick Bellys, numbering 450 lodges, lost their courage and would not attempt the crossing. All the others, however, were unafraid and passed over. They used no boats, but made small rafts of driftwood, laying the ends of the lodge poles on these rude craft and allowing the tops to float on the water behind.

On the poles, a large piece of old lodge covering was spread, and on that were piled the domestic belongings, the edges of the skin being gathered up and tied at the top to protect the load from splashing water. Perched upon this bundle rode the old women and the children. Two young men grasped the manes of strong swimming horses and swam along by their side, towing the raft across. Behind, holding to the ends of the lodge poles, swam the young women, clad only in a short skirt reaching from waist to knee.

*Tries His Knee. Crow. 1908.*

glad to swallow anyone thus showing his friendship with the thunderbird.

## Two Crow Creation Myths

*How Itsi Made the World*—In the beginning, water covered the earth. Itsi, He First Made All Things, wandered about on the water, hunting for thoughts, looking for land. He called to a loon flying overhead: "Come here, my brother; dive under the water and see if you can bring up mud. With that, we will make land." The loon dived three times unsuccessfully, but the fourth time he came to the surface with a little mud in his bill. Itsi laid it in the palm of his hand and kneaded it; then he blew it out of his hand, and it scattered over the water and became the land. With his thoughts he created streams and mountains.

Itsi pondered deeply, and from a lump of the newly formed land he made four small images, which he rocked four times, singing slowly.

The fourth time he sang the song, he cast the images from him, and as they struck the earth, they sprang up living creatures of human form and size, two men and two women. The two pairs were placed in different valleys and commanded to multiply. Thus the human race began.

For food, Itsi made plants, roots, and berries of many kinds to grow. Then he molded clay in the shape of animals with four legs and with a hump on the back. "Live!" he commanded, and buffalo filled the prairies. The Deer People and other animals he made in the same manner, and the birds, to whom he said, "You shall give songs to the people, and supernatural strength to those who fast and cry."

Then the creator thought, I have made everything, but out of this earth come creatures that I do not know. He looked closely and saw that they were ants, and their bodies became tobacco seed. He thought, The people I am making shall live over all the earth, but those to whom I give this plant shall be few, and it shall make their hearts strong.

It was a time of great merriment and fun making, yet one not without its serious side, for a tottering old woman gazed long at the swirling river and, declaring that she was not afraid to die but feared the water, stabbed herself and fell lifeless.

The crossing occupied four days, for the current was swift, and many who had no horses were compelled to wait for assistance from their relatives. Before going into the water, men and women painted red stripes about waists, wrists, and ankles, for protection against the water monsters that were believed to inhabit all large streams. Necklaces of white beads were never worn in the water, for beads of that sort were believed to be hailstones, the symbol of the thunderbird, a deadly enemy of water monsters, which therefore would be

As the people multiplied, he scattered them and gave them different tongues and a desire to fight with one another. To the Apsaroke, he gave tobacco seed, saying, "When you meet the enemy, this plant will make you as strong as the powerful little ants from whom these seeds came."

*The Seven Stars* — In the long, long ago, a chief had a very beautiful daughter. Her glossy brown hair was like corn silk, and that was what the people called her.

Handsome young men wooed her, but she gave them no encouragement. Neither the greatest deeds in battle nor the most lavish presents could soften her heart.

One day, when she refused the gifts brought by a young man hoping that he might be accepted with them, her brother said crossly, "Corn Silk must be waiting to marry Ishbish."

Ishbish lived far away, and his medicine was so strong that women fell in love with him on hearing his repulsive name of Worm Face. Thus he had married successively three of the most beautiful women from other tribes, but after a short time, he had fed them to his fathers, monsters of the water. So when the brother of Corn Silk spoke the name of Ishbish, her heart left her, and from that time, the thought of him was in her mind constantly.

While her parents and brother were away from the lodge one day, she prepared a soup of turnips and marrow fat and a bowl of choice pemmican and invited several old women noted for their wisdom. Placing the food before them, Corn Silk said, "Grandmothers, tell me something about Ishbish, and where he lives."

They were so amazed that for a moment they could not speak; then one of them said, "We cannot tell you, for your father would kill us." Then, leaving the food and presents, they went out hastily, shaking their heads.

Corn Silk threw herself on some buffalo robes and cried, "Ishbish, no matter where on the earth you are, I am coming to you!"

When her mother returned, she noticed the girl's swollen eyes, and said, "Child, what is the trouble?"

"My heart is bad," replied Corn Silk, "from remembering my brother, whom the enemy killed. It came to my mind and made me sad."

Again when the others were away, she called in an old woman. "Grandmother," said Corn Silk after the old one had eaten and accepted presents, "where does Ishbish live?"

The woman clapped her hand over her mouth. "Hida, hida!" she exclaimed in her surprise. "My pretty daughter, how did you ever think of him? He is a monster who lives in the form of a man and with his invisible arrow steals the hearts of beautiful young women! When they come to him, he throws them to his monster fathers in the water. Ishbish lives far toward the rising of the sun. How far, I cannot say, but beyond that hill, in a little

*Holds the Enemy. Crow. 1908.*

draw, covered with rosebushes, is a lodge where lives a family of old women who can tell you. Take this root digger, which will protect you from harm. Kick this ball before you, and its speed shall be yours."

Now Corn Silk became very lighthearted. She made pemmican, and moccasins for herself and Ishbish. She wore a beautiful dress of mountain-sheep skin, embroidered with colored porcupine quills and fringed with rattles of deer hooves. One day, when her preparations were completed, she stole away. From the top of a high hill, she looked back at the great circle of lodges over which her father was chief; she thought of the many suitors she had had, some of whom had even lost their lives trying to win her—and now she was going to a strange land to marry a man she had never seen! She turned again to the east and kicked the ball toward the land of Ishbish, and its mysterious and wonderful power carried her through the air with it.

When she stopped, she looked back and found herself in a strange land. Nearby was a lonely tepee; an old woman was gathering sticks. As Corn Silk approached, the old woman saw her and scurried into the lodge. Corn Silk could hear others asking, "What is the matter?" and the answer, "Corn Silk is far from her home. What can it mean?" She entered, and saw that they were old women of the Mice People.

"What can we do for you?" asked one of them.

"I wish to go to the country of Ishbish," she answered.

"Hida!" they exclaimed. "We cannot tell you anything about it, but in the second draw from here live the White-Breasted Mice, who perhaps can help you."

So Corn Silk traveled on and was directed by the White-Breasted Mice to the lodge of the Gophers, who said to her, "You are going in the right direction, but the Mole People in the next coulee can tell you just where to find him." At the end of the fourth day, Corn Silk came to a dirty little lodge, discolored by the smoke of many winters. The old women who dwelt there were blind, and they traveled under the earth. One of the oldest said, "My daughter, listen well; do as I say and you

will come to no harm." Then she explained carefully what Corn Silk was to do.

Corn Silk kicked the ball, and again she flew through the air toward the home of Ishbish. When the sun rose, she was standing on the top of a hill, looking down upon a great village in a beautiful valley. Men were playing the hoop-and-pole game, and they seemed to know her quest, for they remarked as she passed, "Ishbish will have another wife." She asked the way to the lodge of the chief, and when they pointed out a miserable smoky little lodge near the water, her heart was heavy and she sat down to rest. A mole came out of the ground and said, "Corn Silk, don't forget what we told you." That cheered her a little. Ishbish was not at home, but when he returned later in the afternoon,

*Hoop on the Forehead. Crow. 1908.*

Corn Silk found him so handsome that she was delighted. "You have come," he said. "I sent for you long ago; you have worn my patience." But she threw her arms around his neck, and he treated her kindly.

In the early morning, she awoke, and, stirring the embers of the fire, she was terrified to see that her husband's face was covered with worms.

"It is not morning; come back to bed," he said impatiently.

She lay there thinking sadly about all the handsome young men, her tribesmen, who had wanted her.

"On the fourth day, I shall give you to my fathers for thinking what you are thinking," said Ishbish. He always seemed to know her thoughts.

In the morning, he was again handsome; only at night was his face repulsive.

On the morning of the fourth day, the crier went about shouting, "Ishbish is going to throw away his fourth wife. All people come and witness the sacrifice!"

Everyone rushed to the heights. Ishbish came leading Corn Silk by the hand, and he addressed the water far below the bluff: "Fathers, because you asked it, I have destroyed three of the handsomest women in the land. Here is Corn Silk, who considered herself better than any other woman of her tribe."

The water heaved and waves dashed against the rocks below.

"Stand on this," he commanded, pointing to a whitened buffalo skull near the edge of the bluff.

But Corn Silk retorted quickly, "I will not; I am to die, anyway," and she kicked it over the brink.

Before the skull could strike the water, one of the monsters leapt upward for it, baring his long white teeth. Corn Silk stepped on the spot where the skull had rested, and she sank into the earth to her ankles, for the Moles had dug away the earth beneath, and all the underground people laid firm hold of her moccasin strings. Ishbish pushed her three times. The fourth time, he threw all his weight against her. Then the ground gave way and Ishbish plunged over the edge of the bank and was swallowed up by one of the monsters below.

The people shouted and opened a pathway for

*Bear Cut Ear. Crow. 1908.*

Corn Silk, who ran back to get her ball and stick. Then, taking her husband's sacred red paint, his porcupine-tail comb, four sacred arrow shafts, and his arrow straightener, she hurriedly left.

"Brothers," said the creature that had swallowed Ishbish, "I am sick. I think I have swallowed our son," and he vomited him up on the land. Then he ordered Ishbish to chase after Corn Silk and bring her back to them.

The medicine power of the ball was almost exhausted, and Ishbish was gaining when Corn Silk scattered the sacred red paint in his path. It became a fog, so dense that he was lost. As the fog settled, he picked it up piece by piece and it turned back into paint in his hand.

Again he approached, and Corn Silk threw back the stone arrow straightener, which became a high wall extending across his path in all directions. He searched for a place where he might climb over, and at length he scrambled to the top, but on the opposite side there was no foothold. So he shut his eyes and leapt. He picked himself up, sorely bruised, and, looking back, saw only the little stone arrow straightener, which he recovered, and started on.

As he once more shortened the distance between himself and Corn Silk, she threw the porcupine-tail comb behind her, and it turned into a great forest, the trees so close together that he could not force his way through. He climbed one of the trees and crawled over the top to the other side. When, at last, he reached the ground, he found only the porcupine-tail comb behind him.

"I shall catch you and feed you to my fathers!" he shouted. But Corn Silk threw back the arrow shafts, and a whirlwind carried them just above his head. Ishbish followed them, springing up into the air in order to reach them. They took him back a long distance before they fell to the ground.

By this time, Corn Silk had reached the stone lodge of the eight brothers, of whom the Mole Woman had told her. She called out, "My brother, let me in. Ishbish is behind me, and I have run a long way!"

A voice replied, "Run around the lodge four times and enter."

She did so, and the stone doors closed behind her just as Ishbish came up and stood outside, breathing hard.

"Corn Silk," he called, "come out! Ivak, open the door!"

Ivak was a dwarf, who received the name of Greasy Chest from his habit of dipping the tail of a wildcat into a kettle of soup and licking off what did not drip down upon his chest.

"If you do not send her out," threatened Ishbish, "I will kill you!"

But Ivak continued to eat his soup, pausing now and then to shoot an arrow at a mark on the ground. Ishbish continued to storm and threaten, and at last the little man said, "I shall go outside and throw him to the ground. But first I will tell you what to do after I have overpowered him."

*Forked Iron. Crow. 1908.*

Then he rushed out and grappled with Ishbish. After a fierce struggle, he threw Corn Silk's husband to the ground. While they were fighting, she covered them with wood and lighted the pile. The sparks flew up; she caught them and threw them back into the fire. Finally, only ashes remained. Corn Silk stirred them with a stick and found a small hard lump. This she rubbed with grease, painted it red, and rolled it up in the robes of Ivak. At once, the dwarf stood before her, boasting, "I have killed Ishbish!"

After a while, they heard a noise, and he warned Corn Silk: "Hide yourself, sister; my brothers are coming." She crouched behind a pile of skins, and soon she heard the rumble of deep voices as the seven brothers entered and threw off their packs of game.

Black Wolf, the eldest, had noticed the bare spot where the contest had taken place, and he murmured, "Haaaaan! Ivak is always doing something. He must have found someone with whom to play!"

While the meat was boiling in the stone pot, the brothers sat around the fire, telling of the day.

"I do not care what you killed," said Ivak, "I have something very beautiful."

"You must have stolen one of my arrows," said one.

"I make better arrows than you," replied Ivak.

"I left my eagle feathers up on the rock; you must have taken them," said another.

"I can catch all the eagles I wish," retorted the little dwarf. Then he called out, "Sister, come here!" and Corn Silk stood before them, her long hair gleaming in the firelight, her eyes downcast before their gaze. They leapt up, each one eager to marry her, all except Black Wolf, who said, "You are all fools; she is our sister!" And so it was settled; she would remain a sister to them.

Now the next time they went on a hunt, Ivak said, "My sister is here and she can guard as well as I," so the seven took him along. Before they started, he said to Corn Silk, "If any strange woman comes near here, tell me at once when we return."

They had not been gone long when Corn Silk heard a woman's voice singing the name of Black Wolf. Soon the voice was in front of the lodge. "Corn Silk, my daughter, I have heard about you and have come to see you," it said. Then an ugly old woman, very bony and with white hair, entered the lodge. It was Red Woman. Corn Silk gave her a dish of buffalo tongues. She greedily devoured them and then the old woman departed; from a distance came the sound of her weird song.

The eight brothers returned and Corn Silk made their supper, but she was so busy, she forgot all about Red Woman.

Three times, while the brothers were away on a hunt, Red Woman visited the lodge; and each time Corn Silk forgot to tell them about her. After the fourth visit, she wrapped a strip of deerskin about a stick and put it in her hair to remind her that she must tell Ivak.

While they were hunting that day, Black Wolf noticed that Ivak was gloomy, and he said, "My brother, why are you sad?"

"Because in my dreams I see our home being ruined," he said despondently.

When they returned that evening, he saw the stick in his sister's hair, and he knew that something had happened.

"Corn Silk, what have you in your hair?" he asked.

She drew a sharp breath and clasped her hands. All the brothers stopped eating and looked up.

"Has Red Woman been here?" demanded Ivak.

"Four times," said Corn Silk. "But her medicine caused me to forget."

"We can live here no longer," said Ivak. "Our home has been ruined. Red Woman can now do us harm."

He told his brothers and Corn Silk to stand under the smoke hole of the lodge and to hold one another tightly. Then he shot one of his four medicine arrows, and the arrow went up the smoke hole and they went with it. The arrow fell a long distance from the lodge and Corn Silk and her brothers got up from the ground.

"Now, Ivak, which way shall we run?" asked Black Wolf.

"Of all animals, the swiftest is the antelope," he answered. "Let us become antelopes. Our sister shall keep watch on this high hill, and when she sees a cloud come from the east, she will know it is Red Woman, and she can warn us."

So Corn Silk sat upon the hill, her eyes fastened on the clear blue sky. Her gaze wandered, and when she again looked up, a heavy cloud was almost over her. She started up and ran swiftly to the antelope in a little green valley through which ran a clear stream fringed with willows and birches.

Black Wolf said, "Rather than die upon some barren hill, let us remain here." Then they resumed their human form.

Red Woman came up to them and cried tauntingly, "O Black Wolf, shoot me through the heart; it is right here," and she placed her hand on her left side. Black Wolf shot her through the breast, and

*Does Everything. Apsaroke. 1908.*

she said, "How good that feels. Shoot me in the eye, Black Wolf." He sent an arrow into her eye, and she mocked him: "Now the other eye!" And when he had shot that eye, she leapt toward him and beat him to death with her stick.

The other brothers rushed to his rescue, but she killed them in the same manner. Then Ivak, who was the last brother left, saw a meadowlark nearby. "Her heart is on her head," the bird said. Looking closely, the dwarf now saw a bit of eagle down floating above Red Woman. It was held by an almost-invisible thread of sinew.

"Of all men, Ivak is the most clever. I fear he will kill me," said Red Woman, cackling.

"Yes!" cried Ivak. "It is really so!" And he let an arrow fly at the thread of sinew. Red Woman knew he had discovered her secret, and she turned

to flee, but his second arrow severed the thread, and she dropped lifelessly to the earth.

Then Ivak built seven sweat houses in the shape of the stars of the Dipper, and in each he placed the body of a brother, and by the sacred sweat, he restored life to them. After which, he explained, "All things on this earth perish, my brothers. You shall dwell in the sky and be called the Seven Stars, and at night all people shall use you as a guide. I shall be a screech owl."

Before they separated, he told Corn Silk that her home was toward the east. "On your way, you will meet four children. Do not touch them, for if you do, disease will come upon your people." Then as the seven brothers went up into the sky and Ivak flew away in the form of a screech owl, Corn Silk started on her way. She passed three of the youngsters in safety, but the fourth, a pretty child, ran after her, calling, "Mother! Mother!" She thought, Perhaps I can take this child home and people will believe it is mine. So she carried him on her back in her blanket.

The people rejoiced at her return, and her father made a great feast in her honor; he was happy, for now he had his daughter to lighten the burdens of old age. Soon after this, when all was still one night, the child arose and, passing up through the smoke hole, went to another lodge in a distant part of the village and killed all the people in it by sucking out their hearts.

The next night, another family was mysteriously killed, and the people were much alarmed. The chief summoned all the medicine men to consider these strange happenings. Now, one of these medicine men had a wonderful arrow, which helped him to discover hidden things; if one of the feathers became loosened, he would look through the aperture between the feather and the shaft and behold things that others could not see. He took this arrow and threw it in the buffalo trail, where it would be trampled and the feather loosened, and the spirit that was doing the mischief would suspect nothing.

The third night, the child put his head out of the smoke hole of the lodge when everyone was asleep and looked carefully around. He caught sight of the arrow. He saw that one of the feathers was loose, and he dodged back, exclaiming, "He sees me!"

In the morning, the medicine men assembled again, and the owner of the arrow said, "The one we are seeking is among these lodges. He saw that this feather did not quite touch the shaft in the middle, and he dared not come forth."

That day, it rained and the shaft swelled so much that the feathers fitted tightly to it, leaving no opening, and at night when the child looked at it, he saw all the feathers close to the shaft, and he ventured out to kill a third family. The medicine men were as greatly puzzled as ever, for the mysterious arrow, of course, could tell them nothing. But the bad weather continued and caused the sinew that held the feathers to the shaft to loosen, and so there was a very small space between the shaft and the feather next to the ground. When the child

looked out of the smoke hole that night, all seemed the same to him, for the loosened feather was hidden from his sight. So he went out and destroyed a fourth family.

The next morning, the crier called all men to the lodge of the medicine man of the arrow.

"How is it?" they asked.

"The child that Corn Silk brought is destroying us," said the medicine man. "He is an evil spirit, a disease in the form of flesh."

They resolved to burn him alive, and the women were told to gather wood and place it in a huge pile in the center of the village. They came to Corn Silk and said, "Is this your child?"

"Yes, it is my child." She wept.

"You are lying!" they said. "If you do not tell us the truth, we will burn you with him!"

So she told them how she had found the child and brought it home and pretended that it was hers.

They burned the child until only ashes remained; then the lodges were struck and the people moved to a far place, and Corn Silk was disgraced forever. No one would talk to her, and in spite of her youth and beauty, she lived alone, poor and forsaken, in a solitary lodge by the river.

*Goes Ahead. Apsaroke. 1908.*

## Sioux History

The term Sioux—a French abbreviation of the Chippewa Nadoweisiw, signifying Little Adders, or Little Enemies—designates seven tribes: Mdewakantonwan (Mdewakanton), Mysterious Lake Village; Wahpekute, Shoot Among Deciduous Leaves; Wahpetonwan (Wahpeton), Village of the Deciduous Leaves; Sisitonwan (Sisseton), Village of the Swamp; Ihanktonwan (Yankton), End Village; Ihanktonwanna (Yanktonai), Little End Village; and Titonwan (Teton), Prairie Village. In a time more remote than the furthest reach of definite tradition, these seven tribes were kindred bands composing one great camp in the vicinity of the headwaters of the Mississippi, a community still referred to as Ochetishakowin, the

*Yellow Bone Woman and Family. Sioux. 1908.*

Seven Council Fires. They called themselves Dakota, meaning "allies." Disintegration came. First the Teton, then the Yankton and the Yanktonai left the camp circle of the Seven Council Fires and found new homes in the west, so that the tribes of the Dakota occupied the same relative position as within recent historic times: the four tribes known collectively as Isanyati, Knife Dwellers (anglicized into Santee), remaining in the Mille Lac region of eastern Minnesota; the Yankton and the Yanktonai, leading a seminomadic existence farther west; and the Teton, roaming the boundless prairies beyond them but centering about Big Stone Lake of Minnesota River.

Much has been written of Sioux warfare with the white man. In August of 1867, a band of warriors under the watchful eyes of Red Cloud met a small command of soldiers. These were thirty-two men, well armed with breech-loading rifles and having abundant ammunition. Here, then, is an account of Captain Powell's encounter, a prime example of warfare without honor, of fighting without coup.

There were more than three thousand warriors, and the women and children assembled on the hills to witness the annihilation of the little band. A force of five hundred warriors, magnificently equipped and mounted, dashed forward. Powell ordered his men to remain silent until the Indians were within fifty yards; then the firing commenced. The execution was terrible. Indians had never faced such guns before. Their line reeled, many dropped to the earth, and the survivors scurried back to the main body, where Red Cloud began another movement by sending out a swarm of sharpshooters to prepare the way for another attack.

Six charges were made, each time with dire result to the Indians. Dismayed and alarmed, the living began the work of recovering their dead. As reinforcements arrived from the fort, Powell's men were escorted to safety. In the first charge, Lieutenant Jenness and one soldier had been killed and two soldiers wounded. This was the extent of the loss by the troopers. Captain Powell estimated that he had killed 67 and wounded 120, while his men asserted that the Sioux had lost from 300 to 500. The Indians themselves are usually reticent as to the extent of their losses in this engagement, and when they do speak of it, their statements conflict. The exact number will never be known.

This famous treaty that followed in 1868 was impossible to fulfill. Its violation, therefore, caused the wars with the Lakota that scarred the plains. The enormous reservation created under the treaty provisions consisted of that portion of the present state of South Dakota lying west of the Missouri River. As the white settlers crowded and clamored for more land, it would have been difficult, but still possible, for the government to keep faith by preserving that great empire for the Indians. It would have been possible to keep faith in the agreement as to annuities in money and goods, and in the additional services offered. But the most impractical article of the treaty, reads as follows:

The United States hereby agrees and stipulates that the country north of the North Platte River and east of the summits of the Big Horn Mountains shall be held and considered to be unceded Indian territory, and also stipulates and agrees that no white person or persons shall be permitted to settle upon or occupy any portion of the same; or without the consent of the Indians first had and obtained, to pass through the same; and it is further agreed by the United States that within ninety days after the conclusion of peace with all the bands of the Sioux nation, the military posts now established in the territory in this article named shall be abandoned, and that the road leading to them and by them to the settlements in the Territory of Montana shall be closed.

Thus was the valuable game preserve saved for the Indians, but its promise was of brief duration. The withdrawal of this stipulated protection, and the disappearance of the game, provoked disturbances that continued at intervals until the fighting strength of the Lakota had been completely overcome.

This occurred nearly thirty years later (after the Sioux triumph of the Little Bighorn) when an unlooked-for catastrophe occurred at Wounded Knee. When Big Foot's band, fleeing to the badlands, was overtaken by Major Whitside's command on December 28, 1890, the chief asked for a parley, but, refused in this, he surrendered on demand. Captives and troops moved to Wounded Knee Creek, twenty miles northeast of Pine Ridge, and General Brooke sent additional forces under Colonel Forsyth, who now assumed command of the total force of 470 men, as against 106 captive warriors.

The next morning, the troops began to disarm the captives, but the task proved a slow and tedious one. While it was in progress, Yellow Bird, a medicine man, encouraged the warriors to resist, blowing on his eagle-bone whistle. While he was inciting them to action, the troops began to search for arms under the blankets of the braves. Suddenly, Yellow Bird threw a handful of dust into the air. At this signal, Black Fox fired at the soldiers, who at once responded with a deadly volley. Before the slaughter was over, three hundred Indians, men, women, and children, were dead. The bodies of women and children were found two miles from the scene of the first assault, indicating that revenge had impelled some of the troopers beyond all reason. The unfortunate occurrence was followed by a terrible snowstorm, but three days later, a detachment was sent out to rescue the wounded, if any survived, and to bury the dead. Strange to say, a number of women and children were found still alive, in spite of the fury of the three-day blizzard that had raged about their unsheltered bodies.

A long trench was dug, and in it were piled the frozen corpses. The thirty-one soldiers who had fallen had already been buried at Pine Ridge. In the summer of 1907, the outline of that huge grave of the Sioux could still be

*In the Shadow of the Cliff. 1905.*

traced in the grass at Wounded Knee. The Indians had placed about it a neat fence and had reared a monument on which may be read the names of forty-three of the victims and this inscription:

> This monument is erected by surviving relatives and other Oglala and Cheyenne River Sioux Indians in memory of the Chief Big Foot Massacre, December 29, 1890. Col. Forsyth in command of U.S. Troops. Big Foot was a great chief of the Sioux Indians. He often said, "I will stand in peace till my last day comes." He did many good and brave deeds for the white man and the red man. Many innocent women and children who knew no wrong died here.
>
> The erecting of this monument is largely due to the financial assistance of Joseph Horncloud, whose father was killed here.

The four thousand Indians at Pine Ridge, who had prepared to follow the path of peace, fled in anger at the news from Wounded Knee. It looked as though a war had now begun in earnest, but the soldiers were too numerous. General Miles knew personally all the leading chiefs and had their confidence. He promised to have army officers appointed as agents and to use his full power at Washington to have the wrongs of the Indians adjusted. It was midwinter, the Ghost Dance craze was subsiding, and by January 16, 1891, the Indians had all surrendered and the last Sioux disturbance was at an end.

*Stinking Bear or Smell the Bear. Oglala Sioux. 1905.*

westward. They reached the Missouri, forcing the Arikara southward and penetrating as far as the Black Hills. Within recent years, they have held the region west of the Missouri River and north of the Platte, extending permanently as far west as the Black Hills. In addition, their occasional parties went as far west as central Montana, where they met the country of the Blackfeet. Along the northern line of Wyoming they attempted to take up their abode even beyond the Bighorn. This, however, was the land claimed and held by the Apsaroke, or Crows, who, notwithstanding their smaller numbers, more than held their own and forced the Lakota to the east of Powder River.

The permanent crossing of the Missouri River began from 175 to 200 years ago, or between about 1700 and 1725. As to their habitat before the passing of the Missouri, folktales and winter counts enable us to trace them back to Mille Lac, Minnesota, around 1680; beyond this point, tradition grows more vague, yet it does raise some interesting questions and speculations. "Big Water," of course, could have been the Great Lakes, but according to some of the old men, that water was "bitter." Large shells that could have come only from the sea are mentioned. The argument may reasonably be made that these could have been obtained by barter, but the Sioux insist that their source was the water beside which their people lived.

No tribe that the writer has studied is so lacking in traditional knowledge of its original home and early migration. In fact, no creation and early migration legend worthy of the name has been found to exist among any of the western Sioux tribes. On the other hand, other tribes of Siouan stock, the Apsaroke, Hidatsa, and Mandan, have definite creation and migration stories, which make it clearly evident that at one time they had their

## Lakota Sioux

Long ago, the Lakota, or Teton Sioux, occupied the region near Big Stone Lake, in western Minnesota, whence they moved gradually

home on the South Atlantic seaboard, where Siouan tribes are known to have lived well within the eighteenth century, and where indeed the remnant of the Catawba still survives.

If it can be admitted that the Apsaroke, Mandan, and Hidatsa migrated from the South, it is safe to assume that the Plains Sioux came from the same general locality. Sioux tradition indicates that in their western migration, the Sioux passed north of the Great Lakes. This being so, and their origin on the South Atlantic being clear, their migration has been an exceedingly long one, probably following the line of the Atlantic Coast. The very length of their journeying may reasonably account for the lack of a definite migration tradition.

The Hidatsa legend of the creation tells of a land where the birds always sang and the trees were always green. Thence the people moved slowly northward, passing into a land of ever-increasing cold, until they came to a large lake, where they found a tribe speaking a language much like their own. They declared, "These people must be our brothers; henceforth we will live together." Feeling that the winters were too rigorous, they journeyed southwestward and southward until they reached the Missouri, where they found the Mandan, who had been living there a long time. The probable route of the Hidatsa and Mandan was far shorter than any possible one the Sioux could have taken, and the fact of their slow movement and their long residence in fixed places may well account for the early traditions of these two historically sedentary tribes.

Inasmuch as the Teton, as their name (Titonwan) indicates, have been prairie dwellers for centuries, they must be considered as such, disregarding their earlier forest life. It is without doubt that the vast herds of buffalo were the cause of their westward movement. Their life was so closely associated with the bison that with the disappearance of the herds, the Teton were left pitiably helpless. For generations, they had depended in great measure on the buffalo for food, clothing, shelter, implements, and utensils, and because of its neces-

*Two Charger Woman. Oglala Sioux. 1907.*          *Jack Red Cloud. Oglala Sioux. 1907.*

sity in supplying these physical needs, it became also a factor of surpassing importance in the religious life of the tribes. Their divine teachings were brought them by a sacred buffalo cow acting as messenger from the Mystery. In every ceremony, the bison played a part, and its flesh was invariably used in the rituals of their worship. But, alas for their religion as well as for their temporal needs, the herds were swept from the earth as in a twinkling. So sudden was the disappearance that the Sioux regard their passing as *wakan* ("mysteri-

*Good Day Woman. Oglala Sioux. 1907.*

ous"). The old men still ask what became of them, and nothing can convince them that the herds have passed forever.

It is doubtful that any people were ever brought more suddenly to such a radical change in their manner of living as the Lakota. The enforced change in diet alone so undermined them physically that they became an easy prey to every ill, particularly the diseases introduced by the white man. Their dwellings changed from the warm but well-ventilated portable tepees of skins to flimsy ones of cotton cloth, or, worse yet, to small, close,

ill-ventilated, permanent log cabins, the floors of which soon reeked with disease-producing filth. The comfortable robes of the buffalo were superseded by trade blankets and unsuitable cast-off garments given to them by kindly but ill-informed people. One day they were proud; the next they were paupers; "wards of the nation," we call them. The old life was an ideal one: It gave the Sioux every necessity of life with a minimum of effort. His principal labor was that of the chase, which in itself was a pleasure. And on the warrior's return from hunt or raid, the women of the household waited on him as though he were indeed a lord. Even the thought of wasting old age was spared him, for the man whose life was the warpath and the hunt knew full well that a quick death was apt to be his. He preferred it thus; it was better to die while strong and happy than to grow old and suffer long.

Nor was the life of the women the one of drudgery so often depicted. It is true they did the menial work of the camp, but, strange as it may seem, the task was usually a pleasure rather than a hardship. It is difficult to imagine how the work of the camp could have been more equitably divided. Owing to the perilous existence of the men and the consequent high death rate, polygyny was a necessary institution, causing several women to share the burdens of the domestic establishment, and thus lightening the labor of all. Physically, the women are equal to any task, however hard. Observed at work, they seem even stronger than the men. Among the hunting tribes, the life of a woman made for the greatest physical strength. There is thus little differentiation in the endurance of the sexes.

The natural disposition of the Lakota woman is full of cheer, particularly when she is seen in the home and with her children. When strangers are present, however, the code of ethics decrees that the woman should be retiring in manner. To her husband, she is noticeably affectionate and attentive, waiting upon him constantly, seeing that every article of apparel is brought to him as needed, often literally dressing him as she would a child. And, indeed, why should she not derive pleasure from such personal attentions? Has she not with her own hands made every article of his apparel—

*Sioux Child. 1905.*            *Red Elk Woman. Sioux. 1907.*

permitted to accompany his first war party, and after he had accomplished some worthy deed and thus attained to years of discretion, he was at liberty to marry.

Having decided upon a girl whom he would make his wife, he places himself by some secluded path where she is likely to pass at nightfall. As she comes along the shadowy trail, the young man slips into view to meet her. He is shrouded in a blanket, his dark eyes peering out from its folds. The girl may not fancy his attentions and soon pass on, perhaps to meet other suitors. If she is extremely proud, several summers may pass in evening courtship before her heart is won.

With her consent to marry, the lovers exchange the marriage token—a ball of sweet grass wrapped in deerskin with long fringes, to be tied in the hair at the ends of the braids. She then names the time when her lover is to come for her. When he goes to her tepee, he cautiously raises the cover at the place where she is sleeping and touches her. She rises quietly; the two steal forth.

The young man then takes his sweetheart to his parents' tepee. In the morning, the youth's father summons the village crier, bidding him announce that his son has taken a wife. At the same time, a horse is given to some poor person whom the crier publicly names. Thus the two are married. It was never the Lakota custom for a young man to take the girl away from the village and live apart with her for a time as a form of honeymoon. Such has occurred recently, but only when there was parental opposition to the marriage.

At other times, the marriage was more conventional. Let us say that the suitor has already been accepted. His parents would then send presents to the parents of the girl, and they would signify their consent by sending gifts to the youth's family in turn. If these consisted of horses, the girl was

dressed the skins, dyed and fashioned them into form, and with infinite patience embroidered them in beautiful designs with colored quills or beads? And with every stitch, there has gone into the work her affection for the man who is to wear the garment.

From earliest childhood, Lakota children were taught in the way that would make them strong and useful members of the tribe. Long before they were large enough to sit unaided on a horse, they were securely tied on the back of a quiet animal, and there they would sit, riding along with the moving band for hours, and even days, at a time. The boy was early trained to care for horses, driving them in from the ranges to water and then out again to the grazing lands, and when he had reached his tenth or twelfth year, his father usually took him on short hunting trips, instructing him in killing game.

The father would drive a young buffalo from the herd and show the boy how to shoot the animal just behind the shoulder; then followed object lessons in skinning and dressing. Thereafter, he was allowed to single out a calf for himself, and when he had brought it down, he was made to dress it without help. Even as early as the age of thirteen, seldom later than seventeen, a boy was

*Lucille. Sioux. 1907.*

Polygyny was common, the number of wives being limited only by the man's ability to obtain and support them; and the more wives he had, the richer he became, as there were that many more workers to prepare skins, which among the Sioux constituted a large part of the wealth. With the consent of his wives, a man often married a younger sister of one of them, and usually presents were given to the girl. All lived together in the same tepee, and if a deposed favorite should create discord by reason of her jealousy, she was soon sent away. The divorced wife, returning to her parents, married again when opportunity offered. A runaway wife was more than apt to be killed by the husband, and a meeting between the woman's husband and her new lover was likely to result in a fight with fatal consequences.

Sioux culture is based primarily on two concepts: first, that medicine is derived from the mysterious forces of nature; and second, that one must have a courageous heart. A man desired that his mystery power be stronger than any he was to encounter. Many a warrior cried out to his people that his medicine was so great that no arrow or bullet could harm him. Then, singing his medicine songs, he charged recklessly into the camp of the enemy and struck them right and left. Often, such supernatural strength proved itself on the battlefield. For example, Gen. George Crook, considered one of the best rifle shots in the army, said that on one occasion he had shot at Crazy Horse more than twenty times without effect.

In camp, the chiefs and warriors would meet around the council fire and recount stories of the warpath. As each deed was related, a stick from the bundle kept by the chief would be laid before him. The French-Canadian word *coup*, of such common

placed upon the finest. She was then borne to the tepee of her lover, where she was received by the women of the family. They spread a large buffalo robe on the ground for her to step upon in dismounting. Both forms of marriage existed side by side until within recent times. It is, however, self-evident that the latter method was the one followed by daughters of the more important families.

*Rosa Lame Dog. Sioux. 1905.*

usage in speaking of Indian deeds of valor, has not been adopted by the Sioux; their term is *toka-kte* ("kill enemy").

A coup could be won by actually killing an enemy, or by striking the body of an enemy, whether dead or alive. It might also be won by capturing a horse, a band of horses, or by taking a scalp. Honors were counted on each hostile warrior by the first four who struck him, the first in each case winning the greatest renown, an honor called *tanyan-kte* ("kill right"). Thus, if twenty men were struck or even touched in an encounter, twenty honors of the first grade were won by the victors. But the greatest exploit of all was to ride into the midst of the enemy and strike a warrior in action without attempting to wound him. When a man had led four war parties and in each achieved a first honor, he was eligible to chieftainship.

If, in addition to the recognized coups, a man had been wounded (or his horse wounded and/or killed), he was considered an accomplished warrior. This entitled him to wear a scalp shirt, on which his exploits were recorded by various insignia. The breast feather of the eagle, dyed red, represented a wound. A white breast feather signified that the wearer had been a member of a scout-

ing party. A yellow feather denoted a captured horse. Each tuft of human hair that gave the shirt its name indicated a coup. An eagle's tail feather was usually worn in the hair for each honor counted. Wounds to man or horse were indicated by marks painted on the body over the injured spot. A man who had killed the first enemy in a battle also painted his face black.

Another aspect of Sioux culture similar to coup counting in its humanity is their policy with regard to the adoption of captives. Chief Minihuha never heard of a case in which the Sioux had tortured one of their captives by burning, though he had once been told that the Pawnee burned at the stake the Sioux Paints His Face Red, after having killed his entire family. Discussing the treatment of captives, Minihuha related the following incident:

"When I was a young man, my father was with a small party that happened to come upon a single tepee of the Shoshoni. The occupants were killed, all except one little girl, who was captured alive by my father and brought home. My sister had died a short time before, and the little Shoshoni girl was adopted in her place and given the name Zintkala-washte-win, Pretty Bird Woman. She was about twelve years of age and lived with us more than a year. Then through the Arapaho, who were friendly with the Sho-shoni, we heard that her father was alive and was searching for his daughter. My father thought the matter over; then he came to me and said, 'My son, are you willing that your sister should be sent back to her people?'

"I said, 'She has been with us so long that she seems like one

*Oglala Child. 1907.*

of our people and of our family, but I suppose she ought to be sent back if she wishes to go.'

"So my father provided new clothing for her, and three horses, and I gave her my best suit of clothing and my fine racehorse, and at the appointed time she was sent off to her own land."

According to the lore of the Teton Sioux, the Lakota, their teachings—religious, social, ceremonial, and medicinal—are divine law revealed by the White Buffalo Woman, acting as emissary of the Great Mystery. As indicated by their mythology they were, before the coming of this divine messenger, a people with slight knowledge of how to live or to worship. The palladium left with them by White Buffalo Woman was the sacred Calf Pipe, now in the keeping of Elk Head, a member of the Sans Arc band living on the Cheyenne River Reservation. Elk Head's version of the myth agrees with the versions obtained from other sources. He has been the keeper of the pipe for thirty-one

years, having received it the year following the Custer fight in 1876; and he names six other keepers, beginning with Standing Buffalo, who is said to have received it directly from White Buffalo Woman.

The next keeper was the brother of Standing Buffalo, Red Hair. The pipe then descended to Elk Head, who was succeeded by his brother, Bear's Ear. Then followed in order Rising Sun, Hollow Horn, and the present guardian, Elk Head.

If Elk Head is correct about the number of pipe-keepers, the myth is of comparatively recent origin. A proper rendering of High Hawk's winter count places the date 368 years ago. This would require each of Elk Head's predecessors to have been the guardian of the pipe for fifty-six years. There may have been keepers of whom Elk Head has no knowledge, but it is more likely that the winter count is in error, due to the attempt of the annalist to record events that occurred in the misty past.

*Meditation. (Medicine Rock, Cheyenne River.) 1907.*

*Slow Bull. Oglala Sioux. 1907.*

To the Lakota, the pipe is most holy. During the tribal journeying, a virgin, carefully guarded by a priest, bore it in advance of the band, and but one instance of the opening of the bundle during Elk Head's priesthood is known. That was when it was taken from him by the Indian police at the command of the resident agent and opened by that official, but the people made such an outcry against the sacrilege that the pipe was quickly restored to its keeper.

*Little Hawk. Brule Sioux. 1907.*

| **Lakota Creation Myth** | |
|---|---|

*The White Buffalo Woman* — Many generations ago, when the Lakota still dwelt beside the lake far away in the east, they experienced a winter of terrible severity. The snow lay deep on the ground, and the streams were frozen to their very beds. Every day the sharp crack of trees was heard as the frost gnawed at their hearts, and at night the piles of skins and the blazing fires in the tepees scarcely sufficed to keep out the cold. Game seemed to have deserted the country, for though the hunters often faced the hardships of the winter chase, they returned empty-handed, and the wail of hungry women and children joined with the moan of the forest.

When spring came, it was decided to leave that country because of the anger of Spirit of the North. Now they sought a better homeland in the direction of the sun.

There was little enough to pack besides tepees and fur robes. What few dogs had not been eaten were soon harnessed to the travois. Two young scouts were sent out first. These two were quite different young men, however; one was brave and unselfish, while the other thought only of himself.

The scouts were soon far ahead of the men and women, who were bent under heavy burdens that their dogs normally carried. Late in the day, the scouts shot a deer. Thinking the people would make a night camp there, they left the deer where it had fallen. Then they continued on. There was a mist that rose above a little hill. Pausing to look at it, the two youths saw the outline of a woman. As they gazed, the cloud lifted.

She was beautiful, and she wore a short skirt, wristlets, and anklets of sage. In the crook of her left arm was a bundle wrapped in red buffalo skin. On her back was a quiver, and in her left hand she held a bunch of herbs. Straightway, the young man whose heart was selfish wished to possess the beautiful woman. His companion, however, said to him, "She might be a messenger from the Great Mystery."

"No," said the other. "She is not holy, just a woman, two-legged, like ourselves. I must have her!"

Then he ran toward the woman, who at once warned him that she was a sacred being. He went closer and she told him to stop. Still he advanced; she then put her burden on the ground and came toward him. The mist lowered and covered the mysterious woman and the bold youth. Then came a fearful sound of rattling and hissing. It was as if thousands of angered rattlesnakes were suddenly present. The scout was about to run when the cloud lifted as quickly as it had descended. There on the ground were the bleached bones of his former friend. The beautiful virgin stood calmly beside them. She spoke to him gently, telling him that he was chosen to be the greatest shaman of his nation.

"I have many things to say to your people," she said. "Go now to the place where they are camped. Tell them of my coming. Build a great circle of green boughs with an opening to the east. In the center, put up a council tepee, and over the ground inside, spread the sage thickly. In the morning, I shall come."

The young man hastened back and delivered the message of the holy woman. Under his direction, her wishes were obeyed.

In the morning, gathered within the circle of green boughs, they waited for the messenger of the Great Mystery.

She entered the tepee and at once spread open her red buffalo skin bundle. The people saw tobacco, the feather of a spotted eagle, the skin of a redheaded woodpecker, a roll of buffalo hair, a few braids of sweet grass, and, most important of all, a red stone pipe with the carved image of a buffalo calf on its wooden stem. Then the holy woman told them that the Great Mystery had sent her to ex-

*Saliva. Oglala Sioux. 1907.*

plain his laws, to teach them how to worship so that they might become a great and powerful people.

During the four days she remained with them in the tepee, she showed them many sacred customs. If a man wanted great power, she said he had to go into the high mountains and fast for many days. Only then would he see visions and gather strength from the Great Mystery. She showed how to punish the evil heart who makes the innocent suffer. She revealed how young women were to be treated at maturity, and how to care for the sick. She taught the people how to worship the Great Mystery by selecting, in the summer of each year, a virgin who should go into the forest and cut down a straight tree; this was to be set up properly for the Sun Dance, before which all the virgins in the camp were to come and touch the pole. In this way, they were to proclaim their purity. A false declaration, she explained, was to be challenged by the young man who was able to testify to the transgression; in such a case, the young woman would be driven away in derision. A young man wishing success, in war or love, was supposed to paint a rock and make a vow that in the coming dance he would offer himself to the Great Mystery; after this, whenever he saw the rock, he would be mindful of his vow.

Then she taught them the five great ceremonies. These were the Foster Parent Chant, the Sun Dance, the Vision Cry, the Buffalo Chant, and the Ghost Keeper. The sacred pipe, she gave to the young scout she had chosen, with the admonition that its wrapping should be removed only during extreme tribal necessity. From the quiver on her back, she took six bows and six arrows. She gave them only to young men who were known for their bravery, their kindness and truthfulness. These, she told them to use after she had gone. They were to find the summit of a certain hill, where a herd of

six hundred buffalo were waiting. In the midst of the herd would be found six men. The buffalo and the man were destined to die at the hands of the fine warriors. Afterward, they were to cut off the men's ears and attach them to the stem of the sacred pipe.

"So long as you believe in this pipe," she said finally, "and worship the Mystery as I have taught you, you shall prosper. You will have food in plenty. You will increase and be a powerful nation. But when you, as a people, no longer show reverence to the pipe, then you will cease to be a nation."

With these words, she left the tepee, went to the opening at the eastern side of the camp circle, and disappeared. The people, crowding forward to see what had become of her, beheld only a white buffalo cow moving gracefully over the prairie.

*Eagle Elk. Oglala Sioux. 1907.*          *Red Dog (Shunka Luta). Sioux. 1907.*

# III—THE PLATEAU

The people of the plateau include the Nez Percé, whose land embraced Idaho, Oregon, and Washington, and the Flathead and Kalispel, whose country lay roughly between the Rocky Mountains and the Cascades, and south of the Canadian border.

Curtis's text, in part, is a lamentation, particularly of the fate suffered by the Nez Percé under the wise but tragic leadership of Chief Joseph. In these eloquent pages, one imagines Curtis attempting to tell the truth, as it had not been told before. He speaks of the so-called invisible law of the tribe—that the earth is the supreme law of nature and that native ground is sacred and cannot be defiled. Considering the time in which this was written, shortly after the turn of the century, Curtis's plea, like that of the Indians themselves, is especially eloquent. And, to make it hit home more clearly to his Euramerican audience, Curtis invokes the Bible to prove that the Earth Mother religion of the American Indian is also the belief of the Rechabites, "the original Yahveh cult."

The reportage on the Flathead and Kalispel, though less impassioned than that of the Nez Percé, offers a fine representative myth on the transgressions and rectifications of the great universal spell-maker, Coyote. In the myth itself is a history of its own. Humorously told, it describes the fragility of life and the certainty of death.

# NEZ PERCÉ

*Nez Percé
History*

The Nez Percés, dwellers of the Columbia River Basin, made a marked impression on explorers, traders, missionaries, and army officers. From the day they were first seen by Lewis and Clark in 1805 to the close of the Nez Percé war in 1877, all who met them remarked that they were an exceptional people.

The territory of the Nez Percés embraced parts of Idaho, Oregon, and Washington. It is a region of forested mountains and numberless clear streams. Here and there are broad, undulating, upland prairies, offering a good supply of edible roots and abundant forage for horses. The lower courses of the streams flow through pleasant, narrow valleys completely shut in from the cold mountain winds, forming ideal spots for wintering. Deer, elk, and mountain sheep were obtained without great difficulty, and the rivers were alive with fish, particularly salmon, which formed the principal food of the Nez Percés.

*A Young Nez Percé. 1910.*

The Nez Percés were a loosely associated group of local bands, each possessing its own territory and its own chief, yet they had a collective name for these bands, *Nimipu*, meaning "we people." Lewis and Clark first visited them in September 1805, reaching one of their villages on a headstream of the Clearwater. The explorers spent about two weeks among the Nez Percés on Oro Fino Creek while recuperating from the hardships of their passage across the mountains and constructing canoes for the voyage to the Pacific. They found the people well supplied with horses—herds so plentiful, in fact, that the date of their original acquisition must have been several decades before the beginning of the nineteenth century. One of the chiefs was said to own so many that he was unable to count them.

The history of the Nez Percés shows that there was absolutely no course, policy, or conduct available that ensured fair treatment from the U.S. Government. Nor was there any avoidance of the grasping encroachment of settlers. The inert, unorganized Indians of Southern California were literally crowded from the earth. The fact that they, with their pacific disposition, made no resistance had no modifying effect on the covetous settler; nor did it cause the government to reach out a helping hand in appreciation of such pliant behavior. They suffered through good conduct. It was left to the haughty tribes of the plains to turn their long-smoldering resentment into a white-hot flame, which, in the end, brought on more suffering of the same kind.

The Nez Percés were friendly from their first contact with white men, and as a tribe they always desired to be so. Their history since 1855, and particularly in the war of 1877, sadly informs how they were repaid for their loyalty to the white brother.

For a true premise from which to consider the Nez Percé war and the events that led to it, we must consider the componency of the group. Each village or band had its own chief, and when any one of these village chiefs presumed to be head chief of the different bands, it was merely assumption on his part: He mistook political ambition for fact.

The Nez Percés were only seminomadic. Their habitat through traditional and mythic times included the same valleys, which the United States took from them by right of might. By the fact that they had always dwelt in these beautiful valleys and by reason of their Earth Mother religion, the Nez Percés were attached to the land to a greater degree than the average tribe. All the Shahaptian groups speak of the earth as mother, but the Nez Percés seem to have been the high priest of Earth Mother religion. This was their ever-ready argument in all councils: "The earth is my mother. Can I sell her body? You ask me to plow and plant. How can I tear up my mother's flesh?"

The prejudice against parting with land and tilling the soil was not a mere whim, but was based on deep-rooted faith, what the Nez Percés called "invisible law," or the supreme law of nature. This was what placed them on the earth, and it was also what made them so strongly oppose any demand that they give up their native ground and move to one reservation. The belief of rootedness, so inherent in Nez Percé belief, is common to the teachings of other Indian prophets, dreamers, and medicine men, who, through fasting and abstinence, became the spiritual leaders of their people. It was the plea

*Last Home of Joseph Nez Percé. 1910.*

of Tenskwatawa, the Shawnee prophet, and of his brother, the remarkable Tecumtha.

The doctrine that man should not "use" the soil but that he should subsist by the natural growth of the earth is a parallelism, perhaps, to the Hebrew Bible. Dr. Paul Carus, in an article on the development of the "God thought," particularly comparing Yahweh of biblical tribes with the great spirit of the American Indian, cites many instances where divine instructions are given against all tilling of the soil:

The religion of the Rechabites is apparently the original Yahveh cult, whose most obvious feature is a religious consecration of the nomad life in the steppes with an outspoken aversion to all civilization as an aberration from the God-ordained estate of life.

"We will drink no wine: For Jonadab the son of Rechab our father commanded us, saying, 'Ye shall drink no wine, neither ye, nor your sons for ever: Neither shall ye build house, nor sow seed, nor plant vineyard, nor have any: but all your days ye shall dwell in tents.'

"'And if thou wilt make me an altar of stone, thou shalt not build it of hewn stone: for if thou lift up thy tool upon it, thou hast polluted it.'"

Even in the days of Gideon, the Israelites did not live in cities and houses, as did the Canaanites, but in tents, and Gideon selected for his band those who would spurn the use of the hand as a substitute for a drinking vessel, and lapped the water like dogs.

"And the Lord said unto Gideon, 'Every one that lappeth of the water with his tongue, as a dog lappeth, him shalt thou set by himself. . . .' And the Lord said unto Gideon, 'By the three hundred men that lapped will I save you, and deliver the Midianites into thine hand.'"

Among no Indians with whom the author is acquainted was the religious concept that the soil should not be tilled so manifest as among the Nez Percés. It was constantly expounded by their shamen, who made it their supreme argument.

It is said that Chief Joseph was ill-tempered and despondent when informed that the President had finally opened the Wallowa Valley to settlement. He soon took new courage, however, no

*Nez Percé Warrior. 1910.*

doubt feeling that as the matter had been so long in abeyance, there was yet hope that he might retain his much-beloved homeland. But the government's response was a command, stating that the people were to be placed on the reservation. General Howard had his orders, and he had no choice but to move them, or kill them for not complying. That the latter occurred was, no doubt, more a matter of accident than deliberate.

In early March 1877, Howard began his movement toward the military occupancy of the Wallowa Valley. The inception of this maneuver was, of course, known at once by the Nez Percés, who quickly expressed a desire for a council to discuss the situation but asked that it be held at the Umatilla Agency, for they did not trust the church Indians and the interpreters at Lapwai. At the Umatilla interview, on April first, Lieutenant Bell attended as Howard's representative. Alokut was there, but not Chief Joseph, and at the request of the latter, General Howard was to meet Chief Joseph and the other chiefs at Walla Walla on April nineteenth.

*Head Carry. Plateau. 1900.*          *Black Hair. Plateau. 1905.*

their creator. Howard had slight patience with this religious contention, and he insisted that they cease discussing their beliefs and come to business matters. The second day's council was like the first, largely a protest by the medicine men against releasing the land. Howard states:

> Joseph simply introduced White Bird and his people, stating that they had not seen me before, and that he wished them to understand what was said. White Bird sat demurely in front of me, kept his hat on, and steadily covered his face with a large eagle's wing. They then put forth an old Dreamer of White Bird's band, Tooschul-hul-sote by name—a large, thick-necked, ugly, obstinate savage of the worst type. His first remark was about the law of the earth: That there were two parties to a controversy, and that the one that was right would come out ahead. We answered that we were all children of a common government, and must obey. The old man replied that he had heard about a trade between Indians and white men, bargaining away the Indians' land, but that he belonged to the land out of which he came.

At the appointed time, Alokut appeared with a delegation of headmen, but Chief Joseph was ill, and at the request of the Indians, it was arranged to have a large council at Lapwai on the third of May. The principal headmen participating in this council were Chief Joseph, Looking Glass, White Bird, Tuhulhutsut, Shorn Head, Hatalihkin, Kaliwit, Poyakun, Tukalikshima, and Yellow Pelican.

The Indians at the outset asked that they be allowed a long talk, thus indicating that they had not yet fully grasped the fact that the decree was final and words were to no avail. Howard informed them that they might have any reasonable opportunity to talk but that whatever they had to say could not in any way change the situation.

He informed them: "I am here to put you on the Lapwai Reservation, and this I shall do or fight you. There is no use talking about the Wallowa Valley. I am already sending my soldiers there to take possession of it." The first day's council on the third of May did not enter seriously into matters, Chief Joseph asking that they await the coming of White Bird, who was on his way and would arrive that night. The medicine men or priests, called by Howard "dreamers" and "drummers," were forceful with their view against crossing the laws of

Howard's prejudice was such that his report is filled with the words of a hot-tempered Christian argument. Chief Joseph, desiring that the meeting be postponed until Monday, was granted the request; obviously, this gave Howard's troops more time to draw closer to their objective.

In the war that followed, the Nez Percés showed remarkable skill as fighters, but in the end, the superior arms and supplies of U.S. soldiers overcame them. In the final retreat, the Nez Percés traveled only eight or nine miles a day, spending much of their time hunting buffalo. This dilatory action on the part of Looking Glass enabled Col. Nelson A. Miles to overtake his warriors in the Bear Paw Mountains, sixty miles from the sacred "Old Woman's Land."

On the last day's march, they traveled only about five miles. Then, coming upon a large herd of buffalo, they stopped and spent the day hunting, making camp, and the next morning Looking Glass, despite the warning of his scouts, remained in camp to dry the meat and prepare the hides. Even then, Colonel Miles was close upon them—so close that the attack began at about eight on the morning of September thirtieth.

For three days, the bitter struggle continued. One by one, the chiefs fell in a hopeless battle against heavy odds. Tuhulhutsut, the medicine man who had so long held out for the land, was one of the first to be killed. Then Alokut, the younger brother of Joseph, fell and died. Pile of Clouds, the medicine man who had, from the beginning of the campaign, urged Looking Glass to fight, exclaimed, "Death is behind us; we must hurry; there is no time to cut lodge poles or hunt!" He fell early in the conflict. Then Looking Glass, who had led his people for so long, dropped into the pit where he had stood his ground.

Poor Looking Glass: He possessed so many good qualities and displayed so much skill that one is forced to the belief that had he been given a little more time, the history of his tribe might have had a different ending. And while one must appreciate the remarkable record made by the Nez Percés under his leadership, one must also lay the failure of the retreat largely, if not wholly, to his lack of purpose.

The first day's fighting in this final battle was very severe, and practically all of the great leaders were killed during that day. By the second morning, the Indians had dug pits for themselves, which gave them a fair protection, and Miles simply continued the siege, not desiring to waste lives in a charge. Had he realized how fearfully weak they were, he no doubt would have made a charge and closed the battle. On the third day of fighting, Chief Joseph, now the only chief left, went to Miles's camp for an interview. He was kept there two days as a prisoner, and at the same time the Indians were hold-

ing Lt. L. H. Jerome, whom they had captured. An exchange of prisoners was made halfway between the lines, and on Chief Joseph's return to his own camp, he ordered the people to prepare for more fighting; he had not liked the words of Colonel Miles, and he said he would not surrender.

Firing was resumed for a time, but then yet another effort was made by Miles to arrange for peace. Chief Joseph's men, in the meantime, were saying they should give up the struggle, the continuance of which would only cause the death of more women and children, who were now freezing in the snowy pits. White Bird, with many followers, had already escaped to the north. In Chief Joseph's camp, there remained thirty warriors, twenty of whom were disabled. Huddled in miserable holes dug with bare hands were 350 women and children, many of whom also were wounded. It is

*The Wife of Ow High. Plateau. 1905.*

small wonder that the men urged that the fight be brought to a close.

Previous to the surrender, Howard joined Miles and was a witness to the capitulation. There has been much discussion of the ruthless breaking of this agreement. That Miles did assure Joseph that he should return to Idaho is unquestioned, and it is equally certain that every promise made by him was disregarded by the government. That the promises were violated was nothing more than might have been expected, for we, as a nation, have rarely kept, unmodified, any compact made with the Indians. In justice to General Miles, it should be said that he was untiring in his efforts to have the captives returned to Idaho, and he was instrumental in finally bringing about that end.

Following the surrender, the Nez Percés were

*Sitting Eagle. Plateau. 1905.*

taken first to the Yellowstone, thence to Bismarck, North Dakota, and from there to Fort Leavenworth, Kansas, where they were kept for the remainder of the winter. From Leavenworth, they were transferred to Indian Territory, placed on low malarial ground, and furnished such scant protection from the weather that by the end of the first year's captivity, one-fourth of the people had died from disease and despondency. This unfortunate condition continued for eight years, when, in 1885, the last of the survivors were sent north, some being taken to the Lapwai Reservation in Idaho, but Chief Joseph and somewhat more than a hundred of his people were sent to Nespilem, on the Colville Reservation in eastern Washington.

Chief Joseph, for the rest of his life, would launch one hopeless plea after another for the Wallowa Valley; one of his last attempts was a journey to Washington. Perhaps it was discouragement—more likely, it was intuition—but somehow he knew that his life was drawing to a close. While returning to his home, he said that he would make no more journeys; that he would soon be gone. And so it was. The following year, September 21, 1904, his life's fight closed.

The summer following Chief Joseph's death, the writer visited Nespilem, to be present at the Joseph Potlatch—the giving away of all his earthly possessions. A large longhouse, made of many tepees joined together, was put up for the occasion. Here were gathered all the things the old chief had collected during the last years of his life. Owing to Chief Joseph's prominence, he had received many gifts from both white people and Indians. In addition, his relatives from Lapwai brought a great number of new blankets, that the occasion might be a credit to the family. The collected belongings made a formidable heap at one end of the lodge. It took two days to distribute them.

Chief Joseph's widow sat at one side of the pile, and, taking up the articles singly, she handed them to the crier, at the same time announcing through him the name of the intended recipient. This was continued until every possession was given away, even to the trifling articles in the widow's work basket and the simplest household utensils.

This was the closing act in the drama of the life of Chief Joseph, the last of the Nez Percé non-treaty chiefs. To employ words in condemnation of the great wrong that his people suffered would be useless, for it was but one of the countless iniquities heaped upon the Indians since the landing at Plymouth Rock.

*Nez Percé Man. 1899.*

| *Seven Nez Percé Medicine Myths* | In the plateau region, as in other areas of North America, songs are the essentials of myth. An individual owns personal songs, and to him they |

are the most important possession of his life. They determine his spiritual as well as his temporal existence. The music of the songs is rhythmic and entrancing, emotional and hypnotic. So striking is the aboriginal music and imagery that a number of them are gathered here. Following each set of lyrics is the translation, literally recorded, of the picture that each creates in the mind of the listener. In these unique medicine songs, here are words the author has not seen elsewhere. They often seem fantastically formed, varying combinations on original roots and phrases. All of the translations, of purely native origin, are set here in quotations.

### Song of the Sun

*The dawn keeps coming.*
*Keeps coming, keeps coming.*
*Over the mountains the sun shines and lights the*
*    earth.*
*Keeps coming, keeps coming, keeps coming.*
*Keeps coming, the dawn.*

*Translation:* "Day breaks, and the dawn begins to overspread the sky. At this moment, the Sun, still under the earth, begins to sing. Each day he sings this song, because he has so far to travel. Soon Sun appears and sheds his light more and more on the earth, and everything, even the darkest crevice in the mountains, is illuminated. The sound of his song moves ahead of him, and when he almost reaches the zenith, the ocean begins to roll and roar.

"All creatures feel happy when the Sun passes over them. All the birds of the sea have feathers, which have been drifting from one part of the ocean to the other, and these drifting feathers feel the sunlight and come to life. They have been lying under the water and some have never seen the shore, but all have the life of the Sun as they move toward the land. Along the shore, the feathers that already lie there are dry. These, too, feel the light and come to life. The harder the sea rolls, the farther the feathers are carried to the land. We feel the cold wetness these feathers have felt, and the gladness they now feel when the warm Sun comes and dries them."

*The Scout. Nez Percé. 1910.*

*The Old-Time Warrior. Nez Percé. 1910.*

### Medicine Song of the Pelican

*In company seeking the summer;*
*In company seeking the summer;*
*Flying, he longs for his mate,*
*Wings outstretched, wings outstretched.*

*Translation:* "When cold weather comes at the lake in the north, the birds are flying round in a circle, preparing for their journey southward. They are coming, one party after another. The female Pelican has already come on ahead, and the male follows. As he flies, he feels that his mate is already there, and he sings. His heart is lonely. Even though he is among others, he does not think of them: His heart is with the one who has gone before.

"The Pelican song has traveled ahead; has touched the high peaks of the mountains, which answer; their song is clouds the color of his feathers—gray, red, black, yellow. These curl about their summits, and as Pelican passes over them, they begin to rise, as if to meet him. He flies close over them.

"Now all the little birds on earth hear his song and begin to sing their own songs. They fly into the air and settle back, the ducks and other waterfowl.

In passing over from the northern ocean to the southern, Pelican gathers these songs. On the foot of the mountains, the deer rise and sing. By going over them, Pelican makes their places clean and plain. He takes their songs with him. Near the end of his journey, a bank of clouds the color of his feathers gathers. They make just enough room for his people to pass through; then they close behind him. Before these clouds reach the ocean, a heavy fog covers the water; this is the answer to Pelican's song."

### Song of the Grizzly Bear

*Hiya! Dawn! Hiya! Dawn is moving and passes me,*
*    going!*
*Hiya! Dawn! Hiya! Dawn is moving and passes me,*
*    going!*
*Hiya! Dawn! Hiya! Dawn is moving ————!*

*Translation:* "Grizzly Bear is wounded so badly that he is unable to live another day. He sings, meditating whether he will live to see the sun rise. At the same time, he fears to see it, because a wound is at its worst just at sunrise, and at noon, and at sunset. At those times, one feels hotter in the wound. So

Grizzly Bear fears the sunrise because it will dry his wound and the bad blood will not run out. His back is against a tree, and he looks to the east. He sees that the sun has already struck the top of the mountains. He sees the beautiful rays on the summit, then they begin to come down the mountainside, striking the tree against which he rests. As they reach the top of the tree, they become of various hues—some the color of his blood, others the color of the rainbow. The sun has passed over him many days, and each time he has become weaker. A part of his life has gone, little by little, each day."

### Song of the Eagle

*Tilting on wings, flapping, flapping, flapping, tilting on wings*
*Circling by way of song, flapping, flapping, flapping, tilting on wings.*
*Soaring, tilting on wings, hunting.*

*Translation:* "The sun is low, so that it strikes the upper part of the canyon wall. In the bottom of the canyon, the deer are browsing. When Fawn sees Eagle soaring above, he starts to run. Eagle begins to sing. When Fawn gets some distance ahead, Eagle sings and Fawn stops to listen to the song. Eagle soars over him, circling. Eagle swoops down on Fawn. Small birds of prey flock to the feast."

### Song of the Morning Star

*Has been coming, has come moving.*
*Has been coming, has come moving, moving.*
*Has been coming, has come, has come moving, moving.*
*There he is coming in this direction.*
*Crippled, he moves.*
*What the Stars sing, he has been saying.*
*Has been coming, has come moving.*

*Translation:* "The Morning Star rises, and as he goes, he strikes his foot on something in his path,

*No Wings. Nez Percé. 1910.*

and light flashes from his feet. At this, he becomes crippled. The little stars hear of his coming and gather on each side of his path, shedding the bright light through which he passes."

### Song of the Buffalo

*Aiyaiya! Traveling warily, wearily.*
*Traveling warily, traveling warily, traveling warily.*
*Wearily, I discover it is I the wolves seize and hurt.*
*Going, gone—my flesh.*
*Aiyaiya! Traveling warily, wearily, I go.*

*Translation:* "Before starting out on his journey toward the north, Buffalo blows his breath, which forms a fog that goes upward to the sky. With his hooves, he throws his dry dung up, and it becomes a heavy wind from the south, so that as he travels, the wind is behind him. The cloud accompanies him and constantly hangs over him. As he travels,

he looks carefully from side to side, with lowered head. Little whirlwinds begin to form, here and there, and create a heavier wind; the thick dust rises. His own cloud still hangs over him. All at once, unexpectedly, wolves begin to nip at his heels, and he sings, 'I have just found it is I the Wolves are after!' He begins to feel lame and sore. He continues singing and goes on, sometimes stopping to throw up more dung whenever the Wolves press him too closely. Thus he succeeds in passing them in the cloud. In the north, a long cloud comes; it is the color of his hair. He moves straight to this cloud. The only way he can escape is by going under it. Some of his flesh has been torn off. While he sings, he shakes his body side to side; blood runs from his wounds."

### Song of the Elk

*Elk! Eagle moving. Elk! Eagle moving.*
*Feet planted deep in the ground! Eagle moving.*
*Elk! Eagle moving. Elk! Eagle moving.*
*Elk! Eagle moving.*
*Tips of horns touching the ground! Eagle moving.*

*Translation:* "Eagle, and all the other predators have forced Elk into a corner. There he turns and makes his song. Above him is Eagle, wings outspread. The wolves and the other animals are pressing about Elk, trying to kill him. His legs are spread, his feet deep in the ground. His head is lowered so that his horns touch the earth. He will not die without hurting somebody. Eagle holds himself motionless in the air, watching and waiting for a chance to swoop down and take the best part for himself. Elk stands with bloody legs, torn by the wolves. His back is up against the cliff."

*Nez Percé Girl. 1910.*

Tribes of the plateau inhabited the country lying between the Rocky Mountains and the Cascades, and south of the Canadian border. The Flatheads, for example, controlled the portion of Montana in which lie the valleys of Clark Fork of the Columbia and its tributaries. The Flatheads sometimes called themselves Sinchitsuhtetuqi (Red Willow River), the name of the stream on which they lived.

There is no evidence either in history or in tradition that the Flatheads ever lived elsewhere. The tribal memory reaches back no further than the time of the head chief Skutihla, Big Hawk, at the close of the eighteenth century. He was of the Tunaha, a tribe (probably Salishan) that was nearly exterminated by smallpox. The few survivors, including the boy Big Hawk and his mother, came to live among the Flat-

*Que Que Tas. Flathead. 1905.*

heads. Big Hawk is said to have been treacherously killed by the Piegan, who first stole his bow in an apparently friendly meeting, then murdered him when he returned to recover it. This occurred in the buffalo country on the upper Missouri, and there the Flatheads remained inert for many days without a leader. Then they selected a new chief, Chehle-skaiyimi, Three Eagles. He held this position when his people first saw white men, who were the members of the Lewis and Clark Expedition. On September 4, 1805, at the head of Bitterroot River, the expedition found a camp of thirty-three lodges sheltering about four hundred inhabitants. The native recounting of the meeting is interesting:

The two captains advanced and shook hands with the chief, who commanded his people to refrain from any evildoing toward them. The white men removed the pack saddles from their horses and sat down on the ground. The chief said, "They

have no robes to sit on. Some Indians have stolen them. Bring
them robes." Buffalo skins were
brought, but, instead of sitting on
them, the white men threw them
about their shoulders. One of
their men had a black face, and
the Indians said among themselves, "See, his face is painted
black! They are going to have a
scalp dance."

Flathead horses were abundant. A herd of about five hundred belonged to them, and the
white men, after accepting the
hospitable offer of a share in
the Indians' berries (their sole
diet at that particular moment),
purchased fresh animals for the

*The Peace Officer. Kalispel. 1910.*

arduous crossing of the Bitterroot Mountains. Because of their numerous horses, the Flatheads were
constantly attacked by enemy war parties.

The country of the Flatheads
is a mountainous region, with
valleys, forests, and broad, clear
rivers. Dotting the plains and
hidden in the shadow of the
mountains are lakes. The pine
forests are scattered with sunny
glades. While they spent much
time in the buffalo country, they
relied on the game in the mountains and the fish in the streams.

The Flatheads continued to
live in their valley, and some of
them cultivated little farms, but
white men were quick to see the
desirability of the land, and they
began to settle there in ever increasing numbers. In 1871 President Grant issued an executive
order setting forth that "the Bitter Root
Valley . . . having been carefully surveyed and examined . . . has proved, in the judgement of the

*Kalispel Camp. 1910.*

President, not to be better adapted to the wants of the Flathead Tribe than the general reservation provided for . . . it is therefore ordered and directed that all Indians residing in said Bitter Root Valley be removed as soon as practicable to the reservation."

Lewis and Clark first estimated the population of the Flatheads proper at four hundred persons in thirty-three lodges. Sometime later, in 1875, there were reported eighty-one Flatheads on the reservation. More recent figures are meaningless because of the impossibility of properly classifying the children of intertribal marriages. The remnant of the Flathead tribe is probably a more heterogeneous group than any other in the Northwest. Its representatives are the offspring of marriages not only with such kindred tribes as the Pend d'Oreilles, Kalispel, Coeur d'Alenes, Spokan, Colvilles, and others, but with the Nez Percés, Shoshoni, Piegan, Tunaha, Delawares, Iroquois, and white men of various nations. Father Ravalli, who first became acquainted with the Flatheads in 1844, declared that there was not a single person in the tribe of unmixed lineage.

The Kalispel lived in northeastern Washington, in the valley of Clark Fork. Formerly, the Kalispel traveled down the river in June to spear and trap salmon at the falls below Box Canyon. In the late summer or early autumn, a party started for the buffalo country, proceeding up the stream in canoes. Boys, traveling overland, drove the horses.

The canoe trip occupied about eight days and the journey on horseback about nine. The winter was spent in the buffalo country, and in the spring the hunters started homeward with as many robes and as much meat as they could carry.

Like the Flatheads, the Kalispel were reckless fighters when aroused. In the buffalo plains there were frequent encounters with Blackfeet, Apsaroke, and Sioux. Many of their horses were obtained by raids into the territory of the Coeur d'Alenes, the Nez Percés, and the Yakima, and they were at enmity also with the Kutenai, who sometimes invaded their country for horses. It was from the Flatheads that they acquired the custom of scalping.

In 1844 Father Hoecken established St. Ig-

*A Flathead Chief. 1910.*

natius Mission at the mouth of Mission Creek and began to teach the Kalispel the meaning of Christianity. In 1854, on account of the annual floods in the valley, the mission was moved to Ravalli, Montana. The majority of the two hundred or more Kalispel accompanied the priests.

Cabins dotted the valley on the eastern side of the river for a distance of some fifteen miles southward from Mission Creek. Timothy planted by the priests took possession of the meadows, which yielded the hay upon which the people depended. Each summer, they pitched small lodges in a meadow opposite Cusick, Washington, where some semblance of their former life could be observed. The smoke curled upward from a dozen tepees.

*Flathead Horse Trappings. 1910.*

Women, old and young, scattered over the fields plying their root diggers and filling their baskets with camas bulbs. A bark canoe would slip silently through the water toward the paddler's favorite fishing ground, and on the sloping grassy bank, among other upturned canoes, another boatman would bend over his craft, deftly caulking its seams with spruce gum.

*Two Kalispel Myths*

*The Origin of Death*—Coyote's daughter fell sick and died. As he wandered about mourning, he came to a little hill, from the top of which he saw a stream below and signs that someone was living there. Going down, he saw two long lodges on the other side and heard the sounds of a gambling game. He called out, "Take me across!" But no answer came. Then he lay down on the shore and became sleepy. He yawned, and someone hearing him said, "Somebody is calling."

Still no one paid any attention to him. He continued to lie there, wondering, How am I going to make them hear me and bring me over?

Now, the next time he yawned, people looked out of the lodges and said, "Someone is calling. Go and bring him over." Coyote then saw someone start out from the other side. When the person got to him, he saw that it was his own daughter, the one who had recently died.

"What are you doing here?" she asked as he stepped into the boat.

Coyote saw that the canoe was merely a framework of bark. His daughter told him to close his eyes. He obeyed, but halfway across the stream he thought, I should like to know how things are going. He opened one eye, and the boat began to fill. His daughter said sharply, "Shut that eye or we'll sink." He did as ordered, and soon they landed and went to the lodge. It was empty; the gamblers were playing in the one near to it. Coyote was most curious to see how the game was played, but his daughter told him he should not look at it. He answered, "Don't worry, I'll stay here with you."

However, as he said this, he was thinking that he would go look at the game. Shortly, he fell asleep, and when he awoke, sometime later, he again heard the sounds of the game. By now, it was daylight. Now, since his daughter was still sleeping, he got up quietly and went into the other lodge, where he saw that there were two groups of people. Both had their hair tied up on their heads, with some sort of weed in the knots. Seeing that one side had no good players, he decided to join them, and he sat down in the crowd, but they paid no attention to him.

Coyote wondered why the people ignored him. Then he decided to make himself look like they did by tying a piece of weed in his hair. By and by, his side was almost beaten, and Coyote began to make the right guesses, choosing the correct hand each time it came up.

When it was his turn, he started the song and juggled the bones, and at last, he had all the counters except one. However, it was at that very moment that his daughter awakened and heard her father's voice. She came in just as the team opposing Coyote guessed and lost their last stick, at which time they all fell over dead.

Coyote's daughter cried, "Those are my children and your grandchildren whom you have killed. Why did you not obey me when I told you not to come over here? You have killed them. If they had won, you and your side would have died, and then we would have escaped from this place of the dead."

After saying this, she called Coyote to her lodge and showed him a large bag. She told him he must go home and take the bag with him; also that he must not open it before getting to the top of the hill on the other side of the stream. Coyote promised, and putting the bag on his back, he started for the canoe. Once on the other side of the stream, Coyote put the heavy bag on his back and set out; however, something was in it that hurt his shoulder.

On the way up the hill, feeling hot and sweaty, he stopped to rest. Sitting there, he wondered what was in the bag. Finally, he untied it. "I will just peep in and tie it back up again," he said. But the moment the bag was opened, a child leapt out and ran off. Coyote followed as fast as he could. The child was too fast, however, and Coyote went back to the bag, only to see another child jump out. This one, too, he pursued but could not catch. Returning again to the bag, he saw a third child leap out, and a fourth, both

*Flathead Buffalo-skin Lodge. 1910.*

*Shirt. Kalispel.
1910.*

*Chief of the Land.
Kalispel. 1910.*

*Kalispel Maiden.
1910.*

of whom got away. This time, when he got back to the bag, he found it empty. Now he decided that he had better go back to his daughter and tell her what he had done. So he returned to the stream and looked across. But he could see nobody there, nor could he hear a sound. At the landing place, he called loudly, but he received no answer. A second shout brought his daughter from her lodge, and she called, "Didn't I tell you not to look into the bag?"

And that was how poor Coyote released Death's children into the world.

*The Whippoorwill*—Coyote was once coming from the buffalo country, and near Flathead Lake he found a camp, whose people said, "There is a dangerous place down below, where you are likely to be killed. You had better go around it." "No," Coyote said, "I would rather be killed. I will go through."

Continuing his journey, he came to some thick timber, and he plucked a large tamarack to carry with him. This he bore crosswise on his back. Shortly, he came to the end of a narrow gulch. There, the tamarack on his back got caught. Coy-

ote turned, loosened it, and went on. Then he met some people, who told him that he had been swallowed by a dangerous monster. "What monster?" he asked. "We have all been swallowed by this creature," they explained. "You see, it takes the form of this gulch we're standing in."

Now Coyote knew he was really in trouble, and he began to cry. But the others said, "Coyote, you are wise. You ought to know some way to get us out of this." "I will do something," he said, and after that, he went a little distance and deposited his medicine spirits (his feces) on the ground in four places, and the four turds sat there and said to him, "You are dying because you are in a dangerous place."

"What can I do?" Coyote asked.

The fourth turd, the wisest, said, "I am going to be a sharp spear."

The third said, "I am going to be a drum."

The second said, "I am going to be a large hoop."

Then the first said, "I will be yet another hoop."

So Coyote went back to the people and proposed a war dance. Soon, the dance began. After placing two hoops in position, one at each end of the evil gulch, Coyote found the monster's heart, and he told the people that as soon as he thrust his spear into it, they should run out of the gulch as fast as they could.

Then Coyote began to leap around, lunging three times at the gulch's heart. With a quick jab, he pushed the spear into it and shouted, "All run out!" Everyone escaped except Wood Tick, who was caught in the rock jaws of the creature as the hoop in its mouth slipped. Still, Wood Tick managed to squeeze out, and ever since that day, he has been thin and flat.

After the gulch beast was dead, he turned into a huge whippoorwill. Coyote stood by, and, raising the enormous dead bird, he said, "In the future, you shall not kill people. And when you sound your voice, which shall be only at night, the women will say to their children, 'Be quiet, or Whippoorwill will come for you!'"

Then he threw the bird across the river. The rocks where it fell began to turn yellow. After this, Coyote took the branch off his back and planted it in the ground. "There," he said, "you will be Tamarack Tree."

And that bristly, friendly tree is still there, the only tamarack in that part of the world.

# IV—THE NORTHWEST COAST

The Coastal Salish and Kwakiutl tribes that Curtis visited and recorded were, in a sense, within his "neck of the woods," as his studio was located in Seattle. He enjoyed the Puget Sound country very much, and these people were an extension of it, their territory covering the island shores and spruce coasts of Washington and British Columbia.

As he explains here, the tribes of the coastal Salish surrounding Puget Sound spoke a dialect of Nisqually, one of the principal tribes of this group. It is fitting, therefore, that the myth thus presented is Nisqually. A story of ancient days depicting a visit into the land of the dead, the world of ghosts, the narrative bears much resemblance to other northern tales of the area, namely the Tsimshian.

Curtis's passion for Kwakiutl tribes is well known, since he nearly lost his life filming a "living myth" on the open waters of a Kwakiutl village. The fjorded coast intrigued him, serrated, as he said, with its irregular flow of toothlike islands separated by channels of deep, clear water. Here, during his lifetime, the ancient rhythms were yet alive and well, the heartbeat of some lost time still palpably near.

The myths of the Kwakiutl are serene, heroically dramatic, and intensely poetic, and Curtis captured them with the consummate grace of the familiar observer. In fact, the ease with which he writes of these people gives the impression that no language barrier existed between him and his tribal informants. In addition, his anthropological interest in Kwakiutl cosmetics, clothing, diet, and ancestral house building gives a rare glimpse into a culture that has since lost its way into the debilitating vagaries of the modern world.

**Coastal Salish History**

The country of the Coastal Salish extends over 250 miles from north to south, and a hundred miles from east to west. It follows the low-lying shores of Shoalwater Bay (Willapa Harbor) and Grays Harbor; the lofty prairies between Cowlitz River and the head of Puget Sound; the deep waters of that inland sea and the maze of islands between the Strait of Juan de Fuca and the Strait of Georgia; the lowlands of the deltas of such rivers as the Skagit, the Nooksack, and the Fraser; the serrated coasts of British Columbia beyond the Fraser and of the lower eastern portion of Vancouver Island. Everywhere the land is clothed in huge fir, spruce, cedar, and a dense, matted undergrowth of vines and bushes.

The sandy beaches slope back to the forest from the desolate tide flats with their wheeling squadrons of screaming gulls,

*Hami. Koskimo. 1914.*

and the snow peaks, far above the timberline, point at the sun.

In a land of such variety, a certain diversity of habit in its people is to be expected. Thus the bands living about Shoalwater Bay and the Cowlitz on Cowlitz River intermarried with the Chinook, their neighbors on the south, and were considerably influenced by the culture of that tribe. The Quinault, on the contrary, though closely related to the Shoalwater Bay people, differed considerably from their relations in that they were the only whaling tribe of the Salishan stock. They acquired this hunting skill from the next tribe on the north, the Quilliute, who in turn had it from the Makah of Cape Flattery.

The myriad tribes on the shores and the tributary streams of Puget Sound, Hood Canal, and the waters immediately northward were quite homogenous in their habits, yet the Nisqually, on the river of that name, found in their grassy prairies an incentive to acquire horses. Alone among the Coastal Salish, they—without abandoning their aboriginal aquatic pursuits—developed a culture that was part equestrian. Finally, the Cowichan group on Vancouver Island bears many resemblances to the Kwakiutl tribes, who possess a culture quite markedly different from the normal Salishan one.

A host of small bands of Salish Indians inhabited the country surrounding Puget Sound, its islands, and the valleys of its tributary streams, as well as the shores immediately north of Puget Sound. All spoke variations of what is known as the Nisqually dialect (so called from one of the principal tribes using it), yet in spite of the close linguistic, geographical, and cultural relationship, there were no political ties among them. Some of these tribes still exist; others, extinct, have left a memento of themselves in geographical names; some are known only as names recorded by an early traveler or remembered by an aged survivor of the native population. Prominent tribes of this group were the Squaxon, Sahewamish, Suquamish, Nisqually, Puyallup, Dwamish, Samamish, Snoqualmu, Snohomish, Stillaquamish, and Skagit.

In December 1854, at the Council of Medicine Creek, the Squaxon, Nisqually, and Puyallup entered into a treaty with the United States, ceding all their lands to the government and accepting as their reservations Squaxon Island, two sections of land on Puget Sound at the mouth of McAllister Creek, and two sections on what is now the site of Tacoma. On these reserves, comprising an area of less than four thousand acres, were to be assembled a population estimated by Governor Isaac I. Stevens, the Indian superintendent and treaty commissioner, at about twelve hundred people. Ludicrously inadequate in area, these lands were, for the greater part, totally unsuited to the needs of the Indians. This was especially true of the proposed Nisqually Reservation at the mouth of McAllister Creek, a heavily wooded tract at the top of a high bluff.

Now the Nisqually gained their livelihood by two principal industries: They obtained clams and other marine foods in the waters at the mouth of their river; on the inland prairies of its valley, they pastured a considerable number of horses. To give up those lands and move within the narrow confines of the wooded bluff assigned them meant the loss of all their wealth, and was little better than self-destruction. The Nisqually, therefore, pro-

*Masked Dancer. Cowichan. 1912.*

tested, and their chief, Leschi, after vainly opposing the plan, angrily tore up the commission as
chief that the governor had given
him, hurled the pieces to the
ground before the governor's eyes,
and left the council.

The treaty was signed, and the
third name is "Lesh-high." Nevertheless, to the day of his execution,
Leschi firmly maintained that he
had never signed that treaty, and
all the other Indians who were
present affirmed then, and the survivors have never ceased to affirm,
that such was the case.

It is not intended to assert here
that the name of the Nisqually
chief was forged to the document
with the knowledge or consent of
Governor Stevens, although such
a thing has been done. The following is significant:

*Family Party. Puget Sound. 1912.*

"Senator L. F. Thompson, who at the time lived
within two miles of the council grounds when the
treaty was made, wrote: 'After the treaty was over
the Indians came to me and said that Leschi would
not sign the treaty for the Nisquallys and
Puyallups. They were the Indians Leschi represented. But Leschi was told that if he did not sign
it, it would be signed for him. From what the Indians told me at the time and from what the whites
told me, I am positive that Leschi never signed the
treaty.'"

A month after these events, in January 1855,
the Duwamish and Snohomish, and the Skagit, as
well as the more northerly Samish, Lummi, and
Nooksack—all the tribes, in fact, between Duwamish River and the Canadian border—entered
into a treaty at Point Elliott, Washington. Governor Stevens was somewhat more liberal than he
had been at Medicine Creek, apportioning reservations embracing about 2,800 acres among some
five thousand people. The lands reserved were,
moreover, much better adapted to Indian use.

But though the treaty was more generous, it
stated that ultimately all these tribes would be concentrated on Tulalip Reservation. This was in the
very heart of the territory of the Snohomish and
the Snoqualmu, warlike tribes, and hostile toward
the bands of Duwamish River and its tributaries.
Of these the principal bands, besides the Duwamish, were the Muckleshoot and the Stukamish,
who in addition to their fear of the Snohomish and
the Snoqualmu felt reluctant to leave their streams
and exchange a hunting life for marine pursuits
with which they were unfamiliar. It was here that
the first act of hostility west of the Cascade Mountains was perpetrated.

As a direct result of Governor Stevens's treaty
with the interior Columbia River tribes at Walla
Walla, war broke out, the first act being the assas-
sination of three miners by members of the Kittitas
tribe, a Salish group near the head of Yakima
River. Shortly after this, a detachment of volunteers went to arrest Leschi and his brother, in the
belief that this course would restrain the Nisqually
and perhaps altogether avert war on the coast. But
the chiefs, probably apprised of the movement,
hurriedly left their home, abandoning a plow in the
furrow and their herds of horses on the prairie.

One of the volunteers, reconnoitering the position of a camp on White River, near Seattle, was shot, and on the following day, October 28, 1855, several families of settlers on that stream were massacred. Hostilities continued into March of 1856. There were several minor encounters, including an abortive attack on the well-guarded village of Seattle. The difficulties of campaigning in the dense, wet forests of western Washington in a Puget Sound winter can hardly be imagined. Once again, if the Indians had possessed the fighting nature of the Plains Indians, they could easily have cleared the territory of every white inhabitant.

Leschi counseled the Nisqually to scatter in small bands among the

*Going for Clams. Quinault. 1912.*

mountains, and with his brother, Qaiemuhl, he took refuge among the tribes of Yakima Valley. Gradually, the Indians, under the promise of amnesty, were induced to return to their homes, to be gathered on temporary reservations. But for Leschi and Qaiemuhl, Ktsap, the Muckleshoot chief, and Stehai, the son of Leschi's aunt, no pardon was offered. Governor Stevens requested the army officers to arrest these leaders, but they refused to do so. Then a reward for their capture was offered, and the lure was effective. Leschi and Qaiemuhl had recrossed the mountains, intending to return to their home as soon as it appeared safe, and their whereabouts were known to the Indians. Two men, Sluggia and Wapoati, determined to win the reward. The former was related to Leschi. They visited the chief, intoxicated and bound him, and delivered him to the authorities. Qaiemuhl, hearing of his brother's capture, gave himself up at Olympia, where, during the night, his temporary prison was entered and he was fatally stabbed by an unknown man. After two trials and a bitter and protracted controversy between the military and the civil branch of the government, Leschi was convicted of murder and hanged in February 1858. It is of some satisfaction to note that the traitor,

Sluggia, was killed by Yelm Jim, a friend of Leschi's. The avenger was imprisoned for a while, but he escaped further punishment.

In the end, adequate reservations were proposed for the Nisqually and the Puyallup, and a small tract on White River was set aside for the Muckleshoot and the Stukamish.

## A Nisqually Myth

*The Girl Who Married a Ghost* — In ancient days, on a sheltered bay near the ocean, there was a small, well-kept village. The man of greatest wealth and highest rank was no less renowned for his thrift and force of character than for his three beautiful daughters. The eldest was the most beautiful, and, therefore, the most sought in marriage. From near and far came parents and relatives of ardent suitors seeking the consent of the chief to the marriage of his daughters. However, to all promises of lavish gifts, the old man turned a deaf ear; he was happy with his family, and as for wealth, he needed no more than he had.

Thus, matters continued until the hatred and

enmity of the surrounding villages were aroused. It became an openly expressed wish that something dire might befall the stubborn chief. In fact, when he had last refused to part with his eldest daughter, the visitors had angrily denounced him and said they hoped the ghosts would come and buy her and carry her to the land of the dead. To this, the old man gave no heed. But not long afterward, from out on the ocean one night, came the sound of voices singing gay, rollicking songs. The sounds drew nearer, and the chief and his family saw many canoes laden with people—a bridegroom's wedding party. They landed, made known their wishes, and so great were their numbers and so rich their proffered gifts that the chief was unable to refuse them. Thus he gave consent for the marriage of his eldest daughter to a handsome, richly dressed young man.

The wedding ceremony occupied the greater part of the night, yet long before dawn the visiting multitude and the bride embarked and paddled away into the darkness, singing exultantly. Out across the waters, they paddled until lost from sight and sound. Whither they were bound, nor who they truly were, the chief and his family did not know, yet strangely they felt no misgivings.

Before many hours, the wedding guests approached land. They disembarked and went their various ways. To the girl, it was yet somewhat dark; still she could readily distinguish objects. On every hand were groups of people playing games, some gambling with marked bones, others with wooden disks, some playing shinny, and others shooting arrows at a rolling hoop. As far as she could see, there were people everywhere, all boisterously happy. She accompanied her husband to a great house in which dwelt many besides himself. Side by side on the raised platform around the base of the walls slept great numbers of children. The portion of the house to which her husband led her was screened off by broad rush mats; soft mats and many blankets covered their bed. It was time to sleep, her husband said; and indeed, after the long night of excitement and travel, she was glad to retire.

When the young wife awoke, the sun was several hours high, but not a sound greeted her. She thought this odd, recalling the crowds of people she had seen, and she turned to look at her husband, whose head rested on her arm. To her unspeakable horror, she found herself gazing into the empty sockets of a grinning skull. What had been a handsome young man was a skeleton. Without moving her arm, she raised herself on her elbow and peered about. The rows of sleeping children were now rows of whitened bones. Was she dreaming? The bedding was dirty and old and worn to shreds. The great house was smoke-begrimed and almost ready to fall; only her own apparel remained as it had been when she went to sleep.

*Warrior's Feather Headdress. Cowichan. 1912.*

*A Cowichan Mask. 1912.*

But the sight of the water gave her hope: She would take a canoe and paddle away, and in time find her home. So thick were the bones on the ground that she had occasionally to push them aside with her foot that she might avoid treading on them. She could see the prows of canoes above the line of beach gravel, and to them she carefully threaded her way. However, now she discovered that the crafts were old, weather-seamed, decayed, moss-grown, and full of holes. One after another, she pushed them into the water, only to see them fill and sink. Then her heart broke and she collapsed on the gravel and sobbed bitterly. The crying relieved her feelings and she arose more resolute, if not less bewildered. She bathed her face and dried it and then looked about. Far down the beach where a point of land jutted into the water, a wisp of whitish smoke curled upward. A ray of hope lifted her heart; the girl turned and went toward the smoke. All along the shore, beside canoes, on beached logs, and on the gravel reefs above high tide, rested the bones of the dead. She wondered if life existed anywhere on that terrible shore. The hope of this, however small, emboldened the girl and she made her way carelessly, stepping on bones, kicking them out of her way.

She proceeded slowly, at best, and the distance was greater than she expected. The sun, it seemed, had long fallen on a downward course when she finally reached the spot above which the smoke was rising. There she found a small old woman whose back was turned toward her as she sat weaving baskets from hair. A basket cap was on her head. Without looking up, the little woman remarked, "You are the one they brought down yesterday, aren't you, child?"

The voice the girl heard was Screech Owl's. Meanwhile, not turning around, the old woman's fingers flew at their work. In despair, the poor girl started to cry. And, once again, the old woman spoke in her shrill owl's voice. "You do not understand," she said. "You do not know where you are or what to do. This is the land of the ghost people, to which come those who die upon the earth. When you came, it was night upon earth, and that is the time when the ghosts are active. At sunrise, they go to sleep. They have no bodies at night, and by day

Slowly, it dawned on her that she had been entrapped by some evil magic, and she began to think of escape. She feared to look again at what had been her husband, nor dared to disturb it; yet she must escape. Slowly, carefully, she moved her arm until it was free, and as the skull slipped from the crook of her elbow, it dropped upon the blanket and turned on its side. Then she arose and dressed hurriedly. With difficulty, she picked her way among the bones and the musty utensils and clothing to the doorway. There she was greeted by another gruesome sight. Strewn about in groups were endless numbers of skeletons—bones, everywhere bones, up and down the shore as far as she could see—at whatever game and in whatever position the ghosts had been overtaken by daylight.

they lie about as bones. You must do but one thing: Sleep when they sleep and wake when they wake, and all will be well. You see, you woke too soon — when you should have slept. All these people whose skeletons you have stepped on will soon begin to move about. Their time draws near."

Now the girl passed the rest of the afternoon with Screech Owl Old Woman, learning much about the people among whom she had married. As the sun sank and shadows deepened into twilight,

*Carved Figure. Cowichan. 1912.*

the sound of faint voices came from the distance, swelling gradually into choruses of singing and shouting. The ghosts soon noticed her absence, and knowing that Screech Owl Old Woman was the only person she might find to converse with in daylight, they came running down that way.

They found her readily enough, but some of them were incensed, scolding and gesticulating wildly. Their anger, the girl soon discovered, was due to the fact that she had maimed many of the *skaiyu* on her way from the village to the home of Screech Owl Old Woman, for every time she had moved a bone, she had severely injured a ghost, and where she had pushed aside a whole skeleton, that ghost had died. An angry crowd surrounded her. "You have killed so many of us," they cried. "You have sunk our canoes in the water. But worst of all, you nearly killed your own husband by twisting off his head!"

Now the girl was frightened and said nothing. But Screech Owl Old Woman scolded the ghosts for not telling the girl what land this was and not explaining how to live with them. Thus silenced, the angry people turned to go, and the girl quietly accompanied them. They passed many others attending to the wounded. Some were beyond remedy; others had knees twisted, ribs displaced, arms disjointed, feet missing. Her husband was recovering from his own near-fatal mishap. From that time on, though, the girl was careful to listen to the wisdom of Screech Owl.

Time passed, and there was born to the young wife a baby boy, of whom she was most proud. But this arrival of one who was neither *skaiyu* nor human troubled the ghosts. They decided to take the mother and her child back to her earthly home, and accordingly, those who had composed the wedding party again voyaged to the earth.

It was dark when they reached the shore where her people lived, but her parents, apprised by the distant sound of singing, had built a great fire that lighted the whole house. They were delighted to see their daughter and her child. "A fine baby, a pretty boy," they cried as they passed him from one to another. For twelve days, the *skaiyu* told the child's mother, she must not unwrap the baby on his cradle board by daylight, else he would change and would have to be returned to ghost land. After this warning, the ghost people silently withdrew.

For eleven days, the young mother watched her little boy. Each day she went to the woods to gather moss and cedar bark, which she shredded and used as pads for the cradle board. On the twelfth day, she remained absent a long time, and her mother, curious to see whether this child brought from ghost land was like other children, unlaced the wrappings. Raising the blanket, she was shocked to discover the bones of a little skeleton. Then she indignantly cast the bones and the cradle board out of the house.

*Quinault Female Type. 1912.*

At that instant, the young mother began to feel ill, and she hurried home to see what was the matter with her child. When she found the cradle board on the ground and the little bones scattered in the sunlight, she was at once angry and brokenhearted. "Mother," she said sadly, "one more day and my child might have lived happily on earth."

That night, the *ɩkaiyu* came for the mother and child.

"I must go now," she told her parents. But she also told them she would return to earth once more. And she did—one night with many of the ghost people. After singing out on the water for a time, they finally paddled away into the mist and were not seen again.

To this day, the people lament when they think of the child who could have lived on earth or in the country of ghosts. It is sad, they say, that so much should have been lost, all because of a curious old woman. But then they also add, "Anyone might have done it," and they content themselves with listening to the hoarse cries of Screech Owl Old Woman, who, though she is without child, still travels between the worlds of sleep and wake, night and day, life and death.

*Still Life. Puget Sound. 1912.*

# KWAKIUTL

*Kwakiutl History*

Broadly speaking, the name Kwakiutl is used to designate a large number of related tribes on the coast of British Columbia. In the south, the Kwakiutl come in contact with the Salish of Vancouver Island and the mainland north of Fraser River, while farther north an isolated Salish group, the Bellacoola, juts down to salt water in the midst of Kwakiutl territory. In the extreme north, the Kwakiutl are neighbors of the Tsimshian tribes and of the Haida of Queen Charlotte Islands.

The physical characteristics of the region are remarkable. Innumerable fjords cut deeply into the mainland. For the greater part, their shores are steep and rocky, even mountainous. But here and there, usually at the mouth of a stream, there is enough low, level land for a village site. In the fjords and off the mainland coast are countless islands, all rocky and clothed in evergreen forests; they are separated by narrow, intricate

*Nunalalahl. Qagyuhl. 1914.*

channels of deep, clear water. On such islands are many of the Kwakiutl villages. Close to the mainland, from northwest to southeast, Vancouver Island stretches its three-hundred-mile length, protecting the smaller islands from heavy storms and rendering the channels safe for canoes. North of this sheltering landmass, the winds from the open Pacific sweep unchecked into Queen Charlotte Sound and up into Hecate Strait, but the natives find safe passage in the narrow waterways behind the small islands that skirt the shore. Less fortunate are those about the unsheltered northern end of Vancouver Island, who in rough weather must either remain ashore or restrict their movements to the quiet waters of their home bay or inlet. On the mainland, as on Vancouver Island, the mountains come close to the sea, and with few exceptions, the inhabitants are inevitably marine people.

It is an inhospitable country, with its forbidding rockbound coasts, its dark, tangled, mysterious forests, its beetling mountains, its long, gloomy season of rains and fogs. No less inhospitable, mysterious, and gloomy, to the casual observer, is the character of the inhabitants. They seem constantly lost in dark broodings, and it is only after long acquaintance and the slow process of gaining their confidence that one discovers an uncertain thread of cheerfulness interwoven in the somber fabric of their nature.

Until comparatively recent times, the universal garment for both sexes was a scarcely ankle-length robe of woven cedar bark or of fur, worn as a rule about both shoulders and tied at the throat, the edges hanging unconfined. Men sometimes carried the robe in a roll thrown across the shoulder, or wore it wrapped about the waist, with the upper corners tucked in under the roll. At work, men and women fastened the robe at one side so as to leave either shoulder

*At Memkumlis. 1914.*

*Nakoaktok Warrior. 1914.*

and arm free, while a girdle of cedar withes or woven goat-hair yarn held it at the waist. Still in use, though its significance, once literal, long ago became figurative, is the expression "gird yourself"— get ready for work. Not infrequently, men worked stark naked on the beach or in the village streets. Women, however, outside the comparative privacy of the family, were never seen without the robe, except in performing certain dances of the winter ceremony. Furthermore, they always wore a narrow knee-length apron of cedar-bark fringe or goat-hair cords hanging from a girdle of the same material.

Fur robes, which were used only by the "upper class," were made of the skins of such animals as mink, marten, raccoon, marmot, beaver, sea otter, and black bear. Sea-otter skins, which were reserved for persons of the very highest rank, were the only fur used by women. Only in exceptionally cold weather was the fur worn next to the body. A garment of marten skin was expensive and could not be purchased without a partial payment of a slave. The mink-skin or marten-skin robe consisted of three rows of pelts, each row containing seven or eight skins arranged side by side. The four skins at the neck of the garment were unsplit so that they formed a ruff with fur on both sides, and the tails hung free. Marmot skins were highly valued because the fur is full and soft, and, though the animals were numerous in the mountains, the season of prime fur is short.

A seamless waterproof cape of woven cedar bark with a fur-edged opening for the head was worn in rainy weather; and as a shield from rain and excessive heat, both sexes still sometimes use a hat woven from twisted strips of cedar bark. The cylindrical crown and the broad, drooping rim lack the painted designs of the chief's hat, which is covered with conventional figures of the wearer's ancestral crest and, perhaps, of his personal vision spirits. This finely woven spruce-root hat was borrowed from the Haida about the year 1860.

Moccasins were worn only in very cold weather. They were made of single pieces of deerskin or mountain-goat skin and were worn with the hair inside. Hip-length leggings of woven cedar bark were worn by men of the Haqisla and the Bellabella when traveling through deep snow in the woods.

Men had the hair thrown back from the forehead and hanging down the back. At the nape of the neck, it was tied, sometimes with a braid of a sweet-smelling grass, and below this it hung loosely. The present custom is to cut it short. Some remove the beard; others permit it to grow. Most men have little hair on the face, but not a few have a considerable growth. As a bit of ornamental dress, the entire unslit skin of a mink or a marten was worn as a headband, the tail and the head meeting behind.

The hair of women, parted in the middle, down to the nape of the neck, hangs in two braids in front of the shoulders, the ends being tied with fragrant grass or with goat-hair yarn.

Young dandies of the Quatsino Sound tribes brought the hair around from the sides, tied the two strands over the forehead, put a sprig of cedar through the nasal septum, and turned the cedar-bark robe with the opening at the back; and so, holding the edges together with the hands behind the back, they would strut about, singing love songs in order to excite the admiration of the girls.

The most valued ornaments of the wealthy class were ear pendants and nose rings of abalone shell. The former varied in size from a small square bit no larger than a thumbnail to a great piece as broad as a man's hand, while the nasal ornament was a circular ring with a narrow opening that permitted it to pass over the septum of the nose, which was not always pierced. The largest pendants, too heavy to be supported by the ears, were tied to the hair braids. As the abalone shells of British Columbia are fragile and of inferior luster, they are not suitable for this use. Respecting the source of these comparatively rare ornaments, it is related that about 1840 a Tsimshian man sailed to Oahu, Hawaii, aboard a trading ship on which he frequently had served as pilot. When he returned, he brought several boxes of large abalone shells, which he sold among the northern tribes, whence many of them were obtained by the Kwakiutl.

Bracelets, anklets, and necklaces consisted of rows of dentalium shells sewn on deerskin. Bands

*A Koskimo Dandy. 1914.*

woven from mountain-goat hair by means of a set of interlacing teeth cut into two pieces of yew were worn by females from infancy, in order to keep the feet small. Woolen strips are now generally used for this purpose.

Tattooing was not general. It was performed usually on the arm in memory of one's lover, and commonly took the form of one's family crest. A bone splinter and charcoal of tules were used in the operation.

The superstructure of a Kwakiutl house is supported by heavy cedar posts. In the notched tops of the hewn side posts, usually six in number, rest two eave timbers extending from the rear to the front. Another hewn post supports the ends of the gable timbers in the rear wall, and two others perform a similar service at the sides of the door in the front wall. The eave timbers are a handbreadth in thickness and about twenty inches in width. The front end of the ridge timber rests on a heavy crosspiece connecting the tops of two massive columns, while the rear end is supported directly by a single post. These three interior posts stand well inside the front and rear lines of the house. From ridge to eaves extend numerous rafters, which are crossed by a series of battens. The roof boards extend in the direction of the rafters, and formerly were slightly guttered and applied like tile. They are held down only by their own weight, or, in stormy weather, by the addition of heavy stones—being left unfastened in order that they may easily be removed by means of a pole to permit the escape of smoke.

The "poorer class" laid the wall boards horizontally and secured them with cedar withes between pairs of upright poles. Not a few houses are now constructed throughout of mill lumber.

A striking feature of almost every building of the old style is the carving of the interior posts to represent mythical beasts and birds. As late as 1865, houses with carved posts were by no means numerous, and the original of each was believed to have been given by some supernatural being to an ancient ancestor of the family. Carved posts have become increasingly common, the authority to make use of some certain house frame being one of the most valued rights transferred in marriage.

When a man is about to build a new house, he reveals his intention at some public gathering and requests certain chiefs to bring the timbers, which, by inherited custom, it is their exclusive right to provide. Every step in the undertaking is accompanied by a feast and a distribution of presents to workers and spectators. When the materials are brought in, there is a feast. When they are moved from beach to building site, there is a feast. In short, whenever any single portion of the work is accomplished, there follows a feast, and no more labor is performed on that day. He must be a very rich man who can finish a house within four years.

When at length the house is complete, the tribe is invited to a feast and distribution, an occasion that, in allusion to the great blazing fire in the center of the room, is figuratively called "drying the house." Later there may occur a second drying of the house, to which all the tribes are invited. Only

*Naemahlpunkuma-Hahuamis. 1914.*

a man of very high rank can erect a dwelling in this ostentatious manner, and generally he finds himself overwhelmed with debts. On account of the great additional expense, a winter dance very seldom celebrates the completion of a house.

The members of the household commonly sleep on the floor near the fire, or on the platform. In some of the Kwakiutl tribes, the homes of the upper class had a number of small private bedrooms, exactly like a fairly commodious kennel, raised on scaffolds above the floor. These were most frequently the possessions of young men and young women. Other tribes had, and still have, such bedrooms resting on the floor, so that in cold weather they may be carried close to the fire. Not infrequently, the eldest daughter of a family of rank, especially before marriage, had in one of the rear corners a private room walled off from the common quarters. Here she would spend much of her time in proud seclusion.

Most of the Kwakiutl villages stand on the grassy terrace just above the beach gravel of some sheltered cove, with the tangled forest directly behind. Overlooking the water, the inhabitants were surprised by an enemy only with difficulty; but if perchance a sudden attack was made, they could flee through the rear of the houses into the thicket and lie hidden while the raiders pillaged and burned. Nearly every village had a fortified refuge at the top of an inaccessible rocky hill (in many cases an islet), where the inhabitants could dwell in comparative security during the "fighting season"—that is, from about the middle of August until the first of October, when, the water being smooth and the weather usually foggy, conditions were most favorable for war parties.

Of all the arts and industries practiced by the Kwakiutl tribes, none reached a higher development than the art of working in wood. The principal phase of this work—the making of cedar planks—has become obsolete because the necessity that mothered the art no longer exists; but splendid canoes, serviceable, watertight chests, ponderous feasting dishes, ingenious masks, and a host of indispensable utensils are made every day with the most elementary tools.

The manner in which the Kwakiutl approached

*Nimkish Village at Alert Bay. 1914.*

the art of working in wood is a story all by itself. For example, the standing tree from which boards were split was called "begged from," and it is said that, since trees have sentient life, before cutting it, a man would look upward to the tree and say, "We have come to beg a piece of you today. Please! We hope you will let us have a piece of you." The same request was made of a yew tree before cutting off a piece for making tools. But when a tree was to be cut down, it was "killed" without words. Sometimes one sees a great cedar with a circular hole about ten inches in diameter chiseled straight into

*At Kwaustums Village. 1914.*

stern was cut square and was very wide at the top so that two men could sit on it side by side. The prow rose in some cases to a height of eight feet, spreading at the tip into two hornlike projections, with a hooked beak at the front to represent an eagle. Sometimes the beak was omitted, and eagle tails were carved on the sides of the prow. This prow piece, which was a heavy burden for two men, was laced to the hull, and against a head wind the rope stitches were cut and the prow was hauled aboard. The largest craft of this kind held twenty-five men, two on a thwart. This form of vessel was used by war parties, and the high, wide prow afforded good protection.

the heart. This was done in order to test the soundness of the tree. Apparently, little labor could have been saved by this procedure, and the purpose may have been to spare the tree, if it was unfit for cutting, and let it stand to continue making bark.

Canoe making is still a flourishing industry of the Kwakiutl. In a certain myth, we find evidence that the first canoe was a log very slightly hollowed with fire and rudely tapered at the ends. But so unstable was it that a cedar-bark canoe was invented. A large sheet of bark was spread on the ground, and at each end for the width of three fingers the rough outer bark was scraped off. The sheet was then steamed over hot stones until it was pliable, and at each end the edge was puckered and tied. Thus was formed a craft with the rough bark inside. The next form evolved was a dugout with a low prow and a perpendicular cutwater. Some traditionalists say that the stern of this model was cut square; others say that it was like the prow.

Among the tribes of Quatsino Sound, there was in use as late as 1865 the *munka*, a long, narrow craft, the shell of which was so thick that it could not be spread by heated water and steam. The

When a canoe builder works steadily during the summer in order to finish, let us say, four canoes before the winter dance begins, he becomes very thin. It is said that the strong odor of the cedar, especially noticeable in a log that is moist inside, "fills him up," so that he eats only once a day, after returning home in the evening from the woods. Sometimes the exhalations arising from the heart of a moist cedar log will make the eyes water because they are so strong.

It is believed that the spirits of all hunters of the sea—that is, those who wield the spear—become killer whales; hence, nobody in his senses would think of killing one of these mammals. The spirits of land hunters become wolves; hence, no wolf is killed. When anybody chances to find a dead wolf in the woods, he sits down and pretends to cry, scratching his face and praying. An Indian hunter with his steersman once came upon the body of a wolf. He described the incident this way:

"We sat down, one on each side of the wolf, and pretended to cry and scratch our faces, not by moving the hands but by moving the head up and down with the elbows propped on the knees. My steersman said, 'We must bury our friend.' I, being a young man and ignorant of these matters, asked, 'Who is going to put a blanket about him?'

"'You, of course,' he answered. 'You are the spearman.'

"I objected: 'If you do the praying, you will get the luck from him and I will be out of it.'

"'Oh, no,' he replied, 'I will pray for both of us.'

"I took my blanket, the one I wore around my legs in the canoe, and spread it on the ground. He went to the tail of the animal and I to the head, and we pretended to lift it, and the fourth time we really picked it up and laid it on the blanket.

"'Now,' said my steersman, 'we will say the prayer. "Real friend, now you have seen how kind we are to you when we find you with the spirit gone out of you. Now that the living spirit is out of you, we want that lucky part of your body to come to use, in return for what we give you. We are going to bury you. We want you to leave with us the quartz crystal found in the mountains [a piece of which every wolf is believed to carry in his right foreshoulder and which is, in reality, his life]. Leave it with us so that we may have long life."'

"Then we lifted the wolf and put it under a rock and covered it with the blanket and with stones."

The same man related the following experience:

"In my youth, I once shot a killer whale. He was badly wounded, but in reloading I broke my ramrod, so I paddled close to him and drove a

*Sisiutl. Qagyuhl. 1914.*

sharp stake into him near the head. Then bracing myself in the bow of the canoe, I held the end of the stake in the crook of my legs. His spout hole was just opposite my face, and his body stretched behind along the canoe. He spouted continually, and the stench was terrible. He drove straight toward the shore and beached himself in shallow water, and my brother came up and shot him. When the next tide floated the body, I towed it down in front of the village, thinking I had done a great deed, but the old men were much excited and scolded me angrily. They all came to the shore and prayed over the body, imploring the spirit of the killer whale not to be angry with them, for they had not done it. Only one, they reminded him, had done it, and they mentioned my name so that there might be no misunderstanding."

*Two Kwakiutl Myths*

*Raven Makes a Salmon* — The ancient people, who were both human and animal, were hungry and without food. Omehl, the Raven, leaned against a tree and thought. Then he went to his canoe and paddled along close under a rock, and he asked of the dead people, "Is there any twin child among you?" One after another, the bodies of the dead answered no, but after a while he came to one who said she was a twin child. He laid the coffin on the ground, removed the bones, and arranged them in their proper relation. Then he sprinkled the living water four times over them, and they became alive. This woman, Raven brought to Eclipse Narrows, and then he sent all the people in their canoes to bring round stones, which they piled in the rapids at the narrows until the water became shallow. Then Raven said, "Now, young brothers, get split cedar sticks. We will make a salmon trap."

In one day, they had the necessary sticks, and when the weir was complete, they put their basket traps in place. Deer set his in the middle, but being a fool, he did not leave an opening by which the salmon could enter it. When all was ready, Raven commanded his new wife to walk into the water below the weir. As soon as the water reached her waist, the stream was filled with salmon, and the traps were quickly filled. These were the first salmon, and they came from the woman's body.

The woman told the people to throw all the bones and the other refuse into the water so that new salmon would spring from them. It is for this reason that now the refuse of the first catch of salmon is returned to the water. When Raven came home from gathering fuel, the house was filled with fish. He entered the house, but some drying salmon hanging low caught in his hair, and he muttered, "Oh, why do you catch in my hair, you that are from the dead!"

The woman asked quickly, "What did you say?"

"I said, 'Why do you catch in my hair, you that are drying?'"

"No, you said, 'You that are from the dead!'" She looked up at the fish, clapped her hands, and cried, "We!" And all the salmon fell down and rolled into the water, where they at once became alive and began to jump and swim. The woman disappeared at the same time. Then Raven leaned back and thought. He called his fighting men together and said, "We will prepare to fight with some tribe. Get ready your weapons!"

When they were ready, he told them he was go-

*Tenaktak Canoes. 1914.*

*A Fair Breeze. 1914.*

ing to make war on the Salmon People, in order to recover his wife. On the beach opposite the Salmon village, they hauled out their canoes, and Raven crossed secretly to that place, where he came upon the young son of the Salmon chief and abducted him. When the Salmon found that the child was missing, they sent messengers to all the fish people, from the Smelts to the Killer Whales.

Now Raven and his paddlers saw the water behind them boiling with the commotion caused by the canoes of the fish people. Soon the pursuers overhauled them, but Raven's son broke their canoes with his stone club, and the fish people, finding themselves in the water, had to assume their fish forms in order to escape drowning. Raven, standing in his canoe, was seizing this one and that, and throwing them in every direction, exclaiming, "You will be the salmon for this river! You will be the *oulachon* for that river!" And so he designated all the places where the salmon and the other fish were destined to be found.

*Beaver Makes a Flood* — At Qaken (the Salish name of a place on the eastern side of Salmon River, Vancouver Island), there were many women in camp digging clover roots. Among the young men left on the other side of the stream in the Village Hwussam were some who had lovers among the women, and they proposed to one another that they go to see their sweethearts. Marten shouted a request to be taken across, and the women said, "He is a pretty young man; we will get him." So they sent a canoe for him. Next, Raccoon called to them, and because they liked his striped face, they took him.

Then came another call: "Come and take me!"

"Who are you?" came the response.

"I am Snake!"

"Let us get him," said the women. "He is a pretty little man; he has a small face!"

"Come and take me!" came a shout. And the women asked, "Who are you?"

"I am Stone-Worker-with-the Feet, I am land otter!"

*Tenaktak Wedding Guests. 1914.*

"Go and get him," said the women. "He is a pretty little man."

Again came a call across the river, and the women answered with the usual question. The reply was short and gruff: "I am Beaver!"

"What Beaver are you?" they asked.

"I am Tree-Feller!" Beaver was becoming angry.

"Who are you, Tree-Feller?" they asked.

"I am Dam-Builder!"

"Who are you, Dam-Builder?"

"I am Swimmer-Downstream-on-the-Belly!"

"Who are you, Swimmer-Downstream-on-the-Belly?"

"Do you not know the sound of a tree falling on the ground?" shouted Beaver.

Then one of the women called, "You had better stay there, and your belly will grow broader on the ground, you great big-bellied thing!"

Now Beaver became very angry. He walked into shallow water, sat down, and threw water into the air, calling with long-drawn words: "Rain constantly, rain constantly, carry them away by water!"

The women cried derisively, "We have our mats and our blankets with which to cover ourselves!"

Still Beaver splashed the water and called for rain, and soon the sky grew black and the rain fell. The river rose rapidly and carried the women directly across the strait to Blinkinsop Bay, where they became frogs.

*Kwahwumhl-Koskimo. 1914.*

# V—The Northernmost Coast

It is not widely known that Edward S. Curtis spent, off and on, a period encompassing thirty years among the Alaskan Eskimo, and that his transcriptions of their myths is, from an unbiased literary standard, his finest work. How he accomplished this is also not well known, for the people themselves—numbering, as he tells us, some thirty thousand, from the Aleutian Islands to eastern Greenland—were not easily accessible.

The country they inhabited, even in summer, was inhospitable and desolate. The life they lived was austere. Yet, at Nunivak Island and Little Diomede, Curtis discovered a trove of legends, the lure of which would draw him back, again and again, to the tundra lands.

Astonishingly, apart from the diseases conferred upon these people by the white man, Curtis's conclusion is that the natives have welcomed white visitation for quite a number of reasons, not the least of which is their abundant curiosity and their elasticity and inventiveness as a culture. Perhaps this may explain the wealth of myth they shared with Curtis, the quixotic stories rivaling those of Grimm or Andersen.

Further, it is in these tales that we see a people committed to unraveling and weaving together a disparate universe; of making sense of a cosmos of uncertainty. The immoderate warmth that Curtis felt in the people themselves surely transcended the minus-zero temperatures of their environment, lending to their tales an ebullient sense of happy equanimity.

# ALASKAN ESKIMO

In 1927, after a summer spent among the Eskimo of the Alaskan islands, coast, and inland waterways, this text was begun. The Eskimo gain their livelihood from the sea. However, for half of the year, during the Arctic winter, there is little opportunity to obtain food from either land or water. With the coming of temperate weather and the breakup of the great ice fields, they go forth in their skin craft in quest of food, buffeted constantly by sweeping gales and the treacherous, shifting, grinding ice packs. Only the most expert canoe men survive the stress of these Arctic conditions, the acquisition of food in the face of every difficulty. The narratives of hunters who put out to sea in their frail skin kayaks never to return give an idea of the inhospitable region.

Only the fittest, indeed, in such an environment could survive. They number somewhat fewer than thirty thousand, inhabiting the coast and many

*Nuktaya. King Island. 1928.*

islands of North America approximately from the Aleutian Islands to eastern Greenland. The extent of the territory occupied by the Eskimo, with some exceptions, from the coast to the interior, is but a few hundred miles. When this vast territory is compared with the small population, it might be expected that many differences would be found in the various cultures. Although such is the case, the similarities of the Eskimo as a whole are perhaps more uniform than those of the people of any other American cultural group.

The mode of life of the Eskimo depends on the distribution and migration of game; hence, when different groups are dependent on different game foods, variations in culture occur. This is well illustrated by comparing the most important food products of Nunivak and King Islands with those of Little Diomede Island and Cape Prince of Wales. The former islands lie directly in the path of seal and walrus migrations; hence, the people may be characterized as having a distinctive "seal culture." Walrus and whales are most important to the Diomede and Cape Prince of Wales Eskimo, being more numerous than seal within the range of their villages. These groups differ from Kotzebue Sound Eskimo, who hunt beluga and seal on the coast and caribou (now reindeer) along the streams. This variance is reflected strongly in their ceremonies and in certain social customs.

*Holiday Costume. 1928.*

*Ready for the Throw. Nunivak. 1928.*

The work here recorded comes from personal study, travel, and fieldwork of thirty years of experience. During this time, contact with whites and their diseases have worked a tragic change on the Eskimo. A notable exception was found in the natives of Nunivak Island, whose almost total freedom from Caucasian contact has thus far been their salvation. However, within a year of 1927, it was officially reported that the population decreased nearly thirty percent.

Nunivak Island rises steeply from the Bering Sea. It extends east and west about 120 miles, with a distance of fifty miles between its most northerly and southerly points. The shoreline is bluff and rocky, and its few harbors are suitable only for small craft. The harbors offer little real protection and must be navigated with the utmost care. The interior of the island is essentially level, with a few mountains grouped in the southwestern end. The entire area is treeless; the vegetation of tundra—grass, moss, and edible herbs and roots. Over this bleak, cheerless island sweep the heavy winter storms. Few Eskimo have penetrated the interior, which is given over to the recently introduced reindeer and to foxes and other animals. The natives prefer to dwell along the coast, where they are assured of a fairly abundant supply of birds, sea mammals, and other seafood. The broken coast affords a slight degree of shelter.

The villages on Nunivak Island are situated with respect to the accessibility of the food supply. Since the major part is derived from the sea, the inhabitants of each village erect their homes close to the shore, facing the water.

Most of the villages of Nunivak Island are situated on the northern and eastern shores, especially on such prominent headlands as Capes Corwin, Manning, and Mendenhall. The people on each of these capes have at least two villages and camps. These settlements, or groups of villages, scattered as they are along the coast, contain only as many as about forty inhabitants each. A census of the whole island, made in 1926, gave 177 natives; in 1928, only 52 were reported.

King Island, the home of the northern sea cliff–dwelling Eskimo, is barely a dot in the Bering Sea. It thrusts up its head from the watery depths, the sheer cliffs rising about seven hundred feet above sea level. It is flat on top, about two square miles in area, resembling a huge stone cube. This bleak, forbidding, rocky mass supports few varieties of growing things. Mossy vegetation, low bushes, and berries grow among the rocks. Birds flock, breed, and migrate by the millions, dwelling in the almost-inaccessible rocky niches. Walrus and seal are numerous, for King Island is in the direct route of the north and south migrations of these mammals. Berries are gathered, birds are caught, and seal taken, but the natives are primarily walrus hunters, and it is the walrus that has attracted and held this small group of Eskimo to its inhospitable island. At the south side, there is a rock slide, with its talus extending into the sea. This slide, not more than two hundred feet wide and scarcely less precipitous than the cliff itself, affords the only landing on the island for boat or canoe. Few vessels call: An occasional trading ship and the rare visits of the revenue cutter are about the only ones. There is no protection from the sea, and the water is too deep for easy anchorage.

The inhabitants have erected a village of about twenty-nine houses, scattered irregularly on seven terraces. Due to the sheerness of the cliff, the dwellings are built on stilts. On the pole framework sit the two-roomed houses. The exterior sides, roof, and floor are covered with walrus hide tightly lashed in place. Between interior and exterior is a filling of moss, a foot thick, which provides excellent insulation against the cold.

Of late years, the Eskimo of King Island have spent the midsummer months at Nome, leaving their village entirely deserted, except by the dogs, which remain on the island in large numbers, sub-

*Nunivak Youth. 1928.*

sisting on whatever they can hunt or on walrus carcasses left by the natives. While continually fighting among themselves, the dogs were pitifully glad to see the members of the expedition. They leapt, fawned, rolled underfoot, and, in their joy, upset the camera many times.

The hunting of black whale, walrus, sea lion,

and seal takes place in slightly choppy or stormy weather. It is believed that when the weather is calm, the spirits of the drowned will upset the boats of their relatives and drown the occupants.

Between the Alaskan mainland at Cape Prince of Wales and the easternmost Russian outpost, East Cape, Siberia, lie the two Diomede Islands. Little Diomede is a bleak, forbidding shore, ruggedly resisting the gales that sweep through the straits from the vast unbroken Arctic. Interminable fogs envelop it; the great wind-driven ice floes of the Arctic pile against

*A Nunivak Hunter. 1928.*

its granite cliffs. The ice fields of the Bering Sea, borne relentlessly northward by the Arctic drifts, are split asunder by its sheer walls. These waters sport several varieties of whale, walrus, and seal herds. Countless birds flock, breed, and migrate to and from these islands.

Little Diomede, a few square miles in extent, rises from the sea in sheer cliffs. Plant life is limited to a few species of moss and berries. On the western side, a cliff with boulder-strewn slopes extends outward in a gravel spit, then ends in a submerged reef. Legend claims that in former times, seal and walrus herds rested from their long migration on this spot. Today the small village of Eskimo, an aggregation of stone houses on terraces, is situated at a point just above the meeting of slope and gravel spit.

Each family has its own dwelling, large and roomy, the outer walls of which are of boulders.

The chief foods are primarily meat, blubber, oil of walrus, seal, and whale. Fish are caught with nets and hooks, eaten either fresh or dried, or with shellfish. Clams are taken from walrus stomachs and shrimp from whale stomachs. Kelp supplies the remainder of the food staples derived from

the sea. During the brief summer, the rocky land provides a few varieties of berries, of which the salmonberry and blueberry grow in greatest profusion, and also the Alaskan potato. Berries are usually eaten raw. During the nesting and breeding season, birds' eggs are collected in great numbers. Men, women, and children search the rocky slopes for hidden nests and bring back grass bags heavily laden with their find. During the summer months, birds in great number and variety are caught with nets, spears, slings, and bolas. These include, among many, auks and auklets, cormorants, ducks, ptarmigan, and puffins. Much of the catch is stored for winter use.

Ceremonies have to do with whale and seal

*Girl's Costume. Nunivak. 1928.*

hunting, the naming of children, and the first bird or animal catch by a boy or a youth.

In autumn, the whaling season begins. In former years, many whales inhabited these waters, and, considering the character of the equipment used, good catches resulted. In late years, however, beginning with the appearance of modern whaling ships, and especially after the introduction of bomb guns, whales became fewer in numbers and in time were rarely seen. Recently, since the disappearance of the ships, it is said that whales are again increasing and are more frequently observed.

*The Ivory Carver. Nunivak. 1928.*

| *Two Nunivak Myths* | *The Seal Spirits*—A seal suddenly discovered that she was alive. She lay on a woven mat on a rocky bench by the water, |

*The Seal Spirits*—A seal suddenly discovered that she was alive. She lay on a woven mat on a rocky bench by the water, under the ice. Below was water; above was a hole in the ice through which the sky could be seen. As the water rose and covered the bench, she felt the need for air. She popped her head through the hole and saw land nearby. Then, for the first time, she used her flippers and swam close to shore. There was a village, with people moving about. She thought, Those people are not like me. I must keep away from them.

She saw a kayak disappear behind a floe, and when it emerged, the paddler had changed to a white ptarmigan parka and wore a white pointed cap. He resembled a piece of ice. Then the seal saw him put a talisman in his mouth. Immediately, a mist floated from the hunter to her, making her feel very drowsy. The man slowly approached with his harpoon, but then the seal dived down and broke the spell. She said to herself, "That man meant some harm to me."

She swam a long time, following the shore. She ate and slept in the sun on an ice floe. Finally, she arrived at a large seal rookery. A big seal, who had the power to becoming human at will, took possession of her. One day, food became distasteful to her; she was heavier and moved sluggishly. Her mate chose a solid ice floe for her to rest upon, and there a male seal was born to them. At first, the baby made a lot of noise in its sleep and would not wake up. His parents were frightened and thought, If a hunter should pass by here, the baby would be killed.

Then the baby had waking intervals. The parents taught him to swim, and they all moved down the coast, close to land, always so that they could get to sea quickly. They passed a village, but because an unclean woman was there (one in a menstrual period), they kept far out to sea. Many hunters came out in kayaks. One wore a white cap and parka. The man put a talisman in his mouth, and its power made the seal family feel drowsy and helpless. As the hunter was about to cast his harpoon, they dived and escaped. As they looked up, he could be seen with weapon in hand, waiting. The parents instructed, "When you are alone and hunters come out, be very careful, because they throw sticks that tear the flesh and kill. You must always move swiftly. While swimming, keep close to shore, or you may run into nets stretched between rock points."

They came to a clean village where there was no garbage on the shore and the people were neat. The father seal said, "That village and those people are clean. We can go near them."

A kayak approached. The hunter was well

*King Island. 1928.*

dressed, and his kayak was new, with white covering. The father said, "This is a good man. Even if he comes close, let us stay on top of the ice."

The hunter used his talisman, and when he was near enough, he cast his harpoons at all three seals. They came back to consciousness and knew that they were dead. The scratching and tickling of the stone knife as it cut into their flesh made them feel good. They were happy, cut up and stowed in the kayak. On shore, the man's wife carried them to the house on a sled. They were glad, because she was clean. Inside, after lighting a small lamp, she poured water in their mouths, which tasted sweet.

Then she cut off their faces and placed them before the house. Before retiring, the man and wife burned bark and passed it under the seals' noses. This greatly pleased them.

Late in the spring, as soon as someone found an egg on the tundra, the woman put on new clothes and carried the seal flesh in a woven grass bag outside the village. She built a small cache which faced the sun, and stored the meat within, placing on it her "medicine."

This the seals disliked, so they went back to the ocean. Much swimming brought them to a small corner in the bay where a house stood on the shore. They left their skins and became human. The seals entered the home where a woman and her daughter lived.

The young seal married the girl. The woman said to him, "Today you must be very careful, for your wife's relatives are coming."

The young man's parents answered, "You must stay here, but we shall leave."

Soon, two women entered and seized the young man, taking him from his wife. Cunningly, he told them, "Do with me as you will, but first take me to the water."

On the shore, he broke away, where he dived into the sea and became a seal again. Surprised and unable to catch him, the women went away. Then the young man became human and returned. The seal parents took the woman on their backs; the husband took the girl; they all set out for the land of the seals, where they lived together on a never-ending supply of clams, mussels, and fish.

*The Spider Trickster*—There lived in the sky a spider whose neighbors were Seagull and Hawk. When she was alone in her house, Spider rolled aside the log headrest and watched the people on earth. Far below, there was a village where a great hunter lived. The village was industrious, especially in the spring, when the inhabitants were intent with preparations for the seal catch.

The people down below were preparing for a feast. The man she could see clearly, but the wife seemed to be enveloped in a hazy mist. Spider's heart was filled with desire. She muttered, "I wish I could go down there and marry that man. I shall be here alone until my time to die comes. That will be bad. I wish that man was my husband."

Spider saw the Bladder feast being held. The great hunter was transparent to her. She could see through him. There was only one dark spot in his body, which was his stomach. Spider made up her mind. She told her neighbors, Seagull and Hawk, "I have been alone all my life. Now I am going down to earth. You must prepare to help me if I am attacked."

That night, while the people were singing songs in the men's house, Spider swung down on her long thread. When she landed, the women came out of the men's house. Spider hid by the path and killed the great hunter's wife as she passed by. Spider followed the women to the women's house, where she cooked food. She carried a bowl of food to the men's house and laid it at the feet of the great hunter. She lived with the hunter as his wife and nobody noticed that Spider was not his real wife.

One day the hunter said, "You must be very careful in what you do. I know that you are not the wife I had before, and that her relatives are suspicious. She had five brothers and five uncles. The youngest brother is the child who often comes here. Those people wish to know where their relative has gone."

Soon Spider had a child by her husband, and then he warned her, "These people are trying to kill you. You have no chance to get away."

One night, while Spider was walking with her child, she saw something sparkle on the ice far ahead of her. The sparkle traveled toward her, and soon she saw that it was a whale, plowing through the snow as whales push aside water with their blunt snouts. Spider was frightened, and she thought of her neighbor Seagull. As the whale grew near enough to strike, Seagull flew down and harpooned it with his long beak.

The next morning, when she awoke, her husband asked, "How did you escape the uncles and brothers of my former wife? You must be very careful now, for her father is searching for you.

*The Umiak. Kotzebue. 1928.*

Perhaps I had better stay by you while you are in trouble."

"No," Spider answered, "you must stay in the men's house."

That night, Spider tied her child on her back and walked over the snow. Again she saw a sparkle on the snow moving toward her. As it approached, she saw that it was a beast with a serrated back, cutting through the frozen ground as easily as if it was swimming through water. Spider thought, Now I am in trouble and need help.

As the beast was about to strike her, she heard the thunder of wings and the wild screech of a hawk. Hawk swooped down and killed the strange beast with a thrust of his beak.

*Umiak and Crew. Cape Prince of Wales. 1928.*

the sky. You must remain on earth, because this is your home."

The husband felt very badly. He wanted to go with her, because he did not want to be alone on earth. At night, Spider made preparations to leave, lashing the child securely on her back. After much pleading, Spider permitted him to go with her. She went up into the sky, dragging him behind her. There they lived happily, often pulling aside the head log to watch the people on earth. Seagull and Hawk entered the body of the husband and became his supernatural powers.

In the morning, her husband said, "How did you escape the ferocious animals sent to kill you? The relatives of my former wife are very angry, because they all have the power to conjure up beasts and evil spirits. The next attempt will be the strongest."

Spider was so frightened that her teeth chattered. That night, when she opened the smoke hole, all the brothers and uncles of the former wife entered the house. They said to her, "You have killed all the beasts and the evil spirits that we have sent for you. Now we are going to kill you!"

In her fright, Spider thought of Seagull and Hawk. As each relative came to grab her, Seagull and Hawk poked their heads through the smoke hole and killed them with their beaks. They spared only the youngest brother. He said, "I told my uncles and brothers not to kill you, but they did not listen to me."

The boy lived with them until he was old enough to take a wife. Then the husband told Spider, "The boy will try to avenge his relatives and kill you. You must be very careful."

Spider replied, "I am tired of being hunted and of people trying to kill me. Tonight I shall return to

## Three King Island Myths

**The Island** — A man lived on the mainland. One day, while fishing in a river near the Sawtooth Mountains, he speared a large bullhead from his kayak. By lashing its tail violently, the struggling fish widened the river and it formed Salt Lake. The fish towed the kayak swiftly down the stream, and at the mouth the man was able to pull in the line until it was near enough to cast a second spear. The pain-maddened fish flung about so furiously that it formed what is now called Grantley Harbor.

The bullhead towed the kayak away from land before the man was able to make his kill. He towed the monster by passing a line through its mouth. He paddled long and hard. As he tired, he looked about and saw that he had not moved the length of a kayak. Glancing over his shoulder, he was astounded to see that the fish had turned into an island (King Island); the hole where the line was attached can still be seen. The man was frightened, cut the line, and paddled home at full speed.

He said nothing about what had happened, until one day he asked a poor youth to go hunting with him. He related the story, saying that he wished to see if the fish had really become an island. They paddled far across the open sea, and before them rose the rocky cliffs of the island. On shore, the poor youth chased birds for so long that the man, impatiently, set out for home without him. The youth, finding that he was marooned, lived in a cave. With a stone knife, he cut up dead seal and whale that washed ashore. He lived there all winter and spring.

During the following summer, the man grew curious as to the fate of the youth, and he paddled out to the island. The youth hid and did not answer the man's calls. The man thought, The youth must have starved. I will see if I can find his body. As soon as the man had climbed the cliff, the youth jumped in the kayak and paddled away. He heard the man cry out after him, but he shouted back, "You deserted me on this island! Now you can stay and live as I lived. I am leaving a supply of food, although you left me nothing!"

The man starved that winter. When the youth returned to the island the following summer, he was unable to find the body.

The man always brought her meat. The woman decided that her husband was Polar Bear.

Many seal were left for her, which she cut up and stored away. She knew that someone else was hunting, but neither she nor her husband could figure out who. One night, Black Whale in human form entered. He was very angry because Polar Bear had married the woman. The gifts of seal had been from him. The two fought in the house. Polar Bear cried, "There is no room to fight here; let us go outside!"

They struggled on the beach in their own forms. Polar Bear snapped with his teeth and slashed with his claws. Whale lashed out viciously with his tail. Polar Bear lodged himself on Whale's back and sunk his teeth into Whale's nose. With furious energy, Whale vainly tried to dislodge Bear. At last he was exhausted, and he cried, "I can no longer fight. I am giving up!" Whale dived in the sea.

Polar Bear once more became human and lived peacefully with his wife.

*The First Woman* — A woman was the first person to come to King Island since it had been made from a fish. No one knows where she came from or how she got there. The woman built a hut of grass and cut up meat for winter food. After being there some time, she noticed that the carcasses came to life and bled from their noses. Then, each morning on waking, she found part of her parka hood gone. She knew that someone had been with her, but she never knew who it was. At last, she woke suddenly and saw a man beside her. She said, "You have been coming here all fall and winter. I did not see you or know who you were."

"I felt sorry for you," answered the man, "because you were alone, so I stayed with you. You and I are married. Now I must hurry; it is light, and I may be too late to see someone."

*The Gleaming Belt* — A young man who was a fine hunter lived with his parents in a house built on a

*Walrus Boats. Big Diomede in Distance. 1928.*

*Selawik Women. 1928.*

flat rock. His old mother was worn and tired from work, and she said to him, "I am tired. I need a daughter-in-law to help me. You must marry."

While hunting birds on top of the island, the young hunter came to a rockbound pool in which five girls were swimming. He stole their clothing and teasingly refused to return it. To four of the girls, he threw the clothes, garment by garment. When they were dressed, they emerged from the water and flew away as geese. The fifth, too shy to talk, hung her head. She did not even plead for her garments. The man thought, I would like to marry that girl if I could catch her. He returned everything but her belt ornament. She was sad without it, because she was unable to fly after her sisters. He led her to his home, but to her, the smell was so strong that she could not enter or stay inside with-

out holding her nose tightly. The girl could eat no oil or meat. She subsisted on grass seeds and roots that her husband gathered from the pond.

The headman, who had two wives, learned of the girl who had come from nowhere, and he desired her. When she refused to go to him, he sent a messenger to demand four ducks of the young man. The girl said to her husband, "Go to that pond where you found me, and if your power is strong, you will get the ducks."

Although it was winter, he found no ice on the pool, and, armed only with a club, he killed four ducks. He threw them in the entranceway to the headman's house. The headman sent another messenger, saying that if the girl would not come to him, he must have four cranes. Again, the young man obtained them from the pool. The headman was angry at being defied, and at the young man for being able to fulfill the demands. Next, he asked for something that could talk. The wife now said to her perplexed husband, "Somewhere in the world is something that can talk, but I do not know where it is. When you seek it, you must take nothing but my belt ornament. Your father will give you a staff that will show you the way. I shall make extra boots. I cannot go home anymore, and the headman will take me while you are away."

The man set out. Whenever he raised the staff and let go, it fell in the right direction for him to take. When he had gone so far that all his boots were worn out, he came to a mountain so steep that its slopes were unscalable. At his call for help, one of his wife's sisters appeared and carried him to the mountaintop. She gave him food and new boots and sent him on his way. Two other sisters helped him, and the fourth, on hearing his story, asked, "What have you to give in exchange for this thing that talks?"

"Only the belt ornament of my wife, your sister," he answered.

"If your power is strong, you will arrive at a village where the headman lives alone in the men's house. Two men armed with knives guard the door. They kill all strangers who try to enter. Show the ornament to them, and they will be blinded by its gleam. In the entranceway are six more guards; you can dazzle their eyes as well. Inside lives the headman, who possesses the thing that talks."

Just as the man's boots were worn out and he was about to drop from hunger and fatigue, he arrived at the village where the thing that talked was. The two outside guards halted him, and he said to them, "I am too tired to run. You can kill me if you like, but first look at this." When they looked at the belt ornament, the glare dazzled them, and the man was able to pass. Once inside, six men with drawn knives stopped him and asked, "How did you pass the two outside? Nobody is allowed to see our headman."

He replied, "I am too tired to run away from you. You may kill me if you like, but first look at this."

Their eyes were also blinded by the gleam of the ornament. The man easily slipped through the door of the men's house. Here were two more sentinels, who asked, "How did you enter? Our headman, who is in two pieces, will kill us for letting you enter."

"The guards asked me to enter and speak to your headman," he lied.

The headman, who really was cut in two, sat up, scolded the guards for allowing a stranger to enter, and asked the man to sit beside him. "No one can see me. How did you, with no gifts and no wealth, pass by my man?"

"I have something I wish to show you."

"Show me what you have," commanded the headman.

The man dazzled the headman's eyes with the belt ornament. The headman was amazed and questioned, "What is this that hurts my eyes so? I am rich and have everything I want, but I do not have a belt ornament like that. Let me see it again."

After gazing at it covetously, the headman con-

*Selawik Girl. 1928.*

tinued, "If you will give this to me, I shall give you anything you desire. I shall have a house like mine built for you."

"This ornament is all I possess," he replied. "I cannot let it go for a house."

"I shall give you half of everything I own."

"I want nothing of your possessions."

"What do you want? Why did you come to me if you will not accept what I have to offer? I shall give all I own for that ornament."

"Let me see what you have."

"I have offered all my possessions. Now I shall show you my cook."

The headman called loudly for food. Immediately, food was set before them by invisible hands, and a voice announced that the meal was ready. When they had finished, the empty dishes vanished.

*Waterproof Parkas. Nunivak. 1928.*

"Now, will you trade your ornament for my cook?"

"No, it is not enough."

"I shall show you my guard."

The headman lifted a box from a shelf. It contained an ivory figure armed with a knife that hung on a chain. The headman commanded it, "Come out of the box, but do not harm us." The figure walked about the room with its knife ready to strike. The man refused to take it. The headman said, "I have offered you everything. What more do you want?"

"Let me try these things."

At the headman's order, the unseen cook brought food and the guard walked about, ready for his command to strike. Then the ivory figure spoke: "You have bought me and I am yours." The man accepted and then said to his host, "I have at last found that which talks. Let us trade."

When he was ready to leave with his new possessions, he was given a boat by the headman, who said, "Take my kayak. It will carry you anywhere you wish to go, but be sure to send it back."

The boat took him home, the staff directed the way, and the unseen cook served him food. On King Island, he found that the headman had taken his wife. He strode to the men's house. When the headman saw him enter, he rose. "Did you bring for me the thing that talks? Let me hear the voice and I shall return your wife."

The man hid his rage. He ordered his invisible cook to serve them a meal. Then he brought forth the box with the carved figure. To the headman, he said, "Here is the thing that talks. It will speak to you in its own way." To the figure, he commanded, "If you do not like this headman, kill him, but leave the people unharmed."

When the headman tried to pick up the carved figure, it stabbed his hand. Next, it thrust the knife through the headman's heart. Then the man took home his wife and brought along the headman's wives to be his servants.

*Sea Man and Moon Man—* There was a great seal netter who always kept a full cache beneath the floor. He lived with his wife, two sons, and a dog. One winter, the straits were solid with ice. No fishing or hunting could be done, and the people began to starve. The man died, and his family survived only by devouring his seal nets.

One morning, during a cold north-wind storm, the elder of the sons set out with his walking stick to see if he could find anything on the shore that might be good to eat. Far from the village, he found a peculiar conical object on the ice. It sounded hollow when it was struck with the walking stick. A very heavy blow toppled it over, revealing a hole beneath. When he looked through, the young man saw another world beneath the water. While craning his neck, his body slid through and, in spite of frantic efforts to recover his balance, he fell far below, limbs sprawling, until at last he struck the bottom. Lying dazed, he heard the sound of chopping. He followed the noise and came to a house, where, beside the entrance, a man was cutting up wood with an adze. The man invited him inside, and his wife fed the young man whale meat. He ate voraciously, for it was his first meal in a long while.

The man asked, "What are the people doing in your village? How are they getting along?"

"We have no food. The people are very thin and worn. My father starved to death."

"Spend the night here; you can go home in the morning."

The youth remained overnight, although he lay awake a long time, puzzling how he was going to reach the hole far above. In the morning, his host inquired, "How many people are there in your home?"

"Only my mother, one brother, and our dog."

The wife gave the youth a long strip of whale blubber and some meat. The man asked another question: "When your father was alive, how did he hunt?"

"He always hunted seal with nets."

"Your village is surrounded by solid ice, so you cannot fish or hunt. Take this staff, which has an

*The Bow-drill. King Island. 1928.*

ice pick on one end and a scoop on the other. At home, go outside the village, out of sight, and strike the ice with the pick. Something will happen. Spread the net, and if you get something you cannot kill, touch its head with the stick. Do not take this pick home, but bury it under the snow near where you make the holes."

The man brought out a large top. It was as big as a man. The young man, with the pick in hand, grasped the top's pole. Then the host spun the top, which rose in the air and glided through the hole in the ice. The young man dropped the top back through the ice and went home. The family wept for him, for they had thought him to be lost or dead. He removed his parka and cut a small piece from the whale strip. It swelled until it was large enough to provide a huge meal for the entire family. They soon became well and healthy.

One evening, the youth took net and ice pick and went to the north of the village. He chose a suitable place, struck the ice with the pick, and it cracked until there was a large space of open water. Next he scooped ice away from the hole and set the net. As soon as he felt it drag, he hauled in a large seal, which he killed by touching its head with the pick. All night, the youth netted, until he had a great pile of seal. He went back to the village, after hiding his pick near the hole, and had them haul in the catch. All the village, and even the people on Big Diomede, feasted, and soon they were strong again. The youth became a great hunter, always keeping a filled cache and giving away much meat to others. One night, when he went to find his pick, it was gone. There were no tracks; it had disappeared. In despair, he went to where he had fallen to the world below. There, he wept and cried all night. In the morning, the conelike object appeared beside him. This he rolled aside, dropped through the hole, and went to the Sea Man's home. The Sea Man, upon hearing the tale, asked his wife to bring his sealskin hunting bag. From it, he drew a long piece of seaweed. As soon as he flung the seaweed to the floor, it became a boat crew of eight men. Then Sea Man called for his broad-bladed steering paddle. The handle was on a swivel, so that it could be turned in any direction. Set in the handle were two eyes. Sea Man asked the paddle, naming all the villages thereabout, "Is the person who stole my ice pick in any of these villages?"

"No one from these villages stole the ice pick."

"Did Sun take it?"

"No."

"Did Moon take it?"

"Yes."

"Young man, you will have to recover the ice pick yourself. These men will carry you to the moon. When you get there, ask for the pick. If Moon Man refuses to give it back, let my paddle steal his wife and bring her here."

They paddled up through the hole and through the air, toward the moon. Once there, the young man got out, and immediately he saw Moon Man adzing wood.

The youth said, "I have come for my ice pick."

"I did not take it."

"I am told by Sea Man that you took it."

Moon Man denied knowing of the ice pick, so the youth returned to his boat. However, first he threw his paddle into the entranceway of the house. Moon Man's wife, startled by the clatter, rose and bent over the paddle. She saw the eyes staring at her. Curiously, she poked it with a foot.

Her foot stuck to the paddle and she was unable to release it. Desperately, she kicked with the other foot, but it, too, was fixed to the paddle. Then, losing her balance, she fell to the floor. The paddle bore her to the boat, which quickly set off for earth. The youth went home and the boat crew returned to the sea bottom with Moon Man's wife.

Near midnight, the young man was awakened by something striking the smoke hole. The voice of Moon Man called through: "I have brought your ice pick! Return my wife to me!"

"I shall not get your wife. Find her yourself!"

"I shall pay you anything for her. I shall make you the strongest man in the village," offered Moon Man. But the youth only answered as before.

"I shall make you the best hunter on earth."

"No. You must get your wife yourself."

"I shall make you a great medicine man."

"No. You must find your wife yourself."

"Come out and see what I shall give you."

In curiosity, the young man dressed and went out. Moon Man said, "I shall give you this ivory hook. With it, you can reach out and pull in anything in the world that you wish. I shall show you the man from Big Diomede who used to visit your father."

Moon Man reached over to Big Diomede with his hook and dragged back a man who was still sleeping. "This man often came to your father's house. You, too, can do this. I shall put the man back where I got him."

The youth accepted the ivory hook and took back his ice pick. Then he guided Moon Man down to the sea bottom through the hole in the ice to fetch his wife. Sea Man rushed out of his house and began to beat both of his visitors severely, shouting, "What did Moon Man pay you to do this? I told you to refuse all offers from him!"

Sea Man stopped the beating, and Moon Man said, "I gave him an ivory hook with a supernatural power. For my wife, I shall give you this spear. See! There is a polar bear! Watch!"

With the spear, Moon Man reached far away and touched the bear. It fell over dead. Pacified by the offer, and greatly desirous of such a weapon,

*Village at Little Diomede. 1928.*

Sea Man replied, "I shall return your wife for that spear. It will be an easy way to hunt. I shall not take you above; you must get up by yourselves."

Moon Man declared, "Watch us! Something will take us back."

A ladder appeared, reaching far above through the hole in the ice. Moon Man and his wife, dragging the youth by his wrists, climbed. On the earth's surface, before leaving for the moon, Moon Man said: "O youth, now I am pleased. I have my wife again. I gave you the ivory hook. Whenever you want anything, no matter how far away, reach out with the hook and you will get it."

The youth, with ice pick and hook, became a great hunter and married a young woman from Big Diomede Island.

One time, on the far side of the mountain, he caught a mouse by the tail just as it was about to dive into a hole. He skinned it alive and flung down the body. Mouse, in great pain, ran home, where her young ones, frightened, hid. That night, Mouse told her young: "That youth was helped by Moon Man and the man down below."

Then she went to the young man's home, where all were sleeping. Across the entrance, she raised her paws over her head and slapped them so hard on the floor that all arose and looked at her. Immediately, the youth, his wife, and all the family became old people, wrinkled, doddering, and just about at the point of death. She ran over their bodies and went through the entrance and then up the slope behind the village. The youth, with his entire family, followed Mouse over the mountain. Where they went from there, no one knows.

*The Orphan Who Raised the Dead* — The daughter of a wealthy man died and was buried on the mountainside. Although the medicine men did their best to raise her, none was successful. The daughter's spirit went up and down the coast trying to find some good hunter to help her. She found none on the Alaskan mainland, and only two on the Siberian shore who might be of some use. At last, coming to the village of Kuma, on Big Diomede, she found a hunter who could carry out her instructions.

In the morning, this hunter, seeing the weather was calm and the young ice forming, picked up harpoons, carried the coiled line about his neck, and went out. He heard a hair seal blowing through a hole, and he carefully crept over to it. Then, when the seal breathed again, he thrust the harpoon downward. Immediately, he lost consciousness. When he revived, he found himself standing on the sea bottom. A woman was beside him. She explained, "I came here to get you. I died, and my father had many medicine men try to raise me, but none could do so. I have looked for a good hunter to help me. I have found you after a long search. Here, take this harpoon point; it possesses power. There is an orphan in my village, not yet a medicine man, who is to raise me, but you must help."

The spirit woman and man walked far on the sea bottom. Above was ice. As the sea became shallower, the ice drew closer, until it touched their heads. They emerged through an ice crack and went up the mountain to her grave. There she instructed, "This is the grave containing my body. I shall enter, but you must remain here until night. When you see a stirring, roll off the stones and lay aside the boards and wrappings. First, I shall sit up, and then I will stand. You must put your arms about me. Do not be afraid, but remain, even if you are alarmed. No harm will come to you." With these words, her spirit vanished into the grave.

All day, he watched. After dark, he detected a movement in the grave. The hunter was frightened but remained. He thought, I cannot run. I am very far from home. This spirit woman promised no harm would come to me.

The man rolled aside stones, pulled off boards, and raised the body to a sitting position. It fell forward again, breathing out fire four times, and then sat up as if just waking. The girl said, "I am very glad you have helped me, for I shall soon be alive again." He held her in his arms as she rose. Then she exclaimed, "Listen! That orphan is about to begin. I hear drumming and singing in the men's house." They walked toward the village. Meanwhile, the orphan was conjuring, and he said to the girl's father, "I have seen your daughter approaching with someone who walks on the ground. He must be a human. He is wearing an auklet parka and carries a harpoon and line."

The father was pleased and answered, "If you succeed in raising my daughter, I shall give you a kayak with equipment and fill it with seal meat and oil."

On the way down the mountainside, the girl, still part spirit, told the hunter, "The orphan has already seen us. My father offered him a kayak filled with seal meat and oil. The orphan does not know where you are from. Now my father offers more riches. The orphan is telling him we are behind the men's house."

Then the orphan said to the father, "Your daughter and the human are now in the entrance-way. They are coming in."

As the two came up through the entrance hole, the father recognized his daughter and sprang toward her. He was stopped by the orphan, who explained that he was not quite finished with his conjuring to return her to life.

After all was done, the father embraced her. He gave the orphan an umiak, a kayak, half his wealth, and offered his daughter in marriage. The orphan refused her, saying that because the Big Diomede man had done most of the raising, he should have the girl. The Big Diomede hunter married the daughter and took her to his own village. The orphan became the wealthiest and most powerful medicine man in the village.

1868    Edward Sheriff Curtis born February 16, near Whitewater, Wisconsin. Edward's father, Johnson Curtis, lost his health during the Civil War; cannot resume farming and becomes a minister.

1874    Family moves to Cordova, Minnesota.

1887    Family moves to Seattle, Washington. Builds cabin in Port Orchard, a ferry ride across Puget Sound.

1888    Father dies of pneumonia in May.

1891    Borrows $150 and goes into business with partner, Rasmus Rothi. Founds Rothi and Curtis, Photographers at 713 Third Avenue, Seattle.

1892    Curtis at age 24 marries Clara Phillips. Rothi parts company with Curtis. Curtis forms new partnership with Thomas Guptill to form Curtis and Guptill, Photographers and Photoengravers at 614 Second Avenue, Seattle.

1893    First child, Harold, born.

1894    Guptill withdraws as partner.

1895    Edward Curtis's brother Asahel starts work as an engraver at the photo studio.

1895–    Curtis photographs Princess Angeline,
1896    the daughter of Chief Sealth, from whom Seattle took its name. This could possibly be his first photograph.

1896    Second child, Beth, born. Wins bronze medal from the Photographers' Association of America for "excellency in posing, lighting and tone."

1897    Enters business on his own with growing reputation as commercial photographer of romantic portraits, Indian subjects, and landscapes. Studio now called Edward S. Curtis, Photographer and Photoengraver. Gold discovered in the Canadian Yukon. Curtis sends his brother Asahel to Alaska to photograph the gold rush.

1898    While hiking and photographing Mt. Rainier, Curtis discovers a group of lost scientists and leads them to safety. Two members of this group will change the course of Curtis's life forever, Dr. C. Hart Merriam and Dr. George Bird Grinnell. Third child, Florence, born.

**1899** Accompanies E. H. Harriman expedition to Alaska as official photographer, by invitation of Grinnell and Merriam. It is on this expedition that Curtis learns how to approach photography in a scientific manner or method. Curtis wins first-place awards at the National Photographic Convention for three Indian images: *Evening on the Sound, The Clamdigger,* and *The Mussel Gatherer.*

**1900** Stays as guest with George Bird Grinnell on Crow Indian reservation in Montana; decides to devote himself full-time to photographing Indians. Makes first trip to the Southwest later that same year.

**1900–1906** Works as businessman and full-time photographer of Indians, photographing extensively among the tribes of the Southwest, Great Plains, and Pacific Northwest. Establishes basic elements of style and approach to photographing Indians.

**1904** *Lewis and Clark Journal* publishes first major feature about Curtis's Indian work. Curtis envisions photographing all Indian tribes "who still retained to a considerable degree their primitive customs and traditions." To achieve this goal, Curtis hires Adolph Muhr to manage his studio, thus freeing him to photograph. Curtis wins photo contest in *Ladies' Home Journal* and is asked to photograph President Theodore Roosevelt's children. Roosevelt becomes a major supporter of Curtis's project.

**1905** Curtis, again through the help of his friends Merriam and Harriman, has a successful photographic show in Washington, D.C.

**1906** Convinces J. Pierpont Morgan to provide capital loan to begin publication of *The North American Indian,* a 20-volume, 20-portfolio work.

**1907** Publishes volume 1 of *The North American Indian.*

**1909** Fourth child, Katherine, born.

**1909** Runs into financial problems. J. P. Morgan advances Curtis an additional $60,000 and sets up The North American Indian, Inc., to oversee his investment.

**1910–1912** In further attempts to generate funds, Curtis creates a "picture-musical" production, complete with full orchestration of Indian music to accompany his slide lecture.

**1912** Forms the Continental Film Company as another attempt to create funds for *The North American Indian.* Produces a motion-picture documentation of the Kwakiutl people of British Columbia.

**1913** Publishes in volume 9 a memorial tribute to J. P. Morgan. Secures further support from Morgan's son for *The North American Indian.* Moves Seattle studio to Fourth and University. Creates a new photographic process called Curt-tone, or Orotone, a positive photograph on glass.

**1914** Film *In the Land of the Headhunters* is completed. Although well received critically, the film does not bring in the much-needed funding for continued field research.

**1916** Curtis's wife files for divorce, causing even further indebtedness.

**1916–1922** *The North American Indian* is put on hold. Curtis is not able physically or financially to continue his life project.

**1919** After divorce, Curtis moves to Los Angeles and establishes new studio in the famous Biltmore Hotel. With renewed spirit, Curtis enjoys new photo opportunities.

**1920–1936** Curtis starts working for the Hollywood studios, taking still photographs of scenes from such movies as DeMille's *The Ten Commandments.*

**1922** Volume 12 of *The North American Indian* published.

*1922–*
*1926*  With the publication of volumes 13, 14, 15, 16, and 17, Curtis finishes his documentation of the Southwest Indians.

*1927*  With help from daughter Beth, Curtis photographs the Indian people of Alaska.

*1930*  Publishes volume 20 of *The North American Indian*. The project now complete, Curtis is physically and emotionally exhausted.

*1930–*
*1948*  Curtis never totally regains his health. However, he pursues an avid interest in mining and searching for gold.

*1935*  The North American Indian, Inc., after having printed only 272-plus sets but selling just over 200, sells all assets to Charles Lauriat Books of Boston, Massachusetts. Lauriat will spend the next 40 years trying to sell sets of *The North American Indian*.

*1948*  Begins correspondence with Harriet Leitch at the Seattle Public Library and writes for the first time since 1930 about the North American Indian.

*1952*  On October 19, at the age of 84, Edward S. Curtis dies of a heart attack at the home of his daughter Beth in Whittier, California.

# Sources and Notes

## Tewa and Tiwa

SOURCE: *The North American Indian*, vol. 17 (Tewa), 1926; vol. 16 (Tiwa), 1926.

Of volume 17, Curtis comments that his work is based on research conducted by W. W. Phillips, "who made a preliminary field trip in 1905, and C. M. Strong, who spent about eight months in 1909 at the Tewa villages. All the material gathered in these earlier years has been correlated and largely augmented by W. E. Myers, who visited the Rio Grande tribes in 1909 and 1917, and spent the entire summer of 1924 in the same field." In his introduction to volume 16, Curtis mentions the difficulties encountered in trying to gather material of a sacred or ceremonial nature. Considering that he had the same staff working on both volumes, it is possible they—and not he—encountered these reticences. On the other hand, the material thus gathered, while perhaps not as strong mythologically, is fascinating historically.

## Keres

SOURCE: *The North American Indian*, vol. 16 (Keres), 1926.

In his introduction, Curtis speaks of the conflict between the old and the new, "the ancient order of life" as opposed to "the progressive element, composed chiefly of younger men and women." Between these two factions, the gatherer(s) comes; Curtis admits to the fact that "the full story of the Pueblo tribes of New Mexico will never be told."

## Zuni and Hopi

SOURCE: *The North American Indian*, vol. 16 (Zuni), 1926; vol. 12 (Hopi), 1922.

The Zuni introduction speaks of the historical conflict between the Christian teachings brought by the Spanish missionaries and the "native beliefs" that were secretly practiced. As he further states, "With some exceptions the attitude of the Spanish leaders toward the Pueblos was not a beneficent one. . . ." Overall, his conclusion is that "the Pueblos have clung tenaciously to the religion of their fathers, the overlay of Christianity being superficial indeed." The Hopi introduction mentions Curtis's first visit in 1900; further work with them continued until 1919. He is grateful, he says, to have taken pictures "so long ago; for, conservative as these people are, there has been a great change in their mode of life, hence many of the photographs here presented could not have been made in more recent years." One might also add that this would be equally true in the gathering of myths.

## PIMA AND YUMA

SOURCE: *The North American Indian*, vol. 2 (Pima, Qahatika, Yuma), 1908.

Curtis states, "These various tribes have been broadly termed, with the Pueblos, the sedentary Indians of the Southwest." Once again, his commentary in the introduction deals with Christian faith and its imposition on native religion. He concludes: "As a rule the extent of their Christianization has been their willingness to add another god to their pantheon." Curtis also speaks admiringly of the nine tribes treated in volume 2—their hardiness, their adaptability in a harsh and intractable land.

## APACHE AND NAVAJO

SOURCE: *The North American Indian*, vol. 1 (Apache and Navajo), 1907.

Curtis states, "Although much time was expended and much patience consumed before the confidence of their elders was gained, the work was finally successful. . . ." He further remarks that the material given by medicine men was later corroborated "by others until no doubt of its entire accuracy remained." He also speaks of the inception of his work, beginning in 1898, and the "months of arduous labor" spent in trying to gather "a comprehensive and permanent record of all the important tribes of the United States and Alaska that still retain to a considerable degree their primitive customs and traditions."

## MANDAN AND ARIKARA

SOURCE: *The North American Indian*, vol. 5 (Mandan, Arikara), 1909.

In his introduction, Curtis explains that George Catlin, the famous biographer in word and paint of the Mandan, was guilty of "romantic daydreams in which he endeavored to show that the Mandan were Welsh." Theories of American Indian lineage

descending from the Lost Tribes of Israel, for example, were, as Curtis notes, popular in Catlin's day (1850s) and 250 years earlier. Curtis goes on to state that "the present weakened condition of the Mandan Tribe," offered him little opportunity to photograph them as he would have wished. However, he felt that the text, as offered here, "affords a very adequate idea of them and their former mode of life." The Arikara material, he praises as "alive with illustrations."

## ARAPAHO AND ATSINA

SOURCE: *The North American Indian*, vol. 6 (Arapaho), 1911; vol. 5 (Atsina), 1909.

As stated in his introduction, Curtis confirms that "Piegan, Cheyenne, and Arapaho belong to the western division of the Algonquian linguistic family. . . ." Each tribe of the trio has planted its name firmly in the literature and history of the northern plains. He mentions, in addition, that the Arapaho dialect is "quite distinct from that of the Cheyenne," but he concludes that culturally the two tribes are much alike. The Atsina text, according to Curtis, was valuable in that much of what was written about them at the time was derogatory. He hoped to dispel some of the misinformation of his day.

## CHEYENNE, PIEGAN, CROW, AND SIOUX

SOURCE: *The North American Indian*, vol. 6 (Piegan, Cheyenne), 1911; vol. 4 (Apsaroke), 1909; vol. 3 (Sioux), 1908.

Commenting on the Cheyenne material, Curtis says that it "was collected from that branch commonly known as the Northern Cheyenne, now living on Tongue River in Montana." His belief is that the Cheyenne showed "an unequalled struggle against inevitable subjection" and that the press faulted them, along with the Office of Indian Affairs, with "accounts of their hostilities."

The Piegan chapter was, Curtis says, "collected from members of the tribe on the reservation in northern Montana, the inhabitants of which are erroneously termed Blackfeet." His contention is that though they belong to the Blackfoot group, they are also a distinct tribe. Piegan, Blackfeet, and Blood, he continues, are three "westernmost Algonquian tribes" whose association is so close that descriptions of the Piegan might also apply to the Blackfeet and Bloods of Alberta, Canada.

Of the Crow, Curtis points out that they represent "the highest development of the primitive American hunter and warrior." He praises them physically and acknowledges their fine clothes and lodges—the latter being "larger and finer" than those of their neighbors. He gives credit in his introduction to an exceptional interpreter—an elder, Hunts to Die—"from whom was obtained a large part of the information," and he also acknowledges further corroboration from "old men of the tribe," who gave him mythical and tribal lore.

The Sioux text was compiled by Curtis after fieldwork conducted from 1905 to 1908. He gathered material from nine bands of the Sioux Nation "and their ethnically close relatives, the Assiniboin."

## NEZ PERCÉ, FLATHEAD, AND KALISPEL

SOURCE: *The North American Indian,* vol. 8 (Nez Percé), 1911; vol. 7 (Flathead and Kalispel), 1911. In the introduction, Curtis comments that "the Nez Percés are of Shahaptian stock" and that the tribe, due to "missionary influence," had become split into two groups. One of these, he says, "proved more susceptible to religious instruction than perhaps any other group of Indians in the Northwest." The second group "clung to the earth-mother belief and for religious reasons were opposed to parting with the land on which their creator had placed them." In addition, he mentions the Nez Percé war, confirming that "the voluminous writings on this subject have been based largely on false premises. Perhaps the Indians' side of the story will tend to prevent future historical students from likewise going astray." Curtis makes no specific mention in his introduction of either the Flathead or Kalispel. He does say, however, that in gathering material for

the volume, "numerous extended visits were made to the several localities and tribes." He adds that at the close of 1909, "the entire force of the writer's party was engaged in the task of completing the research."

## COASTAL SALISH

SOURCE: *The North American Indian,* vol. 9 (Coastal Salish), 1913.

Curtis opens with the statement that "The dominating cultural influence of the tribes in this volume was their dependence upon seafood" and he further states that "there have been few people who held life so lightly as these coast dwellers." His reasoning is that there were among them "headhunters" and their form of warfare was the most "primitive to be found anywhere." He speaks of them elsewhere in his introduction as being "peculiarly strong of chest and shoulders, but squat in stature." And he further compares them, mentally and physically, "to the more picturesque tribes of the Plains." In no other volume does Curtis speak so critically of his subjects, which is interesting because these were the people of his home state of Washington.

## KWAKIUTL

SOURCE: *The North American Indian,* vol. 10 (Kwakiutl), 1915.

"An unusual amount of time," Curtis explains in his introduction, "has been devoted to the collection of material for this volume, a portion of each field season from 1910 to 1914 having been spent among the Kwakiutl Tribes." He gathered, in fact, so much material that volume 10, since it could not be condensed, was presented on "a somewhat thinner paper." Curtis's main informant for the book was a man named George Hunt, an interpreter of Scottish and Tsimshian parentage; Hunt was born in a Kwakiutl village and lived among them for sixty years.

## THE NORTHERNMOST COAST

SOURCE: *The North American Indian,* vol. 20 (Alaskan Eskimo), 1930.

The fieldwork for this volume was completed, according to Curtis, on the "Alaskan islands, coast, and inland waterways, in 1927." It is fitting that in bringing his monumental thirty-year work to a close, volume 20 should include some of the best storytelling. His admiration of the Eskimo is clearly stated in his introduction; their narratives thus have a seemingly happy voice even when dealing with tragic events. As Curtis states, "In all the author's experience among Indians and Eskimo, he never knew a happier or more thoroughly honest and self-reliant people." He compares them adversely with the North American Indian, "whose attitude, evidently because of the distrust he has learned to engender toward the Whites, is that of contempt." Curtis's conclusion on this matter is that the Eskimo has a sense of "ready adaptability" that permits him to desire, "at least outwardly, the manners of the White men about him." Sadly, he also reports that within one year of his visit with the Nunivak—a tribe that had had almost no contact with Caucasians up to that time—their population decreased (one assumes because of disease) nearly thirty percent.

## TRIBES REPRESENTED IN
## *THE NORTH AMERICAN INDIAN*

Volume 1 (1907): Apache, Jicarilla Apache, Navajo

Volume 2 (1908): Pima, Papago, Qahitaka, Mohave, Yuma, Maricopa, Walapai, Havasupai, Apache-Mohave

Volume 3 (1908): Teton Sioux, Yanktonai, Assiniboin

Volume 4 (1909): Apsaroke, Hidatsa

Volume 5 (1909): Mandan, Arikara, Atsina

Volume 6 (1911): Piegan, Cheyenne, Arapaho

Volume 7 (1911): Yakima, Klickitat, Interior Salish, Kutenai, Flathead

Volume 8 (1911): Nez Percé, Walla Walla, Umatilla, Cayuse, Chinookan

Volume 9 (1913): Salishan tribes of the coast, Chimakum, Quilliute, Willipa

Volume 10 (1915): Kwakiutl

Volume 11 (1916): Nootka, Haida

Volume 12 (1922): Hopi

Volume 13 (1924): Hupa, Yurok, Karok, Wiyot, Tolowa, Tututni, Shasta, Achomawi, Klamath

Volume 14 (1924): Kato, Wailaki, Yuki, Pomo, Wintun, Maidu, Miwok, Yokuts

Volume 15 (1926): Southern California Shoshoneans, Dieguenos, Plateau Shoshoneans, Washo

Volume 16 (1926): Tiwa, Keres

Volume 17 (1926): Tewa, Zuni

Volume 18 (1928): Chipewyan, Cree, Sarsi

Volume 19 (1930): Wichita, Southern Cheyenne, Oto, Comanche

Volume 20 (1930): Nunivak, King Island, Little Diomede Island, Cape Prince of Wales, Kotzebue

# INSTITUTIONS HOLDING COMPLETE SETS OF *THE NORTH AMERICAN INDIAN*

The original intent was to print five hundred sets of *The North American Indian,* which was started in 1907, with the issue of volume 1/portfolio 1. Original subscribers to *The North American Indian* were told it would take Curtis seven years to complete his documentation. However, it took twenty-three additional years, with volume 20 finally printed in 1930. Because of this incredible length of time to document and print *The North American Indian,* it was evident early in the work that not all of the five hundred sets would be printed and sold. Therefore, in 1930, only 214 sets had actually been sold to original subscription holders.

The North American Indian, Inc., sold all of the existing inventory to Boston bookseller Charles Lauriat.

In 1935, Lauriat was offering complete sets at a price of $885, with few buyers. We now know he eventually sold an additional fifty-eight sets, because his subscription list equals 272 names. However, in my attempts to locate all 272 sets, I have found institutions that own complete sets that were unnumbered. I think, therefore, a figure closer to three hundred is more accurate. The following is a list of public institutions that I have located that own a full set of *The North American Indian.* This list should be considered incomplete, and hopefully other public institutions will eventually be discovered. At least this list will allow the reader an opportunity to know where they could go to look at more of Edward S. Curtis's work.

—Bob Kapoun

ARIZONA

Flagstaff: Northern Arizona University, Cline Library

Phoenix: Heard Museum

Tempe: Arizona State University Library

Tucson: University of Arizona Library

ARKANSAS

Fayetteville: University of Arkansas; University Library/Special Collections

CALIFORNIA

Berkeley: University of California at Berkeley Library

Fair Oaks: University of California at Davis Library

Long Beach: California State University at Long Beach Library

Los Angeles: Los Angeles Public Library; University of California at Los Angeles, University Library; University of Southern California,

University Library; Natural History Museum of Los Angeles County Library; Southwest Museum Library

Sacramento: California State Library

San Diego: San Diego Museum of Man Library

San Francisco: San Francisco Public Library, Special Collections Department

San Marino: Huntington Library

Stanford: Stanford University Library

COLORADO

Boulder: University of Colorado Library

Denver: Denver Art Museum Library; Denver Public Library, Western History Department; University of Denver Library

CONNECTICUT

Hartford: Wadsworth Athenaeum; Trinity College, Watkinson Library

Middletown: Wesleyan University Library

New Haven: Yale University Library

DELAWARE

Wilmington: Wilmington Library

DISTRICT OF COLUMBIA

Smithsonian Institution, Special Collection Libraries; National Geographic Society

FLORIDA

Gainesville: University of Florida, University Library West

GEORGIA

Athens: University of Georgia, Hargrett Rare Book and Manuscript Library

IDAHO

Moscow: University of Idaho, University Library

ILLINOIS

Chicago: University of Chicago Library; Field Museum of Natural History; Newberry Library, Special Collections

De Kalb: Northern Illinois University, University Libraries

Evanston: Northwestern University, University Library

INDIANA

Bloomington: University of Indiana Library

Fort Wayne: Allen County Public Library

IOWA

Des Moines: State Library of Iowa

Dubuque: Carnegie Stout Public Library

KENTUCKY

Lexington: University of Kentucky Libraries

LOUISIANA

Baton Rouge: Louisiana State University, Hill Memorial Library

MAINE

Brunswick: Bowdoin College Library

MARYLAND

Baltimore: Johns Hopkins University, Milton S. Eisenhower Library

MASSACHUSETTS

Amherst: Amherst College Library

Boston: Northeastern University, University Libraries Special Collections; Boston Public Library; Boston Anthenaeum

Cambridge: Harvard University Library; Peabody Museum of Archaeology and Ethnology, Tozzer Library

Williamstown: Williams College Museum of Art

Worcester: Clark University, Robert Hutchings Goddard Library

MICHIGAN

Ann Arbor: University of Michigan, Special Collections Library

Bloomfield Hills: Cranbrook Institute of Science Library

Detroit: Detroit Public Library

East Lansing: Michigan State University Library

MINNESOTA

Minneapolis: Minneapolis Anthenaeum

St. Paul: James Jerome Hill Reference Library

MISSOURI
St. Louis: Mercantile Library Association; Missouri Historical Society

MONTANA
Missoula: University of Montana, Maureen and Mike Mansfield Library

NEBRASKA
Lincoln: University of Nebraska; Sheldon Memorial Art Gallery
Omaha: Joslyn Art Museum

NEW HAMPSHIRE
Hanover: Dartmouth College Library

NEW JERSEY
Princeton: Princeton University Libraries

NEW MEXICO
Albuquerque: University of New Mexico Library
Santa Fe: Museum of New Mexico, Center for Southwest Research, Zimmerman Library

NEW YORK
Albany: New York State Library
Hamilton: Colgate University, Case Library, Special Collections
New York City: Pierpont Morgan Library; Cooper-Hewitt National Design Museum; New York Public Library; American Museum of Natural History; Metropolitan Museum of Art, Department of Photographs; New York University, Bobst Library, Special Collections; Columbia University, University Library; New York Historical Society; National Museum of the American Indian, Heye Foundation; Huntington Free Library, Fordham University, Duane Library
Poughkeepsie: Vassar College, Special Collection Libraries
Rochester: University of Rochester, Rush Rhees Library

NORTH CAROLINA
Durham: Duke University, William R. Perkins Library, Special Collections Department

OHIO
Athens: Ohio University, Vernon R. Alden Library
Cincinnati: Cincinnati Art Museum, Department of Prints, Drawings, and Photographs; University of Cincinnati Libraries
Cleveland: Western Reserve Historical Society; Cleveland Public Library; Cleveland Museum of Art

OKLAHOMA
Oklahoma City: National Cowboy Hall of Fame and Western Heritage Center
Tulsa: Tulsa City, County Public Library; Thomas Gilcrease Museum

OREGON
Bend: High Desert Museum
Eugene: University of Oregon, University Library
Portland: Multnomah County Library

PENNSYLVANIA
Easton: Lafayette College, David Bishop Stillman Library
Haverford: Haverford College Library
Philadelphia: Philadelphia Museum of Art; University of Pennsylvania, University Museum Archives
Pittsburgh: University of Pittsburgh, Darlington Library; The Carnegie Library, of Pittsburgh

SOUTH DAKOTA
Vermillion: University of South Dakota, I. D. Weeks Library

TENNESSEE
Knoxville: University of Tennessee, Hoskins Library
Nashville: Vanderbilt University, Jean and Alexander Heard Library, Special Collections

TEXAS
Austin: University of Texas, Harry Ransom Center; University of Texas, Texas Memorial Museum; University of Texas Center for American History
Fort Worth: Amon Carter Museum
Lubbock: Texas Tech University Library

UTAH

Salt Lake City: University of Utah, Marriott Library

WASHINGTON

Seattle: Seattle Public Library; University of Seattle Library; University of Washington, University Libraries, Special Collections; University of Washington, Henry Art Gallery; Museum of History and Industry

Spokane: Spokane Public Library

Tacoma: Washington State Historical Society

WISCONSIN

Madison: State Historical Society of Wisconsin

WYOMING

Cody: Buffalo Bill Historical Center

Laramie: University of Wyoming, American Heritage Center

CANADA

National Archives of Canada, Ottawa, Ontario

National Library of Canada, Ottawa, Ontario

Royal Ontario Museum

University of Alberta, Edmonton

University of British Columbia

University of Calgary

GREAT BRITAIN

The British Library, Bibliographical Information Service, Humanities and Social Sciences, London

Guildhall Library, London

National Library of Wales, United Kingdom

University of Exeter Library, Exeter

# SELECTED BIBLIOGRAPHY

Andrews, Ralph W. *Curtis' Western Indians: Life and Works of Edward S. Curtis.* New York: Bonanza Books, 1962.

Boesen, Victor, and Florence Curtis Graybill. *Edward S. Curtis: Photographer of the North American Indian.* New York: Dodd, Mead and Co., 1977.

Cardozo, Christopher. *Native Nations: First Americans as Seen by Edward S. Curtis.* Boston: Bullfinch Press Book, 1993.

Coleman, A. D., and T. C. McLuhan. *Curtis: His Work. Introduction to Portraits from the North American Indian by Edward S. Curtis.* New York: Dutton, 1972.

Curtis, Edward Sheriff. *The North American Indian.* 20 vols., 1907–1930: vols. 1–5, Cambridge, Mass.: The University Press; vols. 6–20, Norwood, Conn.: Plimpton Press. New York and London: Johnson Reprint Corp., 1970.

———. *Indian Days of Long Ago.* Yonkers-on-Hudson, N.Y.: World Book Co., 1914; reprint Berkeley, Calif.: Ten Speed/Tamerack Press, 1975.

———. *In a Sacred Manner We Live: Photographs of the North American Indian by Edward S. Curtis.* Barre, Mass.: Weathervane Books, 1972.

———. *The North American Indians: Photographs by Edward S. Curtis.* Text compiled with an introduction by Joseph Epes Brown. New York: Aperture, 1972.

Davis, Barbara A. *Edward S. Curtis: The Life and Times of a Shadow Catcher.* San Francisco: Chronicle Books, 1985.

Gidley, Mick. *The Vanishing Race: Selections from Edward S. Curtis's The North American Indian.* New York: Taplinger Publishing, 1977.

Hartmann, Sadakichi. *The Valiant Knights of Daguerre. #38 E. S. Curtis Photo—Historian.* Pages 267–72. Berkeley: University of California Press, 1978.

Lyman, Christopher M. *The Vanishing Race and Other Illusions: Photography by Edward S. Curtis.* New York: Pantheon Books, in association with the Smithsonian Press, 1982.

Pritzker, Barry. *Edward S. Curtis.* New York: Crescent Books, 1993.

Photographs originally printed in *The North American Indian*. Courtesy of Bob Kapoun.

Page xiii: Povi-Yemo ("Flower Falling"). San Ildefonso. 1905. Vol. 17, pg. 132.

5: Tablita Dancers. San Ildefonso. 1905. Vol. 17, pg. 70.

7: Santa Clara and the Rio Grande. 1905. Vol. 17, pg. 18.

8: Oyegi-aye ("Frost Moving"). Santa Clara Governor. 1905. Vol. 17, pg. 36.

9: Tse-ka ("Douglas Spruce Leaf"). Cacique of San Juan. 1905. Vol. 17, pg. 8.

10: Tablita Dancers Returning to the Kiva. San Ildefonso. 1905. Vol. 17, pg. 66.

12: Fo-e ("Snow Child"). Santa Clara. 1905. Vol. 17, pg. 80.

14: A Kiva at Nambe. 1905. Vol. 17, pg. 72.

14: Mowa ("Shining Light") Nambe. 1905. Vol. 17, pg.140.

15: Pose-aye ("Dew Moving") Profile. Nambe. 1905. Vol. 17, pg. 76.

16: A San Juan Home. 1905. Vol. 17, pg. 4.

17: A Tesuque Ancient. 1925. Vol. 17, pg. 148.

18: A Corner of Taos and a Kiva Entrance. 1925. Vol. 16, pg. 28.

19: Old House and Kiva at Picuris. 1925. Vol. 16, pg. 32.

21: Iahla ("Willow"). Taos. 1905. Vol. 16, pg. 52.

21: Pavia. Taos. 1905. Vol. 16, pg. 56.

22: A Taos Girl. 1905. Vol. 16, pg. 54.

22: In the Forest. 1925. Vol. 16, pg. 58.

24: A Taos Maid. 1925. Vol. 16, pg. 40.

25: Kayati-Sia. 1925. Vol. 16, pg. 94.

26: Santa Ana and Jemez Rivers. 1925. Vol. 16, pg. 66.

27: A Santo Domingo Man. 1925. Vol. 16, pg. 126.

27: A Sia Man. 1925. Vol. 16, pg. 96.

28: Timu. Cochiti. 1925. Vol. 16, pg. 78.

28: Tsipiai. Sia. 1925. Vol. 16, pg. 98.

28: A Santa Ana Man. 1925. Vol. 16, pg. 88.

29: Sotsona (Fox). Santo Domingo. 1925. Vol. 16, pg. 128.

30: Santana Quintana. Cochiti. 1925. Vol. 16, pg. 76.

31: Tyooni-Shiwanna Mask. Cochiti. 1925. Vol. 16, pg. 108.

32: Old Cochiti. 1925. Vol. 16, pg. 68.

35: Zuni. 1903. Vol. 17, pg. 84.

36: A Zuni Man. 1903. Vol. 17, pg. 122.

38: Corn Mountain. 1925. Vol.17, pg. 86.

43: The Stairway Trail at Walpi. 1921. Vol. 12, pg. 50.

45: Nova-Walpi. 1906. Vol. 12, frontispiece.

45: Walpi Snake Chief. 1921. Vol. 12, pg. 126.

46: Buffalo Dance at Hano. 1904. Vol. 12, pg. 178.

48: Puliini and Koyame. Walpi. 1921. Vol. 12, pg. 74.

49: The Plaza at Walpi. 1921. Vol. 12, pg. 80.

50: Picking Up the Snakes. 1906. Vol. 12, pg. 148.

50: Guarding the Snake Kiva. 1907. Vol. 12, pg. 134.

51: Flute Boys, Priests, and Maidens. 1921. Vol. 12, pg. 164.

51: Flute Dancers Returning to Walpi. 1905. Vol. 12, pg. 172.

54: Harvesting Cactus Fruit. Maricopa. 1907. Vol. 2, pg. 88.

201: Nunivak Youth. 1928. Vol. 20, pg. 38.
202: A. Nunivak Hunter. 1928. Vol. 20, pg. 56.
202: Girl's Costume. Nunivak. 1928. Vol. 20, pg. 28.
203: The Ivory Carver. Nunivak. 1928. Vol. 20, pg. 86.
204: King Island. 1928. Vol. 20, pg. 100.
205: The Umiak. Kotzebue. 1928. Vol. 20, pg. 190.
206: Umiak and Crew. Cape Prince of Wales. 1928. Vol. 20, pg. 144.
207: Walrus Boats. Big Diomede in Distance. 1928. Vol. 20, pg. 122.
208: Selawik Women. 1928. Vol. 20, pg. 234.
209: Selawik Girl. 1928. Vol. 20, pg. 238.
210: Waterproof Parkas. Nunivak. 1928. Vol. 20, pg. 24.
211: The Bow-drill. King Island. 1928. Vol. 20, pg. 112.
213: Village at Little Diomede. 1928. Vol. 20, pg. 114.

Photographs courtesy of the Library of Congress

Page xvii: Navajo Woman. 1904.
xviii: A Navajo Smile. 1904.
xix: Moki Melon Eaters (A). Hopi Pueblo. 1900.
xix: Moki Melon Eaters (B). 1900.
xix: Moki Melon Eaters (C). 1900.
xix: Moki Melon Eaters (D). 1900.
xix: The Delights of Childhood. 1900.
6: In the Village of Santa Clara. 1905.
7: Whyay-Ring. Santa Clara Pueblo. 1905.
10: Chit Songwi. Nambe Pueblo. 1905.
11: Nahkat Sheb. Nambe Pueblo. 1905.
13: Winnowing Wheat. San Juan Pueblo. 1905.
13: The Fruit Gatherers. San Ildefonso Pueblo. 1905.
18: Wyemah. Taos Pueblo. 1905.
20: Tull Chee-Hah. Taos Pueblo. 1905.
23: Taos Children. 1905.
33: Zuni Girl with Jar. 1903.
34: Zuni Pottery. 1903.
37: Zuni Girls. 1903.
39: Zuni Bread Maker. 1903.
40: Zuni Girl. 1903.
41: Walpi Maidens. Hopi Pueblo. 1906.
42: Burros and Moki Men on the Road. Hopi Pueblo. 1900.
44: Hopi Children. 1905.
47: Nato—The Goat Man. Hopi Pueblo. 1906.
49: Nampeyo Decorating Pottery. Hopi Pueblo. 1900.
52: Maricopa Girl. 1907.
53: Hso-Man-Hai. Maricopa. 1907.
55: Czele/Marie (Schoolgirl). Pima. 1907.
55: Qahatika Maiden. 1907.
56: Qahatika Child. 1907.
59: The Lookout. Navajo. 1904.

60: Apache Dancers. 1906.
61; Ndee-San Gochonh-Thunder. Apache. 1903.
62: Yenin Guy. Apache. 1903.
63: An Ostoho Cowboy. Apache. 1903.
64: An Apache Girl. 1903.
64: Apache Girl and Papoose. 1903.
67: Tsahizn Tsah. Apache. 1906.
68: Jicarilla. 1905.
69: Jicarilla Cowboy. 1904.
69: Visitors at Jicarilla. 1905.
70: Jicarilla Type. 1905.
70: Chief Garfield. Jicarilla. 1905.
70: Jicarilla Girl in Feast Dress. 1905.
72: A Navajo. 1904.
72: An Oasis. Navajo. 1904.
73: Hatali Nez. Navajo. 1905.
73: Navajo Girl. 1904.
75: Giving the Medicine. Navajo. 1905.
76: Many Goats Son. Navajo. 1904.
76: Navajo Belle. 1904.
76: Tobadzischini. Navajo. 1904.
76: Nayenzgani. Navajo. 1904.
77: Tonenili. Navajo. 1905.
77: Lynx Cap. Navajo. 1905.
83: Prayer to the Great Mystery. (Slow Bull. Sioux.) 1907.
86: Good Bear and Family. Hidatsa. 1908.
111: Ben Long Ear. Crow. 1905.
118: Joe Russell. Piegan. 1910.
119: Reuben Black Boy and Family. Piegan. 1910.
119: Spotted Eagle, Heavy Gun, Calf Robe. Piegan. 1910.
123: Flint Smoker's Daughter. Piegan. 1910.
123: Running Rabbit. Blackfoot. 1900.
124: Bull Shoe's Children. Piegan. 1910.
126: On the Custer Outlook. Crow. (Curtis with Crow Scouts.) 1908.
128: Tries His Knee. Crow. 1908.
129: Holds the Enemy. Crow. 1908.
130: Hoop on the Forehead. Crow. 1908.
131: Bear Cut Ear. Crow. 1908.
132: Forked Iron. Crow. 1908.
136: Yellow Bone Woman and Family. Sioux. 1908.
138: Stinking Bear or Smell the Bear. Oglala Sioux. 1905.
139: Two Charger Woman. Oglala Sioux. 1907.
139: Jack Red Cloud. Oglala Sioux. 1907.
140: Good Day Woman. Oglala Sioux. 1907.
141: Sioux Child. 1905.
141: Red Elk Woman. Sioux. 1907.
142: Lucille. Sioux. 1907.
143: Rosa Lame Dog. Sioux. 1905.
144: Meditation. (Medicine Rock, Cheyenne River.) 1907.
144: Slow Bull. Oglala Sioux. 1907.

145: Little Hawk. Brule Sioux. 1907.
146: Saliva. Oglala Sioux. 1907.
147: Eagle Elk. Oglala Sioux. 1907.
147: Red Dog (Shunka Luta). Sioux. 1907.
156: Head Carry. Plateau. 1900.
156: Black Hair. Plateau. 1905.

157: The Wife of Ow High. Plateau. 1905.
158: Sitting Eagle. Plateau. 1905.
159: Nez Percé Man. 1899.
161: No Wings. Nez Percé. 1910.
163: Que Que Tas. Flathead. 1905.

## ABOUT THE EDITOR

Gerald Hausman has been collecting Native American, Central European, and West Indian folktales since his undergraduate days at Highlands University in New Mexico during the mid-sixties. A twenty-year resident of the Santa Fe area, he has also traveled widely among Indian people, learning the native art of storytelling. His interest in Edward S. Curtis began during his childhood when his mother first shared her own anthropological interest, which included a study of Curtis's portraits.

The work involved in bringing this volume to fruition was a labor of love, because, as Hausman has pointed out, "The writings of Edward S. Curtis, piled one on another, stand more than four feet high, and they represent a vast storehouse of words." All of Curtis's mature writing was examined carefully for inclusion in this volume.

Gerald Hausman's other works as a mythologist include *Turtle Island Alphabet: A Lexicon of Native American Culture and Symbol; Tunkashila: From the Birth of Turtle Island to the Blood of Wounded Knee; The Gift of the Gila Monster: Navajo Ceremonial Tales; Duppy Talk: West Indian Tales of Mystery and Magic.*

## ABOUT THE PHOTOGRAPHY EDITOR

Bob Kapoun is a well-respected gallery owner, art historian, and speaker on Native American art and artifacts. After earning his degree in photography from Southern Illinois University in 1970, Bob moved west to Santa Fe and took an active interest in the wealth of vintage photography of the surrounding area. The works of Edward S. Curtis has become his specialty. Bob and his wife, Marianne Kapoun, expanded the already-historic Rainbow Man gallery to specialize in Native American art and artifacts, as well as regional tricultural folk and fine arts. The gallery is now considered a living landmark of Southwest history and it is a regular stop on historic tours of old Sante Fe. Bob Kapoun is also the author of *The Language of the Robe*, a history of the American Indian trade blanket, which has gone through more than five printings. Considered an expert on the works of Edward S. Curtis, Bob has lectured extensively at museum functions, private showings, and for professional groups. Bob and Marianne have five children and eleven grandchildren.